Y0-DJO-268

CITY GUIDE

Istanbul

Halil Ersin Avcı

Published by Tughra Books
345 Clifton Ave., Clifton,
NJ, 07011, USA

www.tughrabooks.com

Edited by Hasan Hayri Demirel
Translations from Turkish by Korkut Altay
English texts edited by Jane Louise Kandur - Ruth Woodhall
Art Director Engin Çiftçi
Graphic design Sinan Özdemir
Page layout İbrahim Akdağ
Maps Mehmet Fatih Döker - Cem Kırlangıçoğlu
Illustrated by Nejdet Çatak
Photographs Halit Ömer Camcı - Metehan Kurt - Mustafa Yılmaz

ISBN: 978-1-59784-206-8

Printed by
Elma Basim, Istanbul - Turkey

CONTENTS

HISTORICAL PENINSULA - 18   **CHAPTER 1**

TOPKAPI PALACE   19

The Fountain of Ahmed III 20
The Imperial Gate 21
Haghia Irene Church..22
The Royal Mint 23
Palace Kitchens 24
The Royal Stables 24
Harem 24
Imperial Council..26
The Gate of Felicity 26
Audience Hall 27
The Treasury...27
The Royal Apartments 27
The Imperial Terrace 27
Circumcision Room 28
Revan Pavilion..28
Baghdad Pavilion 28

Iftariye Bower 28
The Chief Physician's Room 32
Mustafa Pasha Pavilion 32
Mecidiye Pavilion 32
HAGHIA SOPHIA **35**
THE BLUE MOSQUE AND ITS COMPLEX **42**
Sultan Ahmed Square 45
The Serpentine Column...47
The Stone Obelisk 50
Museum of Turkish and Islamic Arts.........................50
The Binbirdirek (1001 Columns) Cistern 50
Little Haghia Sophia 51
The German Fountain...51
THE BASILICA CISTERN **52**
GÜLHANE PARK **56**
The Istanbul Archeological Museum.........................57
EMİNÖNÜ **60**
THE SPICE BAZAAR **60**
THE NEW MOSQUE **61**
THE GRAND BAZAAR **62**
Nur-ı Osmaniye Mosque...66
Column of Constantine...66
BEYAZIT MOSQUE AND SQUARE **68**
Istanbul University...70
SÜLEYMANİYE MOSQUE **74**
Tomb of Sultan Süleyman the Magnificent................76
Tomb of Mimar Sinan 76
Istanbul University Botanical Gardens 77
ŞEHZADE MOSQUE **78**
Tomb of Ali Tabli 80
Valens Aqueduct (Bozdoğan Su Kemeri)...................80
THE FATİH MOSQUE **82**
Kıztaşı / The Column of Marcian..............................87
YAVUZ SELİM MOSQUE **88**
THE MUSEUM OF KARİYE MOSQUE **90**

MİHRİMAH MOSQUE	92
LALELİ MOSQUE	94
PERTEVNİYAL VALİDE SULTAN MOSQUE	96
MURAT PASHA MOSQUE	98
THE MOSQUE OF MOLLA FENARİ İSA	100
HIRKA-İ ŞERİF MOSQUE	102
YEDİKULE	104

HALİÇ-106

UNKAPANI	107
VALENS AQUEDUCT (Bozdoğan Su Kemeri)	108
GAZANFER AGHA COMPLEX	108
MOLLA ZEYREK MOSQUE	109
ZEYREKHANE	109
FENER	110
Greek Orthodox Patriarchate (Fener Rum Patrikhanesi) 112	
ABDİ SUBAŞI MOSQUE	113
Old Gates Around the Neighborhood of Fener 113	
SÜZGEÇÇİ YUSUF MOSQUE	114
DARÜL MESNEVİ MOSQUE	114
MESNEVİHANE / MATNAWI TALKS LODGE	114
HOUSE OF DIMITRI KANDEMİR	115
HAGHI GEORGIOS (Ayios Yeoryios Jerusalem Metakhion Church) CHURCH	115
THE LIBRARY OF WOMEN'S WORKS	116
FENER PORT	116
BALAT	118

SVETİ STEFAN CHURCH (Demir Kilise)	120
TAHTAMİNARE (Wooden Minaret) MOSQUE	121
AHİRDA SYNAGOGUE	121
SURP HRESHDOGABEN CHURCH	121
BALAT (Ferruh Kethüda) MOSQUE	121
BALAT İSKELE (Yusuf Şücaaddin) MOSQUE	122
BALAT WHARF	122
BALAT HOSPITAL	122

EYÜP-124

CHAPTER 3

FESHANE	125
EYÜP MOSQUE and THE TOMB OF ABU AYYUB AL-ANSARİ	129
THE TOMB OF ABU'D-DERDA	131
PIERRE LOTI	132
MINIATURK	133
KOÇ MUSEUM	133
AYNALIKAVAK PAVILION	134

GALATA-BEYOGLU- **CHAPTER 4**
TAKSIM-TOPHANE-136

GALATA	**137**
The History of Galata	138
Galata Bridges	141
ARAP MOSQUE	**142**
GALATA TOWER	**143**
GALATA MEVLEVİHANESİ / WHIRLING DERVISHES' LODGE	**145**
NEVE SHALOM SYNAGOGUE	**147**
THE OTTOMAN BANK BUILDING	**147**
BEYOĞLU	**148**
The Name	150
İSTİKLAL CADDESİ (Avenue)	**150**
FRENCH CULTURAL CENTER	**151**
AGHA MOSQUE	**151**
GALATASARAY TURKISH BATHS	**151**
GALATASARAY HIGH SCHOOL	**151**
SAINT ANTOINE CHURCH	**152**
ANADOLU PASSAGE	**153**
RUMELİ PASSAGE	**153**

AFRICAN PASSAGE 153
HACI ABDULLAH RESTAURANT 154
İNCİ PATISSERIE 154
TAKSİM 155
TAKSİM SQUARE 155
ATATÜRK CULTURAL CENTER 157
THE REPUBLICAN MONUMENT 157
KAZANCI MOSQUE 157
HAGHIA (AYA) TRIADA GREEK ORTHODOX CHURCH 158
TEPEBAŞI AND TAKSİM TURKISH BATHS 158
SİRKECİBAŞI MOSQUE 158
TAKSİM MAKSEMİ (Reservoir/distribution point) 158
TAKSİM WATERWORKS 159
THE FOUNTAINS OF MAKSEM 159
HAFIZ AHMED PASHA FOUNTAIN 159
TAKSİM TOPÇU KIŞLASI / ARTILLERY BARRACKS 160
HARBİYE MILITARY MUSEUM 160
The history of the Military Museum 160
Military Museum Exhibition Halls 161
Public Mehter Concerts 161
NİŞANTAŞI 161
TEŞVİKİYE MOSQUE 162
CİHANGİR MOSQUE 164
YERALTI (Underground) MOSQUE 166
TOPHANE (Tophane-i Amire) 167
TOPHANE PAVILION 168
NUSRETİYE MOSQUE 168
KILIÇ ALİ PASHA COMPLEX 169

BEŞİKTAŞ-170

THE HISTORICAL DISTRICTS OF BEŞİKTAŞ   **173**

Arnavutköy...173

Aşiyan 173

Balmumcu 173

Bebek...174

Kuruçeşme 174

Ortaköy 174

Yıldız..174

DOLMABAHÇE PALACE   **175**

ISTANBUL PAINTING AND SCULPTURE MUSEUM   **180**

YAHYA EFENDİ DERVISH LODGE   **180**

BARBAROS HAYRETTİN PASHA MONUMENT   **181**

TOMB OF BARBAROS HAYRETTİN PASHA   **181**

NAVAL MUSEUM   **182**

SİNAN PASHA MOSQUE   **183**

ÇIRAĞAN PALACE   **183**

ORTAKÖY MOSQUE   **186**

RUMELİ FORTRESS	188
YILDIZ PALACE	190
YILDIZ CITY MUSEUM	194
MALTA PAVILION	196
IHLAMUR (LINDEN) PAVILION	197

ÜSKÜDAR-KADIKÖY- BEYKOZ - 200

CHAPTER 6

ÜSKÜDAR	201
KIZ KULESİ / THE MAIDEN'S TOWER	204
MİHRİMAH SULTAN MOSQUE	208
THE TOMB OF AZİZ MAHMUD HÜDAYİ	209
AYAZMA MOSQUE	212
SELİMİYE BARRACKS	212
BEYLERBEYİ MOSQUE	213
YENİ VALİDE COMPLEX	213
KARACA AHMED	214

Tombstones...214

The tomb of Sultan Karaca Ahmed.........................215

Sadeddin Efendi Tomb 215

Melek Baba Tomb 215
The tomb of Kaygusuz İbrahim Baba 215
The tomb of Hasan Efendi..215
The Hacı Faik Bey Fountain 216
İsa Agha Fountain 216
Ahmed Agha (Karaca Ahmed) Mosque..................................216
Cevriusta (Nuhkuyusu) Mosque...216
İranlılar (Persians') Mosque..216
Miskinler Tekkesi (Cüzamhane) Leprosy Hospital.....................217

ZEYNEP KAMİL HOSPITAL	218
ÇİNİLİ MOSQUE (TILED MOSQUE)	218
ÇAMLICA	218
KUZGUNCUK	220

Beylerbeyi Palace..221
Kuleli Military High School 222

KADIKÖY	226
HAYDARPAŞA TRAIN STATION	230
MARMARA UNIVERSITY MEDICAL SCHOOL	232
İSKELE MOSQUE	232
OSMANAĞA MOSQUE	233
BAHARİYE	233
FENERBAHÇE PENINSULA	234
BEYKOZ	236
ANADOLU HİSARI / ANATOLIAN FORTRESS	237
HİDİV MANOR	238
BEYKOZ MEADOW	239
KANLICA	240
KÜÇÜKSU PAVILION	240
YUŞA TEPESİ / JOSHUA'S HILL	241
ANADOLU KAVAĞI	242

PRINCES' ISLANDS - 244 **CHAPTER 7**

BÜYÜK ADA (Grand Island)	245
HAMİDİYE MOSQUE	246
HAGHIOS YORGİ MONASTERY	247
PANAYIA CHURCH	247
HESED LE AVRAAM SYNAGOGUE	247
BÜYÜKADA GREEK ORPHANAGE	247
HAGHIOS DEMETRIOS CHURCH	248
HAGHIOS NIKOLAOS MONASTERY	248
HEYBELİADA	248
DENİZ LİSESİ (Naval High School)	249
HAGHIA TRIADA MONASTERY AND CHURCH	249
HEYBELİADA SANATORIUM	250
HAGHIOS NIKOLAOS ORTHODOX CHURCH	250
BURGAZADA	251
AYYANI CHURCH	251
HAGHIOS YORGI MONASTERY AND CHURCH	252
KINALI ADA (HENNAED ISLAND)	252

EXCURSION AREAS - 254

GIANT CYPRESS TREES 255
AVCI KORU (WOODS) EXCURSION AREA 255
AYVAT BENDİ (AYVAT DAM) EXCURSION AREA 256
AYDOS EXCURSION AREA.. 256
BAHÇEKÖY NURSERY 256
AZİZ PASHA EXCURSION AREA... 256
BELGRAD FOREST- NEŞET WATER.. 257
IRMAK (RIVER) EXCURSION AREA... 257
BELGRAD FOREST – DAMS 257
FALİH RIFKI ATAY EXCURSION AREA...................................... 258
BEYKOZ – GÖKNARLIK EXCURSION AREA............................ 258
COMMANDER'S EXCURSION AREA...................................... 258
DEĞİRMENBURNU EXCURSION AREA 259
ÇATALCA MAREŞAL FEVZİ ÇAKMAK EXCURSION AREA 259
ÇİLİNGÖZ EXCURSION AREA 259
ELMASBURNU (DIAMOD POINT) EXCURSION AREA............. 259
DİLBURNU EXCURSION AREA.. 259
FATİH CHILDREN'S FOREST-PARK FOREST............................ 260
FATİH FOREST EXCURSION AREA 260

FATİH FOUNTAIN EXCURSION AREA 260
GAZİ STREET EXCURSION AREA 261
GÖKTÜRK POND EXCURSION AREA 261
İMRAHOR POND 261
GÖKTÜRK NURSERY AND EXCURSION AREA 261
HACET STREAM EXCURSION AREA 261
KAYMAKDONDURAN EXCURSION AREA 262
İNCEĞİZ EXCURSION AREA 262
KİRAZLIBENT EXCURSION AREA 262
KÖMÜRCÜ BENDİ (RESERVOIR) EXCURSION AREA 263
MARMARACIK EXCURSION AREA...................................... 263
KURT KEMERİ EXCURSION AREA....................................... 263
MİHRABAD EXCURSION AREA 263
MEHMET AKİF ERSOY EXCURSION AREA 263
ODAYERİ EXCURSION AREA 264
POLONEZKÖY (POLISH VILLAGE) NATURAL PARK 264
SAZAKÇEŞME EXCURSION AREA 264
TAYAKADIN EXCURSION AREA 265
TAŞDELEN EXCURSION AREA 265
BOSPHORUS TOUR–GOLDEN HORN TOUR 265
MUSEUMS   266
SHOPPING MALLS   267
HOSPITALS   268
AMBULANCE SERVICES   269
STATE HOSPITALS   269
TIPS FOR TRANSPORT WITHIN ISTANBUL   269
EMERGENCY NUMBERS   269
AIRPORTS   270
ATATÜRK AIRPORT   270
SABİHA GÖKÇEN AIRPORT   270
BUS TERMINALS   271
ESENLER BUS TERMINAL   271
THE HAREM BUS TERMINAL   271
EMBASSIES AND CONSULATES   272

CHAPTER 1

HISTORICAL PENINSULA

Amount of time recommended for visit: On average 3 to 4 hours for the palace, 1 hour for the Harem, and 40 minutes for the treasury.

Important Note: A separate ticket is required for the Harem section of the Palace.

TOPKAPI PALACE

HISTORICAL PENINSULA

- ◉ Museums
- ● Palaces and mansions
- ◎ Historical buildings
- ○ Historical fountains
- ● Tombs
- ℒ Mosques
- ✝ Churches

500   1.000   1.500   2.000
Metre

Topkapı Palace is open to visitors every day from 9 am till 4 pm, except on Tuesdays. On the first days of the two Muslim holidays (Ramazan Bayramı and Kurban Bayramı), the palace is open from 12 pm to 6 pm.

So, let's set off…

Follow the tour itinerary, and now look in the opposite direction from the point we are standing at; at the end of the road that passes between Haghia Sophia on our

Topkapı Palace

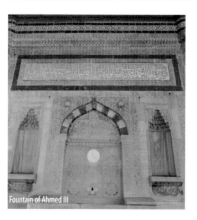
Fountain of Ahmed III

left and the Fountain of Sultan Ahmed III on our right, we can see the Imperial Gate, and the magnificent outer courtyard door of the palace. This gate opens onto the first courtyard of the palace. This door is the main door connected to the walls that surround the Palace and the tower complex.

The Fountain of Ahmed III

The Fountain of Ahmed III is situated in front of the palace and behind Haghia Sophia. It was built during the reign of Sultan Ahmed III

in the 18th century. It is famous for the 14-line poem that is inscribed on it. The most famous line of the poem is *"Drink water in the name of God, pray for Sultan Ahmed."* The niches in the walls of the fountain for birds to drink water from are indication of the Ottoman character. On the backsplash behind the taps, the phrase *Masha Allah* (What wonders Allah has willed/May Allah protect it) is inscribed. On the four sides of the fountain there are four small fountains; on each corner is a tap.

The Imperial Gate

The Gate is vaulted and arched. On both sides, there are engraved *tughras* (monograms) of sultans Mahmud II and Abdulaziz. The

spaces on the sides of the door used to be Janissary quarters. The Imperial Gate was protected by special guards. The gate gives passage to the first courtyard, which is the *Birun* section of the Palace. This part contains buildings such as a hospital, bakery, woodshed, royal mint, etc. As soon as you enter through the gate, the Haghia Irene Church draws your attention.

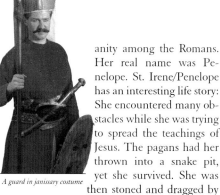

A guard in janissary costume

Haghia Irene Church

The Romans accepted Christianity after the Edict of Milan in 313 and started building churches in a number of places throughout their empire. Emperor Constantine, the founder of Constantinople, built a forum, a palace and a hippodrome that were named after him when he was rebuilding the city in the 330s. With the new religion, in place of the polytheistic Roman temples, Constantine ordered the construction of Haghia Irene, the first East Roman church. The name Haghia Irene literally means Holy Peace. More importantly, Haghia Irene is the name of the female saint who lived during the era of the establishment and spread of Christi-

anity among the Romans. Her real name was Penelope. St. Irene/Penelope has an interesting life story: She encountered many obstacles while she was trying to spread the teachings of Jesus. The pagans had her thrown into a snake pit, yet she survived. She was then stoned and dragged by horses and still she survived. At the end of these miraculous events, the pagans accepted belief in one God and acknowledged her as a saint. Later on, Emperor Constantine named the first church Haghia Irene.

The high walls surrounding Topkapı Palace, which were constructed after Mehmed II had conquered Istanbul, pass between Haghia Sophia and Haghia Irene, leaving Haghia Irene within the palace complex. Even though this church became part of the palace, Sultan Mehmet II did not convert it into a mosque. Because Sultan Mehmet II had knowledge of several Eastern and Western languages and he was aware of the story of Haghia Irene, as a sign of respect to the saint and her accomplishments he did not have the church transformed into a

Haghia Irene Church

Haghia Irene Church

Royal Mint

mosque. Instead, the church was used as storage for the most valuable gains of war, in particular, Ottoman weapons and possessions. The sultans who succeeded Sultan Mehmed II did not break this convention. In 1869, the church became known as the Sultan's Museum.

Further down the road, on your left, you can see the royal mint.

The Royal Mint

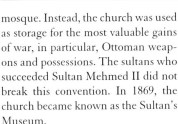

The *Darphâne* or *Darphâne-yi Hümayun*, is what today we would call the royal mint. Currently, the exhibitions pertaining to Istanbul history are not located here.

As we continue down the main road, beyond the ticket booths on the right we can see the palace entrance, *Babüsselam* (the Gate of Salutation). Topkapı Palace is situated on Sarayburnu, the most strategic and open location; this point connects the Sea of Marmara, the Black Sea and the Bosphorus. The construction of the palace started after the 1460s and ended in 1478. After the construction, new additions were made to the structure, according to the needs of following generations. The palace includes approximately 7,000 m² of land. The 5 kilometer-long walls around the Palace were drawn out by Sultan Mehmed II himself. Later, at different times, the walls were damaged by earthquakes and were renovated by Sultan Bayezid II, Sultan Süleyman the Magnificient, Sultan Murad IV and Sultan Mehmed IV. It is said that there were thirteen gates in the walls of the palace. The most famous gates are the Topkapı and Balıkhane gates. There are twenty-eight towers along the wall. The Gate of Salutation is at the end of the first courtyard, which is also known as the *Alay Meydanı* (Parade Grounds). The imperial seals of Mahmud II and Mustafa III are engraved on the gate.

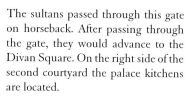

The sultans passed through this gate on horseback. After passing through the gate, they would advance to the Divan Square. On the right side of the second courtyard the palace kitchens are located.

Palace Kitchens

Food to feed 5,000 people used to be prepared in the kitchens. Particularly on ceremonial days, when the Janissaries were given their salaries, and on the fifteenth day of Ramadan, rice, soup and baklava would be cooked. A part of the kitchens was later called the *Helvahâne*. In this section, desserts, jam, syrup, and *majun* would be prepared, as well as aromatic soap. The meals for the Sultans would be prepared in a separate kitchen, known as the *Kuşhane Matbahı* or *Matbah-ı Has*. On the left side of the *Babüsselam*, you can see Beşir Agha Mosque and the Royal Stables.

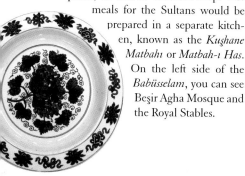

The Royal Stables

The Royal Stables are the buildings where the harnesses were kept as well as the horses of the sultans. The Harem and Divan sections are located on the left of the entrance to the Gate of Salutation.

Harem

The Harem consisted of two hundred rooms. Contrary to the common misconception, it was a training school for palace women. The sultans also lived here with their families; in addition, the palace personnel who served in the palace were trained here. This was a place where future wives of prominent politicians were educated. The Enderun, which provided training for politicians, was very similar to the Harem from this perspective. In the Harem, women were taught music, cooking, knitting and sewing, attributes of a good wife, and religious education. Among the main buildings in the Harem are the Privy Chamber

A room in the Harem

of Murad III, the library of Ahmed III, the Privy Chamber of Ahmed III (also known as the Fruit Room), the Apartments of the Crown Prince, the Apartments of the Queen Mother, the Apartments of Selim III, the Chamber of Mihrişah Sultan, I, and the chamber of Sultan Abdülhamid I. The Harem was one of the best protected sections of the Palace. Only doctors were allowed in this section in order to treat either the Sultan or the concubines. The concubines could only leave the areas under very strict precautions and they would be dressed in such a way that they could not be recognized by anyone. Even the doctors could not see the concubines, and they took the pulse of a sick concubine through a thin layer of fabric.

Imperial Council

The Ottoman *divan* was used as quarters for courtiers. It was also called the *Kubbealtı*, which means "under the dome" in reference to the great dome in the main council hall. Ottoman government officials would hold meetings here to discuss governmental affairs. Most frequently, the grand vizier (*Sadrazam*) would lead the meetings and the sultan would watch the meetings from the *kafes* (grating) right above the grand vizier. The interior of the grating could not be seen when looking up from the Divan, that is to say, no one knew if the sultan would be watching. Therefore, the council acted as if the sultan was always present in the meetings. The sultan intervened in the meeting when inappropriate subjects were discussed. The Imperial Council normally met four times a week after morning prayer until noon. Then,

the grand vizier visited the sultan in the afternoon and after the prayer he would convey the topics on the agenda. Next to the Divan, is the arms collection, which consists primarily of weapons; this is a section worth seeing. After the arms collection, we can see the Gate of Felicity. This gate, at the end of the Divan Courtyard, was witness to many historic events.

The Gate of Felicity

This gate was also known as *Ak Ağalar Kapısı* (the Gate of the White Eunuchs). This gate gives pas-

Imperial Council

sage to the Third Courtyard, which is considered to be the private property of the sultan. No one can pass this gate without the permission of the sultan. The enthronement ceremony and religious ceremonies were held in front of this gate. Also, the Sacred Standard, was entrusted to the commander setting out for war in a solemn ceremony that took place here. After entering through this gate, you can see the Audience Hall, with fountains on both sides.

Audience Hall

The council members of the council met foreign envoys or ambassadors in this hall. Also, it was here that the grand vizier conveyed the matters that were to be discussed and presented in their reports to the Sultan after the council meetings.

Right behind the Audience Hall is the library of Ahmed III, which is famous for its magnificent embroidery and architecture. On the right side of the courtyard, is the Gate of Felicity, the Enderun School, Seferli Koğuşu (the Campaign Dormitory), the Imperial Treasury, the cellar and the dormitories of the eunuchs. One of the most important sections here is the Treasury.

The Treasury

The most precious gold and silver objects of the Palace, such as the throne of Murad IV, the Topkapı Dagger (Topkapı Hançeri), which is a beautiful dagger ornamented with valuable emeralds and diamonds and the Kaşıkçı Diamond (the Spoonmak-

er's Diamond) are placed here. Furthermore, the most valued presents that were sent from India and China are exhibited in this section as well as the sections next to the treasury. The main masterpieces of the Miniature and Portrait Gallery are the portraits of the sultans. These mostly date from the 19th century. In the same section, is the *Padişah Elbiseleri Koleksiyonu* (the sultans' wardrobe collection) with a valuable collection of garments including many precious kaftans belonging to the Sultans.

The Royal Apartments

This chamber houses the Sacred Trusts, such as the Mantle of the Prophet Muhammad. The section was built at the time of Sultan Mehmed II and was altered by Selim I and Murad IV. The Sacred Trusts were brought to Istanbul by Selim I. From that day, the sultans ordered that the Holy Qur'an be read here day and night. This custom continued until the collapse of the Ottoman Empire. The Mantle of the Prophet Muhammad, his sword, his blessed footprints, and a hair of his beard (*Sakal-ı Şerif*) can all be found among the Sacred Trusts; there are also some belongings of Companions and other Prophets who lived before his time. The oldest building of the palace, Fatih Köşkü (Fatih Pavilion) is located in this part of the palace. The apartments overlooks the Bosphorus.

The Imperial Terrace

The main structures of the Fourth Courtyard are the Imperial Terrace, the Marble Pavilion, the large pool on the lower terrace and the Sofa Pavilion. The *Revan Köşkü* (Revan

Pavilion) and the *Bağdat Köşkü* (Baghdad Pavilion), constructed during the reign of Sultan Murad IV, are also located in the courtyard. The adornments of these two structures are similar. The main difference is that the decorations of the golden dome are decorated with plasterwork on the Revan Pavilion while the Baghdad Pavilion has leather decorations. In addition, the Circumcision Room, Chief Physician's Room, the Sofa Mosque, the Mecidiye Pavilion, the İftariye Bower, and Esvap Chamber are other impressive structures in the Fourth Courtyard.

Circumcision Room

The Circumcision Room has a small annex at the back. It was built by Sultan İbrahim (1840–1648). The interior and the exterior are veneered with tiles. Most of the tiles date back to the 15th, 16th and 17th centuries. In addition to the blue and white tiles on the walls, there are fountains that face one another. The room takes its name from the time it was used during the circumcision of the sons of Sultan Ahmed III.

Revan Pavilion

This pavilion was built to commemorate the conquest of Yerevan by Murad IV in 1636. The pavilion is octagonal in shape and has three balconies. The fact that the pavilion is also known as the *Sarık Odası* (Turban Room) in some of the Ottoman sources is related to the fact that the turbans of the Ottoman Sultan were safeguarded here. Also, the Sacred Trusts used to be transferred to the Revan Pavilion when the Has Oda was cleaned every year during the month of Ramadan.

Baghdad Pavilion

This pavilion was built to commemorate the conquest of Baghdad by Murad IV in 1639. It is surrounded by a spacious portico that is paneled in marble. The pillars rest on brass circles. The tiles on the exterior are turquoise and navy blue, while the window frames are star-shaped and the motifs on the dome are in the shape of pomegranate flowers. Formerly there was a red ball hanging within a gold embroidered cage. There are Qur'anic verses on the tiles of the interior. The doors and the cupboards are inlaid with mother of pearl and tortoiseshell.

İftariye Bower

This was constructed by İbrahim I in 1640. The bower is an exceptional place for a view of Istanbul. It is covered by a metal dome that rests on four pillars. The sultan is reported to have broken his fast under this bower during Ramadan, hence, the name (*iftar* being the word for the meal at the end of the fast). When religious holidays fell in the summer, the sultans accepted visitors in this bower and watched athletic competitions from here.

Baghdad Pavilion

CROSS-SECTION: TOPKAPI PALACE & HAREM

Apartments of the
Holy Mantle

Baghdad Pavilion

Revan Pavilion

Imperial Apartments

Ağ

Sofa Mosq

Circumcision
Room

Mecidiye
Pavilion

İmperial
Terrace

İftariye
Bower

Apartments
of the
Favorites

Twin
Pavilions

Harem

Queen Mother's
Courtyard

Pavilion of
Osman III

Terrace of
Osman III

Royal Treasury

que

Audience Hall

Library of
Ahmed III

Display of armor
and arms

Royal
kitchens

arem
ospital

Tower of
Justice

Imperial Council

Harem entrance

Dormitory for
Halberdiers

The Chief Physician's Room

As the 1.7 meter-thick ground floor walls and the depictions in ancient gravures suggest, the structure was originally built as a tower. In its present form, it was used for the preparation and the safeguarding of medications. Another name for the building was the Tower of the Başlala (Head Tutor), because the chief physician worked under the command of the Başlala, who was responsible for the education of the sultan's children.

Mustafa Pasha Pavilion

This pavilion was built by Kara Mustafa Pasha of Merzifon in the 17th century while he was serving as grand vizier. This is the reason why it is known as the Mustafa Pasha Pavilion. When it was renovated during the reign of Ahmed III in 1704, the epigraph referred to the building as the Sofa Pavilion.

Mecidiye Pavilion

The Mecidiye Pavilion is located on the right of the Fourth Courtyard, on the lower ground. The pavilion comprises another section of the Esvap Chamber and the Sofa Mosque. The Mecidiye Pavilion, along with the neighboring Esvap Chamber, was constructed and furnished in the Rococo style in 1859 by Sultan Abdülmecid I. The entrance to the pavilion is through three different wooden doors. The door in the middle leads to the basement. The walls of the pavilions are decorated with portraits of the sultans, signed by foreign artists, with gilded mirrors and furnaces. There are chandeliers on the ceiling with 20–30 branches each.

Dormitory for Halberdiers

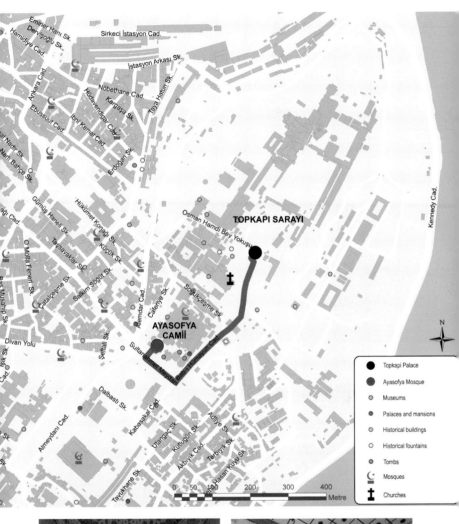

TOPKAPI SARAYI

AYASOFYA CAMİİ

Osman Hamdi Bey Yokuşu

Sirkeci İstasyon Cad.

İstasyon Arkası Sk.

Emine Hanı Sk.
Dervişoğlu Sk.
Hamidiye Cad.
Ankara Cad.
Nöbethane Cad.
Hüdavendigar Cad.
Kargaşa Sk.
Taya Hatun Sk.
Ebussuut Cad.
İbni Kemal Cad.
Erdoğan Sk.

Gümüş Haneli Sk.
Hükümet Konağı Sk.
Taşşsavaklar Sk.
Küçük Sk.
Molla Fenari Sk.
Salkım Söğüt Sk.
Çatalçeşme Sk.
Alemdar Cad.
Caferiye Sk.
Soğukçeşme Sk.
Seftali Sk.
Sultanahmet Meydanı
Babıhümayün Cad.

Divan Yolu

Dalbastı Sk.

Atmeydanı Cad.
Kabasakal Cad.
Utangaç Sk.
Kutuğun Sk.
Adliye Sk.
Akbıyık Cad.
Terbıyık Sk.
İbni Hasan Kuyu Sk.
Tavukhane Sk.

Kennedy Cad.

N

●	Topkapi Palace
●	Ayasofya Mosque
◎	Museums
●	Palaces and mansions
◉	Historical buildings
○	Historical fountains
●	Tombs
☾	Mosques
✝	Churches

0 50 100 200 300 400
Metre

Library of Ahmed III

Audience Hall

HAGHIA SOPHIA

Amount of time recommended for visit: **1 hour**

Haghia Sophia, an unequalled masterpiece and symbol of Istanbul, was erected by Constantinus, the son of the founder of the city, the East Roman Emperor Constantine, in the second half of the 4th century. During a revolt in 404, the first church was set on fire. The second structure was erected on a bigger scale and opened with a great ceremony in 415. In 532, the bloody Nika revolt led to the death of many people and the destruction of many buildings. During this time Haghia Sophia was burnt down. Emperor Justinian, who suppressed the revolt with difficulty, took action to build a place of worship which "no people have seen since the time of Adam and no one will ever see." The construction of the greatest church in the Christian World began on the relics of the former basilica in 532; it was completed in 5 years and opened with a ceremony in 537. The emperor liberally awarded the architects, Isidore of Miletus and Anthemius of Tralles. The construction of the dome was designed according to Roman architecture. The dome, being an eastern architectural structure, is used in Haghia Sophia, and makes it a building that is a product of a cultural synthesis between Roman, Middle Eastern, Mesopotamian, and Asian architecture. Some erroneously translate the name Haghia Sophia (Aya Sofya) as Saint Sophia; however, the church was not dedicated to any person or saint, but to Christianity. The name translates as Holy Wisdom.

The Emperor, who could not hide his excitement during the opening ceremony, dived into the church with his chariot, and he started thanking God and declaiming his superiority to Prophet Solomon, thinking that he had built a greater place of worship. Despite being unprecedented to that date, the structure had some vital flaws. The

CROSS-SECTION OF HAGHIA SOPHIA

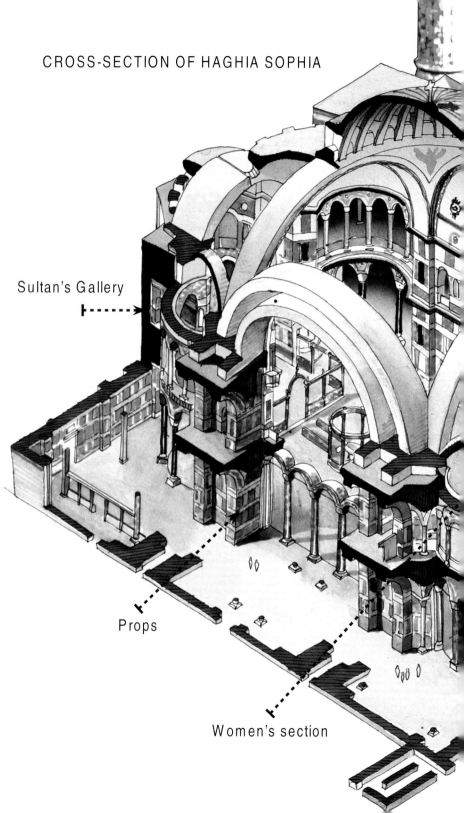

Sultan's Gallery

Props

Women's section

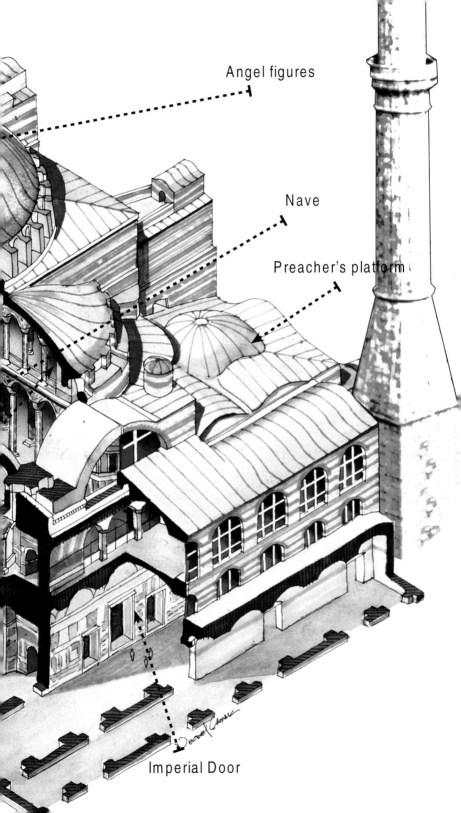

Angel figures

Nave

Preacher's platform

Imperial Door

most important one of these was the size of the dome and the pressure that it applied to its sides. The architectural knowledge, which directed the pressure to the base of the structure, was not yet developed at this time. The walls were forced to open outward and as a result the dome collapsed in 558. A second dome was built higher and smaller; despite this, half of the second dome also collapsed in both the 10th and then the 14th centuries.

A great deal of money had to be spent on Haghia Sophia for it to survive the centuries. For instance, when Sultan Mehmed II conquered the city in 1453, Haghia Sophia was in a state of ruin, as the East Roman Empire at the time did not have the finances to take care of it. After the conquest, it was renovated and converted into a mosque. The buttress walls, added by the great architect Mimar Sinan in the 16th century, the renovation by the Fossati brothers in the middle of the 19th century, renovations in the 1930s, and the iron enclosure of the dome are among the most important restoration attempts. Haghia Sophia served the people of the same God as a church for 1093 years and a mosque for 480 years before it was converted to a museum between 1930 and 1935. The mosaics, which have had the layer of plaster, applied by the Ottomans, removed, are among the most important East Roman works of art.

The museum entrance within the

courtyard is through the original door, still being used after so many centuries. Near the entrance it is possible to see the remains of the former structure. The outer narthex is connected to the inner narthex via five doors, while the inner narthex is connected to the main section by nine doors. The high middle door is the emperor's entrance. The mosaic panel on the top was made in the 9th century. The figureless mosaics on the ceiling of the inner narthex are originals from the Justinian Era. In the main section of the building, the visitor is welcome by a magnificent space. The effect of the dome can be sensed from

dome rests have four angel figures with covered faces. The area of Haghia Sophia is 7,570 square meters.

The capitals of the Haghia Sophia columns are characteristic and classical elements of 6th century Byzantine architecture. The deeply carved marble creates a play of light and shadow. The porphyry columns in the corners, the middle columns made out of green marble from Thessalonica, and the capitals which are made out of white marble with rich engravings are impressive. One can imagine Haghia Sophia in its original form as a church or as a mosque, taking one away from the empty museum of today.

During the last phase of the Ottoman Empire Haghia Sophia was frequently used on special occasions. The structure has managed to survive until today as a result of Ottoman tolerance. As a result of the Islamic belief system, which bans images of living things, the Muslims coated the mosaics and the images with plaster, but they never destroyed them. Haghia Sophia was converted into a mosque on the day after the conquest of the city. The first Friday prayer was led by Sultan Mchmed II himself. In order to make the building suitable as a mosque, there was a great deal of work to be carried out to clean the dilapidated building. A *mihrab* (central prayer niche) and a *minbar* (pulpit) were added at later dates.

the first moment one enters the building. It hangs over the whole structure and encloses it. The walls and the ceilings are covered with mosaics and an explosion of color. The three tones of mosaics are an indication of three periods of restoration that the dome underwent. With the greatness of its diameter and height, this was the largest dome of its time and currently is still one of the greatest. Due to the restorations, the dome is not a full circle. The diameter from north to south measures 31.87 meters, while that from east to west is 30.87 meters. The dome is 55–60 meters high. The four pillars on which the

Four minarets were added to the mosque after a certain period of time. The first minaret is on the east side of the mosque and is reddish in color. It was built by Sultan Mehmed II. The minaret that is in the direction of Topkapı Palace was built by Beyazid II. The other minarets were constructed by the architect Sinan on the order of Murad III. With the restoration work by Sinan all of the minarets began to support the central location of the mosque simultaneously. That is to say, the minarets were attached to the foundation stone, and the collapse of one of the minarets could trigger the collapse of the main dome. Many Ottoman Sultans have made contributions to this structure.

The hanging calligraphic inscriptions of "Allah," "Muhammad," "Abu Bakr," "Umar," "Uthman," "Ali," "Hasan," and "Hüseyin," written on leather, measuring 7.5 meters in diameter, were executed by the famous calligrapher and prominent statesman Kazasker Mustafa Pasha, who lived during the reign of Mahmud II; these signify the importance of Haghia Sophia as a mosque.

Two marble amphorae dating from the Hellenistic period were brought from Bergama in the 16th century and set up on either side of the inside of the door. In the northern nave one can find the "sweating column." In the middle of the column, framed in bronze, is a hole. People considered the hole miraculous and would rub their thumbs over it while making a wish. The column is, therefore, also known as the "miraculous pillar," the "crying pillar," or "the pillar in which Khidr (a holy person) placed his finger."

The famous Ottoman traveler Evliya Çelebi wrote that when Haghia Sophia was being converted into a mosque, a mixture of soil from Mecca and zamzam water was added to the material for plastering the wall in front of this column. The dampness of this mixture caused the column to sweat.

According to another saying, when the church was transformed into a mosque, the qibla was slightly off from the direction of Ka'aba. It is said that Khidr came and corrected the direction by holding onto this column. Thus, it is believed that the hole and the shapes that resemble a handprint around the hole, belong to him. As a result of the importance of this building, many government officials and local notables are buried in the gardens, as well as sultans. The tombs of Mustafa I, Sultan İbrahim, Sultan Selim II, Sultan Murad III and Sultan Mehmed III are located here.

Crying Pillar

THE BLUE MOSQUE AND ITS COMPLEX

Amount of time recommended for visit: **1 hour**

At the exit of Topkapı Palace, the Blue Mosque greets us like a depiction of Ottoman glory. The Blue Mosque (Sultanahmet Mosque) was built between 1609 and 1616 by the imperial architect Sedefkar Mehmet Agha, a pupil of the famous architect Sinan. The construction of the mosque lasted 7 years. It is said that Sultan Ahmed I, who broke the ground for the foundations, carried many rocks to be used in the construction of the mosque. Sultan Ahmed wanted the mosque to be built across from Haghia Sophia. The grand opening ceremony was attended by the great sheikh Aziz Mahmud Hudai. When going from the Sea of Marmara to the Bosphorus, Topkapı Palace, Haghia Sophia and the Blue Mosque complete a united front; this skyline has become associated with Istanbul. The mosque consisted of the Royal Pavilion (Hünkâr Kasrı), the *imarethâne-i amire* (charitable establishment), *sübyan mektebi* (primary school),

darüşşifa (hospital), *darülkurra* (school of reciters) *hamam* (Turkish baths), water fountains, *sipahi* (cavalry) chambers, and the shops. Most of these structures have been torn down. The remaining parts of the mosque complex consist of the tomb and a *madrasa*.

The interior of the Blue Mosque is more attention-grabbing in its design and decorations than the exterior archi-

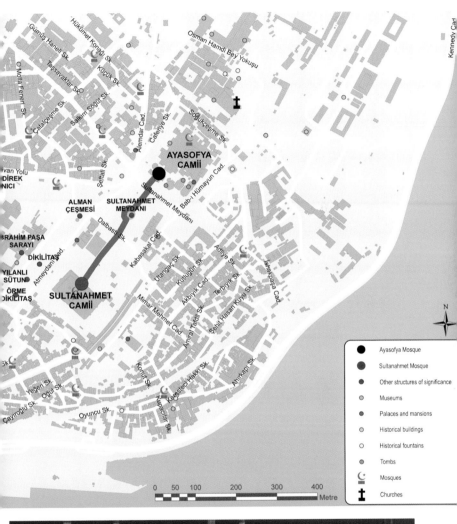

Kennedy Cad

Gümüş Haneli Sk.
Hükümet Konağı Sk.
Osman Hamdi Bey Yokuşu
Taşsavaklar Sk.
Küçük Sk.
O Molla Fenerî Sk.
Çatalçeşme Sk.
Salkım Söğüt Sk.
Alemdar Cad.
Caferiye Sk.
Soğukçeşme Sk.

AYASOFYA CAMİİ

Şeftali Sk.
İvan Yolu
DİREK NİCİ

Sultanahmet Meydanı
Bab-ı Hümayun Cad.

ALMAN ÇEŞMESİ
SULTANAHMET MEYDANI

Dalbastı Sk.

İBRAHİM PAŞA SARAYI

Kabasakal Cad.

DİKİLİTAŞ
Atmeydanı Cad.

YILANLI SÜTUN
Utangaç Sk.
Adliye Sk.

Akbıyık Cad.
Kutlugün Sk.
Tevkiyik Sk.
Sehit Hasan Kuyu Sk.
Ishakpaşa Cad.

ÖRME DİKİLİTAŞ

SULTANAHMET CAMİİ

Mimar Mehmet Cad.
Amiral Tafdil Sk.

N

Yeğen Sk.
Oğul Sk.
Konut Sk.
Çayıroğlu Sk.
Oyuncu Sk.
Kapıcılar Sk.
Keresteci Hakkı Sk.
Ahırkapı Sk.

- ● Ayasofya Mosque
- ● Sultanahmet Mosque
- ● Other structures of significance
- ○ Museums
- ● Palaces and mansions
- ◎ Historical buildings
- ○ Historical fountains
- ● Tombs
- ☾ Mosques
- ✝ Churches

0   50   100   200   300   400
                                    Metre

tecture. The main entrance to the main building is via a flight of marble stairs. The main door is covered by a dome and is embellished with epigraphs. The door that opens into the center is known as the *Zincirli Kapı* (Chained Door). Reputedly, the sultan pulled a chain over the door so that everyone would have to bend down below the chain to enter, as a sign of respect for the house of God.

The courtyard of the mosque is quite large and paved with marble. In the middle of the yard, there is a pool covered by a dome. The mosque is the only one in Turkey that has six minarets. Four minarets, which are of the same height, have three balconies each, and are attached to the four main corners of the mosque. The other two minarets with two balconies are shorter in height. The minarets are fluted. Up until the time of Sultan Ahmed every sultan had a mosque built in his

name with the number of balconies corresponding to their place in the dynasty; Sultan Ahmed was the sixteenth sultan of the Empire, therefore, he constructed the mosque with 16 balconies. However, constructing the Blue Mosque with six minarets posed a problem for the sultan; the Masjid al-Haram, the mosque that surrounds the Ka'aba in Mecca, also had six minarets. As the sultan thought that his mosque having the same number could be interpreted as a sign of disrespect, he had another minaret added to the Masjid al-Haram so that it would remain superior.

The main dome of the mosque is supported by four semi-domes. The central dome is covered with tiles and supported by octagonal columns, known as "elephant feet." The interior of the mosque is illuminated by two hundred and sixty windows, and as a consequence is quite

bright. It has a spacious interior which is 70 meters long and 68 meters wide. The diameter of the dome is 23.5 meters and it is 43 meters high. The interior is covered by 21,043 blue tiles with plant motifs, such as roses, hyacinths, carnations, pomegranates and plum flowers, as well as branches and bunches of grapes. The intention was a naturalistic appearance. The tiles were brought from İznik and Kütahya. In particular, the gilded tiles on the *Cümle Kapısı* (Main Gate) and the *Hünkar Mahfili* (Sultan's Gallery) are great works of art. The mosque is known in English as the Blue Mosque due to the large amount of blue in the interior.

The *mihrab* (central prayer niche) and *minbar* (main pulpit) are exquisite examples of marble carving. The window and door shutters are wonderfully decorated with mother-of-pearl inlay and the *vaiz kürsüsü* (pulpit) is an example of woodwork. On both sides of the *mihrab* there are large chandeliers and a piece

from the *Hajar al-Aswad*. The *Hünkâr Kasrı* is the first of its kind. The entrance to this pavilion, which juts out from the building, has two rooms. The entrance to the second storey is via an elevated platform. The *minbar* is gilded and is made of Marmara marble, and high quality material was used. The sultan would pray the first Friday prayer after ascending to the throne either in the Blue Mosque or in Haghia Sophia. The Blue Mosque was greatly admired by visitors to the city and became one of the symbols of Turkish-Islamic architecture.

Sultanahmet Square

> Amount of time recommended for visit: **30 minutes**

Sultanahmet Square used to be an arena for chariot races, and was the sporting and social centre of Constantinople in the Byzantine Period. In 532, more than 30,000 people are estimated to have

been killed here during the Nika revolt. The square, which maintained its tradition as a hippodrome during the Ottoman Empire, houses three columns that were erected in the East Roman period.

The Egyptian Obelisk

Amount of time recommended for visit: **5 minutes**

The Obelisk was brought from its former location in front of the temple of Luxor in Egypt. It was brought by Emperor Theodosius I by sea and was erected in its current location in the Hippodrome in Constantinople in 390 A.D. Originally, the obelisk was erected for Pharaoh Thutmosis III in 1700 B.C. The tall obelisk, approximately 20 meters high, is made of pink granite and covered on all four sides by hieroglyphic pictograms which recount the glories of Pharaoh Thutmosis III and depict the ancient Egyptian god Amon–Ra. At the very bottom is a marble base which has epigraphs in Greek and Latin while there are scenes retelling the erection of the stone pillar and chariot races on the

other two sides. The obelisk is the oldest monument in Istanbul and is located exactly in the middle of the Hippodrome. The reason for its relocation in Constantinople was, in addition to decorative purposes, to demonstrate the dominance of the East Roman Empire and its superiority over Egypt. One of the two stone pillars in the Hippodrome was brought from Greece, while the other was Roman. The reason for erecting the pillars here was to show that the source of science and philosophy was Byzantium, that is, the superiority of Rome over the former Greek and Egyptian civilizations.

The Serpentine Column

Amount of time recommended for visit: **5 minutes**

This is a unique work of art in Istanbul. The serpentine column consists of three intertwined snakes. Their triple heads once supported a golden tripod. Thirty-one Greek city-states defeated the Persians in the 5th century B.C., and they had the bronze

Egyptian Obelisk

BLUE MOSQUE CROSS-SECTION

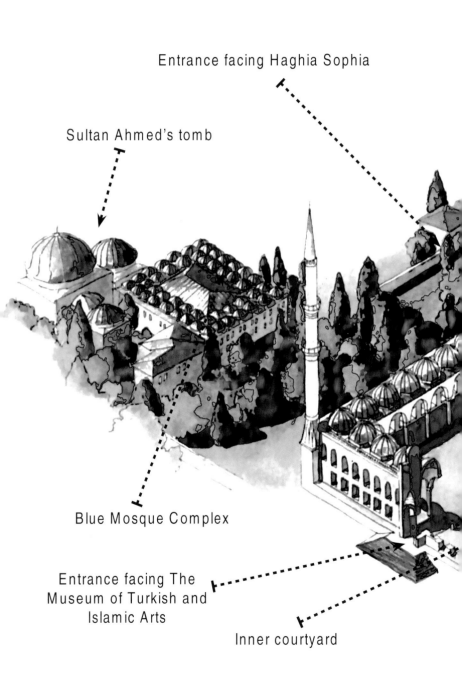

Entrance facing Haghia Sophia

Sultan Ahmed's tomb

Blue Mosque Complex

Entrance facing The
Museum of Turkish and
Islamic Arts

Inner courtyard

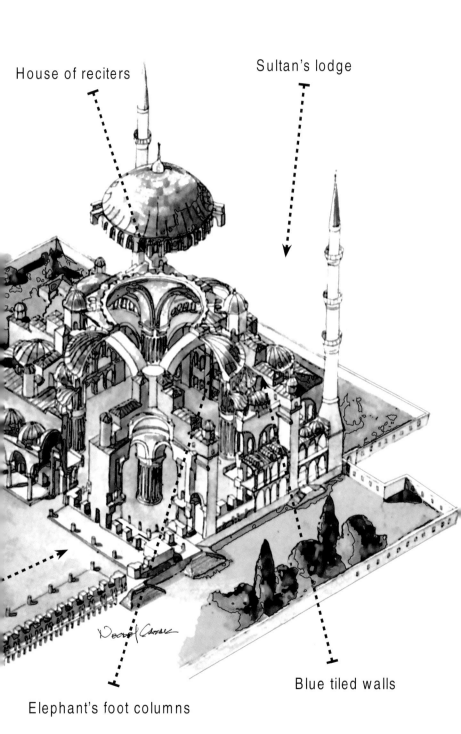

House of reciters

Sultan's lodge

Elephant's foot columns

Blue tiled walls

The calligraphic figure with the names of the Ten Companions of the Prophet, Sultan Ahmed Mosque.

column built from Persian weapons that were melted down. The 8-meter high column was originally placed

next to the altar of Apollo in Delphi. It was later relocated in the middle of the Hippodrome in Constantinople by Constantine I in 324 A.D. The triple snakeheads were in place until the 7th century, but later these were lost. One of the pieces is located in the Istanbul Archaeological Museum.

The Stone Obelisk

Amount of time recommended
for visit: **5 minutes**

The exact date of the construction of this column is unknown. In the 10th century it was covered with gilded bronze and copper plaques by Constantine VII. This obelisk had sunshades attached to it to protect the spectators who had come to watch athletic competitions in the Hippodrome. On competition days, the sunblinds would be opened to provide shade.

However, during the Fourth Crusade in 1204, the gilded bronze plaques were destroyed and looted.

Museum of Turkish and Islamic Arts

Amount of time recommended
for visit: **1 hour**

The İbrahim Paşa Palace has been used as the Museum of Turkish and Islamic Arts since 1983. It is the only palace to have survived, except for the palaces of the sultans. The elevated structure on a vaulted base envelops three sides of the terrace. Stairs lead up to the first part of the museum from the terrace. In the rooms and the lobbies very rare works of art from various countries in the Islamic world are exhibited. Among the most precious samples are fine collections of stonework, terracotta, metal and ceramic objects, glassware, calligraphy, and manuscripts. In the large display section of the grand hall, there are many samples of ancient hand-woven Turkish carpets. This unprecedented collection is the richest collection of carpets in the world. Rare Seljuk carpets from the 13th century and samples belonging to later centuries are displayed with care. The lower section under the carpet section is the ethnographic section, where one can see artifacts of the traditional Turkish way of life of the last few centuries.

The Binbirdirek (1001 Columns) Cistern

Amount of time recommended
for visit: **30 minutes**

The Binbirdirek Cistern is located to the west of Sultan Ahmed Square. After having been cleaned out in recent years, the cistern was connected to the road that lies alongside it, via

chus before being converted into a mosque. The lower columns inside the edifice bear an inscription that state that Emperor Justinian I dedicated the temple to Saint Sergius and Saint Bacchus. The church was transformed into a mosque during the reign of Sultan Beyazid II by the Chief Eunuch Hüseyin Agha, and a minaret was added. The tomb of Hüseyin Agha is in the garden on the left of the mosque. Opposite the mosque, there are a few workshops where examples of traditional Turkish crafts and decorative gifts are produced and sold. One can visit the workshops and have a tea break.

The German Fountain

> Amount of time recommended for visit: **5 minutes**

This fountain was a present from the German emperor Wilhelm II to Sultan Abdülhamid II in 1898 as a commemoration of Turkish-German friendship. It was transported, piece by piece, from Germany and installed in Istanbul. Both of the rulers were present at the opening ceremony. The dome is covered with gold mosaics. In Ottoman times, sweet drinks would be dispensed to the public from the fountain on religious holidays.

an aqueduct. The cistern, which has been converted into a museum, measures 64 x 56. It dates back to the 4th century A.D., and was built during the reign of Constantine the Great. It is recorded that it was built by a man called Philoxenos. Out of the original 224 columns, only 212 have survived. Today the original floor can only be seen in the center of the pool area, which was made during the restoration. Currently, the cistern hosts a number of small sale booths and exhibition stands.

Little Haghia Sophia and the Workshops

> Amount of time recommended for visit: **15 minutes**

The structure of the Little Haghia Sophia Mosque was built by the Byzantine emperor Justinian. It is located at the end of Little Haghia Sophia Street between Cankurtaran and Kadirga in the Eminönü District of Istanbul. This mosque was formerly the Church of St. Sergius and Bac-

THE BASILICA CISTERN

Amount of time recommended for visit: **45 minutes**

One thing the Basilica Cistern proves is that the old maxim still holds true: Nothing is how it seems. Despite the modest outer appearance with its small entrance, the cistern astounds visitors with its palatial interior. It lies next to the left side of Sultanahmet Square and at the southwestern end of Haghia Sophia. As a result of its magnificent atmosphere and the large number of columns, the cistern is known as the *Yerebatan Sarnici* (Sunken Cistern) in Turkey, but was called the Basilica Cistern in Byzantium. It was constructed by the Byzantine Emperor Justinian I (527–565). Prior to construction, there was a basilica in the same location in the 3rd or the 4th century; this was used for scientific and artistic activities as well as to carry out business and legal affairs. Several churches were built in the location of the basilica, which burned down. Eventually, during the restoration of Haghia Sophia after the Nika Revolt in 532 A.D., Justinian I constructed this cistern. It took 7,000 slaves to construct the Basilica Cistern. The cistern is connected by the 971-meter-long Valens Aqueduct, (Bozdogan) named after the emperor who constructed it in 368 to the 115.45 meter long Maglova Aqueduct, constructed by Constantine I. The water from the cistern was brought from the Belgrade

Medusa's head

Forest. The cistern is a large rectangular structure, measuring 140 meters long and 70 meters wide. The cistern, into which you descend via 52 stone steps, has 336 columns, each of which is 9 meters tall. They are arranged 4.80 meters apart from one another in 12 rows of 28 columns each. The columns rise above the water and look like an infinite and en-

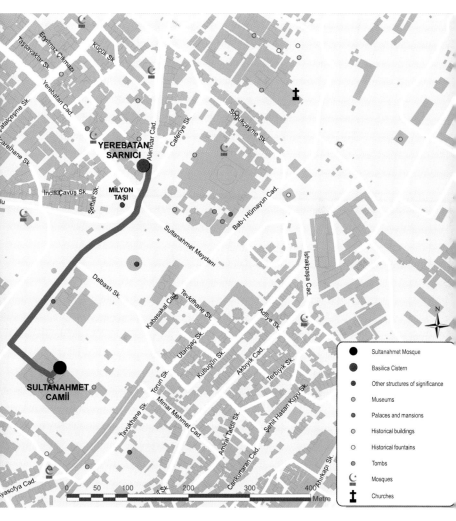

●	Sultanahmet Mosque
●	Basilica Cistern
●	Other structures of significance
◎	Museums
●	Palaces and mansions
◎	Historical buildings
○	Historical fountains
◎	Tombs
☾	Mosques
✝	Churches

chanting forest; it is this appearance that captivates visitors at first sight. The weight of the ceiling is distributed onto the columns via cross-shaped vaults and spherical arches. Many of the columns are built from various kinds of marble, which are said to have been taken from older structures or chipped from granite blocks. While most of the columns were constructed in one piece, some consist of two pieces, one put on top of the other. The capitals are varied. While 98 are Corinthian, some others are Doric in style.

The brick walls of the cistern, 4.80 m thick, and the brick floor were made water-resistant with a thick layer of Khorasan mortar.

This cistern is located on an area that measures 9,800 m^2 and has the capacity to hold 100,000 tons of water. The great majority of the columns in the cistern, excluding a few squared or grooved ones, are cylindrical in shape. The columns that have been engraved with depictions known as "hen's eye," "slanting branches" and "tears" are very interesting. According to tradition, the columns with figures that resemble tears were erected in remembrance of the slaves who died during the construction and to recount their tragedy throughout the centuries.

The two Medusa heads, used as pedestals, in the north-west corner of the cistern at the bottom of two columns are precious examples of statuary from the Roman period. The cistern, from the time of its construction until today, has undergone many restorations, two of which took place during the Ottoman period. The first of these was carried out by the architect Mehmed Agha of Kayseri in 1723 during the reign of Ahmed III. The second grand restoration occurred in the 19th century during the time of Sultan Abdülhamid II (1876–1909).

The Basilica Cistern provided water to the great palace of the Byzantine emperors, which was located on a large area of Sarayburnu; it was also used for a while after the conquest of Constantinople by the Ottomans. For instance, the gardens of Topkapı Palace were irrigated with the water from the cistern. Yet, it is understood that the Ottomans, who preferred running water to still water, did not use the cistern after they had established their own water facilities.

IN THE VICINITY OF THE CISTERN

Million Stone: This was erected by the East Roman Emperor Constantine I. The stone was placed in the center of the city as a mark from which all distances of the Byzantine Empire were measured. This point was also accepted as the center of the earth. In order to make calculations of distance easy, similar stones were erected along the Roman roads. Thus, the Million Stone marks the central point of an extensive road network. Next to the stone is a water level, one of many that were placed along the roads every 60–200 meters. They were used as relief valves to relieve the compressed air in the water that was being carried. (Time Allowed: 1 minute)

CAFÉ / RESTAURANT

Tarihi Sultanahmet Köftecisi, (212) 520 0566
Küçük Ayasofya Cafe

BOOK STORE

Kaynak Kültür Merkezi (212) 519 3911

A two-minute walk along Alay Köşkü Street, right opposite the Gülhane Park's entrance, will take you to Kaynak Kültür Merkezi book center and café (on the left). The foreign editions section provides a wide selection of quality books on Turkish and Islamic culture in English and other major world languages.

GÜLHANE PARK

Amount of time recommended for visit: **1 hour**

Gülhane Park used to be one of the royal gardens attached to Topkapı Palace. Today, it takes pride in housing the Islamic Science and Technology Historical Museum.

The museum features replicas of significant inventions and discoveries by Muslim scientists covering a long period between the 8th and 16th centuries. The items range from instruments used in the fields of astronomy, geography, chemistry and geometry to optics, medicine, architecture, physics and war technologies. The replicas are based on information found in manuscripts by the Muslim scientists who invented them. The museum is the fruit of extensive studies by Fuat Sezgin, who, in 1982, founded the Institute for Arabic and Islamic Studies under Frankfurt Goethe University. Presenting concrete evidence of the often undervalued contributions of Islam to human civilization, the museum is a must-see for all visitors.

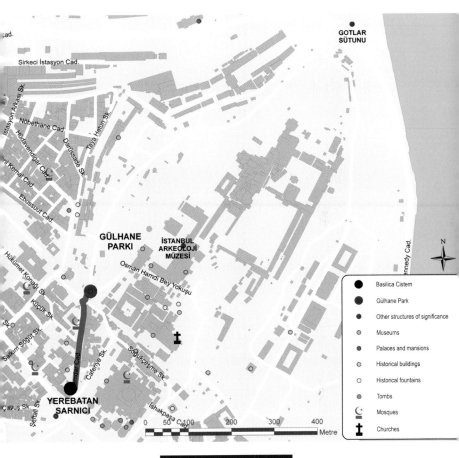

GOTLAR SÜTUNU

Sirkeci İstasyon Cad.

GÜLHANE PARKI

İSTANBUL ARKEOLOJİ MÜZESİ

Osman Hamdi Bey Yokuşu

YEREBATAN SARNICI

İshakpaşa Cad.

0 50 100 200 300 400 Metre

Basilica Cistern
Gülhane Park
Other structures of significance
Museums
Palaces and mansions
Historical buildings
Historical fountains
Tombs
Mosques
Churches

N

IN THE VICINITY

The Istanbul Archeological Museum

Amount of time recommended for visit: **2 hours**

The museum was founded in 1891 as *Müze-i Humayun* (Imperial Museum). Two side wings were added in 1902 and 1908, and in 1991, on the 100th anniversary of its establishment, the museum was enlarged with a new section. The architect of the original building was Alexander Vallaury. On the right side are located the Sculpture Halls of the Antique Age. Unique examples of sculpture from antiquity, stretching up until the end of the Roman era, are exhibited in the halls.

The first hall contains antique carvings and reliefs; these are followed by treasures from the Persian reign in Anatolia; the Kenan Erim Hall is where relics from Aphrodisias are displayed; the room known as "The Three Marble Cities of Ana-

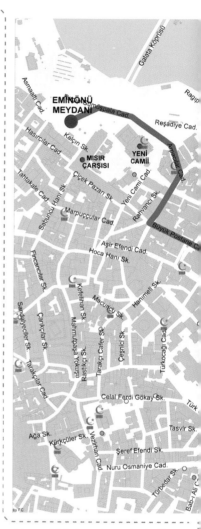

tolia" is where works from Ephesus, Millets and Aphrodisias are found; there are also different sections where visitors can see works from Hellenistic and Roman periods.

To the left of the entrance, after the gift and bookshops, there is the room dedicated to the founder Osman Hamdi. Then, there are the halls which contain the works of art he personally discovered in the royal necropolis at Sayda. The first three sarcophagi belong to the family of the king of Saydan, Tabnit. The unique Lycian sarcophagus and the Satrap sarcophagus are also in this room.

The next section contains the world famous sarcophagus believed to have belonged to Alexander the Great and the Sarcophagus of the Mourning Women. The four sides of this sarcophagus have decorations in relief depicting scenes of the war between the Macedonians and the Persians and hunting scenes.

On the side wall of the entrance to the new annex, the front side of the Temple of Athena in Assos has been reproduced in its exact dimensions.

The Local Cultures of Istanbul section is the first hall in which exquisite artifacts from various ages found during excavations in the vicinity of the city are exhibited in a modern setting. A room containing works of art from the Byzantine period is also located here, as well as Istanbul through the Ages. On the upper floors and in the showroom opposite is the exhibition, Anatolia through the Ages and that of Troy, which contains modern works of art, and the exhibition The Civilizations of Anatolia and Neighboring Countries, which is a chronologically arranged display of works from Palestine, Syria and Cyprus.

The Column of the Goths: This is the oldest monument in the city, having survived intact from the Roman period. It is located in Gülhane Park, towards Sarayburnu. This 15-meter-tall monolithic marble column on an elevated base was erected in the 4th

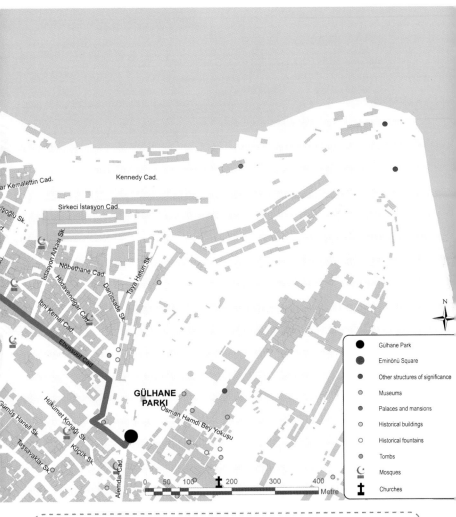

Kennedy Cad.

Sirkeci İstasyon Cad.

GÜLHANE PARKI

Osman Hamdi Bey Yokuşu

⬤	Gülhane Park
⬤	Eminönü Square
●	Other structures of significance
◦	Museums
●	Palaces and mansions
⊙	Historical buildings
○	Historical fountains
◦	Tombs
☾	Mosques
✝	Churches

0   50   100   200   300   400   Metre

century A.D. It has a Corinthian style capital with a coat of arms depicting eagles in relief. It is known as the Column of the Goths due to the epigraph on the column which relates a victory against the Goths.

Sarayburnu: The end of Gülhane Park leads to Sarayburnu (Palace Point), a location that has been witness to many historic moments. The Ottoman navy used to greet the sultans at this point, and military victories were celebrated with cannon salutes. Currently, it is open to the public and is a favorite site for visitors with its cafes and tea gardens.

CAFÉ / RESTAURANT

The tea gardens of Sarayburnu

EMİNÖNÜ

Amount of time recommended for visit: **2 hours**

E minönü used to be one of Istanbul's three centers (the other two being Eyüp and Üsküdar); all three formed the legal and administrative framework of Istanbul during the Ottoman Era. Since the earliest times of history, Eminönü has been known as a region of trade and ports. The district's name, Eminönü ("emin" meaning secure) reflects the fact that Maritime Customs and Maritime Security were located here. Eminönü contains some of the most important historical works from the Ottoman and Islamic Civilizations.

Eminönü was an important site during the Byzantine era as well as for the Ottomans. In the Ottoman era, the district was one of the main export and import centers. The district was also an important administrative center as it housed Topkapı Palace as well as the Bab-ı Âli (the Sublime Porte). Even though Eminönü has not lost its importance, its appearance has changed a lot. Sirkeci and the wharf located at the entrance to the Golden Horn are extremely crowded areas. Still, most people start the Bosphorus tour from Sirkeci.

THE SPICE BAZAAR

T he Spice Bazaar is located behind the New Mosque, adjacent to the Flower Passage. It is one of the oldest bazaars in the city. The Spice Bazaar was constructed on the orders of Sultan Turhan, the mother of Mehmed IV, in 1660 in order to generate funds for the upkeep of the nearby mosque that had been completed on her orders. The architect was Kazım Agha. The bazaar is an "L"-shaped building that consists of 100 small shops or rooms. Originally, the name of the bazaar was the *Valide* (Mother of the Sultan) Bazaar or the New Bazaar. It was later called the Mısır (Egyptian) Bazaar as many spice-sellers who held stalls here imported spices from Egypt. The part of the bazaar closer to the mosque Yeni Cami is covered by a dome. In the section where the two parts of the L-shaped structure meet, is the wooden podium of the guild administrator. The administrator would make announcements concerning the guild from here and take care of any problems. The bazaar was last restored in 1940–1943 by Istanbul Metropolitan Council. (Duration of tour: 30 minutes)

CAFÉ / RESTAURANT

Yunus Balik under the Galata Bridge does not serve alcohol and thus has a more family atmosphere. Eminönü - Istanbul Phone: (212) 519 8591

THE NEW MOSQUE

Amount of time recommended
for visit: 30 minutes

Yeni Cami is located in Eminönü Square next to the Spice Bazaar. One of the most magnificent mosques along the Bosphorus, it completes the Istanbul portrait. The construction of the mosque started in 1597 on the decree of Safiye Sultan, the wife of Sultan Murad III and the mother of Sultan Mehmed III. After 1598, the architect Dalgıç Ahmed Çavuş took over from the original architect, Davud Agha.

The construction, which lasted till 1603, came to a temporary halt with the accession of Sultan Ahmed I and the subsequent ceremonies. The construction was restarted in 1661 by the Queen Mother Hatice Turhan under the supervision of Mustafa Agha.

The mosque was designed as a *kulliye* or complex, and was complete by 1663. The mosque and its complex consisted of a primary school, water dispensers, public baths, a sultan's gallery and a tomb. However, the primary school no longer exists.

The calligraphy that is above the windows is the work of the calligrapher Tenekecizade Mustafa Çelebi. There are two minarets, with two balconies each, on the right and left sides of the mosque. There are three doors leading to the interior, which is a square in shape. The central dome, supported by four large columns, is covered with tiles and four arches; it is supported by four semi-domes. The *mihrab* (central prayer niche) and the pulpit are made from white marble. On the left side of the *mihrab* there is a mosaic panel that is surrounded by precious stones.

The tomb that is inside the mosque complex is the largest imperial tomb; here is the tomb of the Queen Mother Hatice Turhan, five sultans, and other members of the dynasty. The five sultans buried here are Mehmed IV, Osman III, Mustafa II, Ahmed III and Mahmud I. The diameter of the mausoleum is more than 15 meters.

THE GRAND BAZAAR

Amount of time recommended
for visit: **2 hours**

The Grand Bazaar, in the center of the old city, is the oldest and the largest covered market. The foundation of the bazaar was laid in 1461. It is a unique site, and resembles a labyrinth; it was designed on a gigantic scale with more than 60 streets and 3,000 stores. The interior, which resembles a city, has gradually expanded.

The bazaar was built after the conquest of Istanbul on a location that now stands between the Nuri Osmaniye and Beyazid Mosques; it was built in order to generate funds to meet the cost of restoring Haghia Sophia. Since the day of its construction, the bazaar has been an important place for trade. The architectural style resembles that of the Great Mosque in Bursa. It has 20 domes supported by 12 large columns. The bazaar has undergone much restoration due to the number of fires and earthquakes it has survived. The appearance of the bazaar is very complex, with its intricate interior sections.

The names of the sections reflect history, having been named after different craftsmen, such as makers of the fez, mirrors, slippers and so on. According to the guild organization, specific types of occupations were organized in specific units of the bazaar. Only a few of those occupations still exist.

The domes of the Grand Bazaar are covered in lead. In former times the bazaar was known as a very secure place as there were guards who

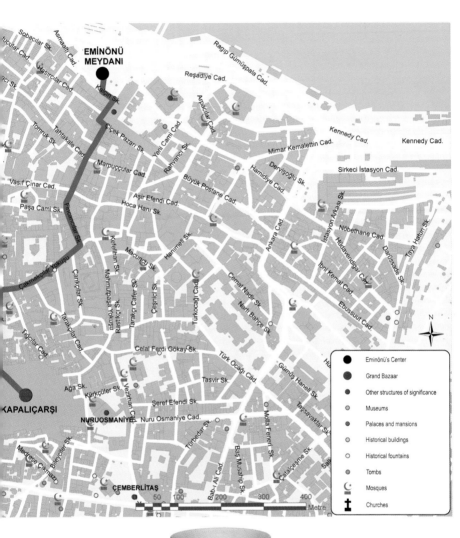

EMİNÖNÜ
MEYDANI

Sobacılar Sk.
Asmaaltı Cad.
Hasırcılar Cad.
Tığlacılar Cad.
Kalçın Sk.
Çiçek Pazarı Sk.
Reşadiye Cad.
Ragıp Gümüşpala Cad.
Tomruk Sk.
Tahtakale Cad.
Marpuççular Cad.
Yeni Cami Cad.
Rahvancı Sk.
Büyük Postane Cad.
Mimar Kemalettin Cad.
Kennedy Cad.
Kennedy Cad.
Vasıf Çınar Cad.
Paşa Cami Sk.
Aşır Efendi Cad.
Hoca Hanı Sk.
Hamidiye Cad.
Dervişoğlu Sk.
Sirkeci İstasyon Cad.
Çakmakçılar Yokuşu
Kefelihan Sk.
Mahmutpaşa Yokuşu
Macuncu Sk.
Hanımeli Sk.
Ankara Cad.
İstasyon Arkası Sk.
Hüdavendigar Cad.
Nöbethane Cad.
Darüssade Sk.
Tarya Hatun Sk.
Fırıncılar Cad.
Çankırcılar Sk.
Raştıkçı Sk.
Tarakçı Cafer Sk.
Çeşnici Sk.
Türkocağı Cad.
Cemal Nadir Sk.
Nefli Bahçe Sk.
İbni Kemal Cad.
Ebussuut Cad.
Tığcılar Cad.
Tarakçılar Cad.
Celal Ferdi Gökay Sk.
Türk Ocağı Cad.
Tasvir Sk.
Gümüş Haneli Sk.
N
KAPALIÇARŞI
Ağa Sk.
Kürkçüler Sk.
Vezirhan Cad.
Şeref Efendi Sk.
Nuru Osmaniye Cad.
Türbedar Sk.
Molla Fenari Sk.
Baş Musahip Sk.
Tassavaktar Sk.
Çatalçeşme Sk.
NURUOSMANİYE
Medrese Çıkmazı
Bileyciler Sk.
Bab-ı Ali Cad.
ÇEMBERLİTAŞ
50   100   200   300   400   Metre

Eminönü's Center
Grand Bazaar
Other structures of significance
Museums
Palaces and mansions
Historical buildings
Historical fountains
Tombs
Mosques
Churches

manned the exits, and as a result, people would leave their belongings here.

The Grand Bazaar has three main gates: Beyazıt Gate, Fesçiler Gate, and Sahaflar

Gate. The other gates are Kürkçüler Gate, Nur-ı Osmaniye Gate, Mahmud Pasha Gate, Mercan Gate, Tacirler Gate, and Örücüler Gate. Today, the bazaar is still a tourist attraction.

Nuruosmaniye Mosque, interior.

IN THE VICINITY OF THE GRAND BAZAAR

Amount of time recommended
for visit: **25 minutes**

Nuruosmaniye Mosque: The construction of the Nuruosmaniye Mosque began on the orders of Sultan Mahmud I in 1748 on the second of the seven hills of Istanbul; it was completed during the reign of Sultan Osman III in 1755. The architects responsible for the structure were Mustafa Agha and his assistant Simeon. This mosque is a unique Baroque masterpiece with its three-dimensional stone ornaments. The single dome has thirty-two windows along the base. One conspicuous element in its interior is the calligraphy around the inside of the dome and along the walls. The two minarets have two balconies each. The Nuruosmaniye Library has more than 5,000 works, both manuscripts and printed works.

Çemberlitaş/Column of Constantine: Known as Çemberlitaş, the Burnt Obelisk, or the Column of Constantine, this column was erected by Constantine the Great in 330 AD in celebration of the dedication of Constantinople, the capital of the East Roman Empire. The column was placed in the middle of an oval square (Forum of Constantine) on the second hill of the city, in the area that is today known as Çemberlitaş; the column was burnt during the great fire of 1779, which destroyed much of the area. The column has lost some of its original height. The column was originally surmounted by a statue of Emperor Constantine represented as Apollo. Over time, due to earthquakes and fire, the porphyry blocks of the column started to crack; they were then surrounded by iron hoops (*çember*) to keep the column from collapsing. The marble base of the column dates to the 12th century, and the masonry base to the 18th century. It is believed that a small chamber under the column housed relics sacred to Christianity. The main road that passes by the column has not changed its course since the time of Constantine.

Çemberlitaş, and Nuruosmaniye Mosque

BEYAZIT MOSQUE AND SQUARE

Amount of time recommended for visit: **1 hour**

Beyazıt Mosque is located in one of the famous squares of Byzantine times, which was called the Forum Tauri. This is the oldest imperial mosque on the right side of the Divanyolu on route to Aksaray. It was commissioned by Sultan Bayezid II in 1505. The architect of the mosque is not definitely known. The complex is the largest after the Fatih Mosque complex.

The mosque is one of the last examples of classic Ottoman architecture. The Beyazıt Mosque complex spreads over a large area and consists of a *madrasa*, tomb, canteen, primary school, *han* (inn), public baths and a soup kitchen. The soup kitchen to the north and the primary school to the east of the mosque are presently used by the Beyazıt Library, while the old *madrasa* is "Vakıflar Hat Sanatı müzesi" (the Foundation Museum of Calligraphy) which contains many precious manuscripts. The sheikh-ul-Islam (head religious authority) used to teach in this *madrasa*. This build-

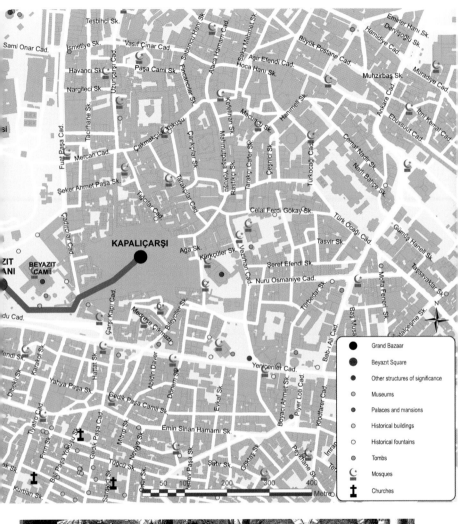

Sami Onar Cad.
Tesbihci Sk.
İsmetiye Sk.
Vasıf Çınar Cad.
Tacirhane Sk.
Havancı Sk.
Uzunçarşı Cad.
Paşa Cami Sk.
Nargileci Sk.
Fuat Paşa Cad.
Mercan Cad.
Çakmakçılar Yokuşu
Fincancılar Sk.
Atafa Hamam Cad.
Saka Mehmet Sk.
Hoca Hanı Sk.
Aşir Efendi Cad.
Büyük Postane Cad.
Emirler Hanı Sk.
Dervişoğlu Sk.
Hamidiye Cad.
Muhzirbaş Sk.
Muradiye Cad.
Ankara Cad.
İbni Kemal Cad.
Ebussuut Cad.
Kefeliham Sk.
Macuncu Sk.
Hanımeli Sk.
Cemal Nadir Sk.
Nafi Bahçe Sk.
Çarıkçılar Sk.
Mahmutpaşa Yokuşu
Rastıkçı Sk.
Çeşnici Sk.
Türkocağı Cad.
Gümüş Haneli Sk.
Şeker Ahmet Paşa Sk.
Tuğcular Cad.
Çadırcılar Cad.
Tarakçılar Cad.
Tarakçı Cafer Sk.
Celal Ferdi Gökay Sk.
Türk Ocağı Cad.
Tasvir Sk.
Tavşavaklar Sk.
Molla Fenari Sk.
KAPALIÇARŞI
Ağa Sk.
Kürkçüler Sk.
Vezirhan Cad.
Şeref Efendi Sk.
Nuru Osmaniye Cad.
Türbedar Sk.
Baş Musa
Bab-ı Ali Cad.
BEYAZIT CAMİİ
ZIT ANI
...du Cad.
Medrese Çıkmazı
Bileyciler Sk.
Çarşı Kapı Cad.
Halıçeşme Sk.
N
...endi Sk.
Dibekli Sk.
Karakol Sk.
Yahya Paşa Sk.
Hattat Sk.
Abidin Daver
Dönem Sk.
Yeniçeriler Cad.
Boyacı Ahmet Sk.
Piyer Loti Cad.
Klodfarer Cad.
İmran...
Tek...
Gedik Paşa Camii Sk.
Tiyatro Sk.
Firin Sk.
Bali Paşa Yokuşu
Gedik Paşa Cad.
Mimar Sk.
Neviye Sk.
Emin Sinan Hamamı Sk.
Fener Paşa Cad.
Şatır Sk.
Gökaş Sk.
Peykhane Sk.
...ak Sk.
Kurban Sk.
Saraylığı Sk.
Tüğcü Sk.

●	Grand Bazaar
●	Beyazıt Square
●	Other structures of significance
○	Museums
●	Palaces and mansions
○	Historical buildings
○	Historical fountains
●	Tombs
☪	Mosques
✝	Churches

50   100   200   300   400   Metre

Beyazıt Mosque, main entrance interior (Zumar 39:53):
Surely God forgives all sins. He is indeed the All-Forgiving, the All-Compassionate.

ing is currently on the right side of Ordu Street when you turn toward Aksaray from Beyazıt. The old structure next to Istanbul University Library is the public baths. These baths were later renamed after Patrona Halil, the bath attendant who started the rebellion which marked the end of the Tulip Era in 1730. This historical edifice is extremely important for this reason

The distance between the two minarets of Beyazıt Mosque is 70 meters; Beyazıt Mosque has the greatest distance between its minarets. The minarets have one balcony each. There are epigraphs on the courtyard gates by famous calligraphers of the time. The U-shaped courtyard is covered by domes that have a diameter of 18 meters and a portico with 20 exquisite columns. The construction of the pulpit, niche, podium, and sultan's gallery was carried out in a unique style. The interior of the mosque is very spacious.

The calligraphic inscriptions on the mosque were written by the fa-

mous calligrapher Sheikh Hamdullah; the same artist also decorated the interior of the dome. The tomb of Sultan Bayezid II is located in the treasury unit of the mosque. The unfurnished and plain tomb, which is the usual octagonal shape, is covered by a dome. Next to this tomb is that of Bayezid II's daughter, Selçuk Hatun. The other tomb, famous for its decorations, is that of the important Ottoman figure, Mustafa Reşit Pasha.

IN THE VICINITY

Amount of time recommended for visit: **45 minutes**

Istanbul University: According to records, the university dates back to 1453, the day of the conquest of Istanbul. The meetings held the day after the conquest, on May 30 1453 and the subsequent construction of a complex at are considered to be the first steps in the establishment of

Entrance Gates of Istanbul University

the university. According to Russian academic, Danishevski, Istanbul University has one of the oldest medical schools in the world.

During the Ottoman Empire, the *madrasa*s established on the orders of Sultan Bayezid, Sultan Selim I, and Sultan Süleyman were considered to be prestigious universities, renowned for their law schools, and studies in literature and the natural sciences.

The process of Westernization, which began after the *Islahat* and *Tanzimat* eras, was reflected in educational institutions, and it was thought that ignorance was the root of Ottoman defeat in all walks of life. A royal decree stating the principle "Progress can only be realized through education" led to the establishment of the *Darülfünun*, a type of university which is now considered to be the date for the establishment of Istanbul University (23 July 1846).

The name of this institution was later changed to *Darülfünun-u Osmani* (Ottoman School of Sciences), and reopened on February 20 1870. The third opening, as *Darülfünun-u Sultanî*, began in the Galatasaray building in 1874, with classes offered in literature, law and applied sciences. After the accession of Abdülhamid II to the throne on September 1, 1890, the fourth *Darülfünun*, called *Darülfünun-u Şahane* was reorganized, now offering courses in mathematics, literature and theology.

Istanbul Darülfünunu (Istanbul Academy of Science): After the Second Reform on April 20, 1912, *Istanbul Darulfünunu* was firmly established; it was given schools of medicine,

law, applied sciences, literature and theology. Its administrative autonomy was granted in 1919 with another regulation.

On April 21, 1924, the Republic of Turkey recognized the *Istanbul Darülfünunu* as a legal entity, and on October 7, 1925, the administrative autonomy of *Istanbul Darülfünunu* was recognized, with the *madrasa*s becoming modern "Faculties."

On August 1, 1933, *Istanbul Darülfünunu* was reorganized as Istanbul University with a new staff and structure. Classes officially began in "the first modern university in Turkey" in 1933, on the 10th anniversary of the Turkish Republic.

The Old Palace used to be located in the current position of the University, during the reign of Mehmed II. Later, after the construction of Topkapı Palace, the Ministry of Defense was moved here.

Beyazıt Tower is located on the grounds of the main Beyazıt campus; it was built as a look-out tower to spot fires for a city that suffered many great conflagrations. The original Beyazıt Tower was rebuilt in its current form in 1828, during the reign of Sultan Mahmud II, by

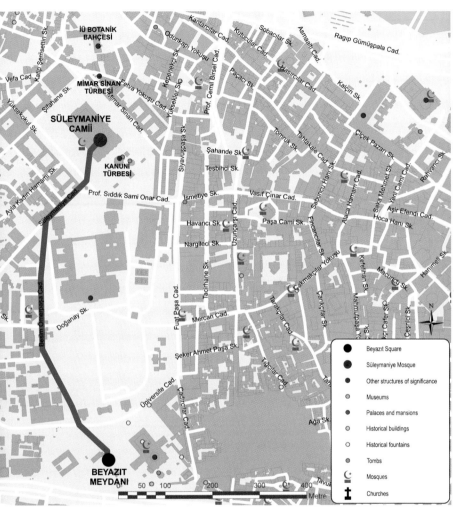

the Balyan family. The 50-meter-high tower is truly a monumental structure.

The tower was used by the military during the reign of Mahmud II, and is currently in use as the office of the rector of the university. The main entrance gate of Istanbul University, which has become the symbol of the university, was built in the 19th century. The inscriptions on the gate, which reflect the architectural structure of the era, were written by the famous calligrapher Kazasker Mustafa Pasha.

CAFÉ / RESTAURANT

Beyazıt Çınaraltı Çay bahçesi

SÜLEYMANİYE MOSQUE

Amount of time recommended for visit: **1 hour**

This impressive complex is located on a large area which constitutes the third hill of Istanbul. The Süleymaniye Mosque was commissioned by Sultan Süleyman I and was constructed by the most famous Ottoman architect, Sinan. The construction took place between 1550 and 1557. The mosque and its complex consist of sections for health, education, and other services. One of the masterpieces of Turkish-Islamic art, its construction was completed in just seven years with massive manpower. Süleymaniye Mosque is one of Sinan's greatest works, which ranks after Selimiye in Edirne. The construction materials came from all over the Ottoman territory. For instance, one of the four interior columns was the Column of Marcian in Istanbul, another from Topkapı Palace, the third from Alexandria and the fourth came from Baalbek, in the Lebanon. All the columns measure nine meters in height and are fourteen centimeters wide. In addition to the columns,

the stones used in the construction came from İzmir and Istanbul, the iron from Bulgaria, and the lead from Serbia. From this perspective, the mosque is a mosaic taken from all the parts of the Ottoman Empire.

It is reported that over all the periods, around 4 million people worked in the construction of this mosque. Throughout the construction, the most famous experts worked here and the architect Sinan led this enormous army of workers.

Reputedly, the complex cost approximately 1 million pieces gold. If we consider that 1 gold piece was worth 80 *akçe* and that a ram cost from 6 to 8 *akçe*, we can see how great the expense of the mosque was in today's terms. The courtyard that surrounds the mosque has ten doors. The door which opens onto the interior is quite magnificent. The interior courtyard is surrounded by porticos which support 28 domes. The arches of the porticos are supported by twenty-four columns. The fountain is made of bronze.

The main interior of the mosque is covered by a dome that rests on four large columns. The main dome is 53 meters high and has a diameter of

*Süleymaniye
Mosque, Fatiha 1:7*

26.5 meters. The glass panels in the mosque were carved by Hasan Çelebi. The air circulation within the mosque is exceptional because it was designed so that the smoke from the candles would be led to special holes in the dome. When the smoke met the cool air, it turned into a liquid, filling the ink holders that were used for the production of ink. As in other works of the genius architect Sinan, the ostrich eggs which hang from the ceiling were meant to prevent spider webs inside the mosque. Interestingly, unbroken ostrich eggs keep spiders away as natural repellents without giving off any smell to disturb people.

Two minarets rise from the corners of the mosque; these have two balconies, while the other two minarets on the east and west sides of the mosque have three. The total number of balconies is 10, signifying that Süleyman the Magnificent was the 10th Ottoman sultan. The four minarets symbolize the four monarchs whose reigns preceded that of Süleyman the Magnificent after the conquest of Constantinople. Furthermore, the four columns inside the mosque represent the four Rightly Guided Caliphs.

The sultan's gallery within the mosque has a simple beauty and is surrounded by eight columns. The door is decorated with rose motifs. The carving on the marble niche and pulpit is exquisite. The shutters over the window are adorned with plant motifs. Leaving Sü-

leymaniye, we find the tombs of Süleyman and of his wife Hürrem Sultan in the middle of the garden, and that of the architect Sinan.

The *madrasa* section of the mosque is currently being used as the library. The building at the southern side used to be an insane asylum. The inn is located on the northwestern corner of the mosque. The soup kitchen has been restored as the Darüzziyafe Restaurant, and the primary school has been converted to a children's library. The caravanserai is located in the southern section of the mosque, which is currently closed. The original nature of the environment of the complex has been kept intact.

Tomb of Sultan Süleyman the Magnificent: The mausoleum is octagonal in shape and faces the *qibla* direction of the mosque. The most significant feature of the mausoleum is that it contains a piece of the Hajar'ul Aswad (The Black Stone from the Ka'ba). It is reported that when the custody of the stone changed during the reign of Sultan Süleyman, it was accidentally dropped and the pieces that broke off from the stone were ordered to be brought to Istanbul. On the order of the Sultan, the largest piece was placed over the entrance gate.

Amount of time recommended for visit: **15 minutes**

Tomb of Mimar Sinan / Architect Sinan: The tomb lies outside the east entrance of the Süleymaniye Mosque. The structure is extremely modest in comparison compared to the masterpieces he designed. Sinan

Mimar Sinan, the most celebrated Ottoman architect, was a true genius.

was born around 1489 in the village of Ağırnas in Kayseri. He was brought to Istanbul during the reign of Selim I as part of the practice of *devşirme*—the levy of boys from Christian families to be trained for posts in the administration and the *kapıkulu* military corps. He became a Janissary during the reign of Sultan Süleyman the Magnificent. Sinan's works impressed the sultan and with the support of Lütfü Pasha he was appointed chief architect. Sinan constructed countless extraordinary masterpieces and reached the zenith of success. Sinan defined Şehzade Mosque as a work which reflects his period of assistance and Süleymaniye as early mastery, and the Selimiye Mosque in Edirne as a work of his true mastery. During his career as an architect, Sinan undertook many different construction projects, not just mosques. He is the architect who helped Haghia Sophia to survive until today. He constructed 84 mosques, 52 small mosques, 7 Qur'an schools, 20 tombs, 17 minarets, 3 *darüşşifa* (hospitals), 5 canals, 20 caravanserais, 36 palaces, 8 aqueducts, and 48 public baths. In total,

Sinan left behind 364 structures. He also constructed his own tomb in a very plain fashion, with a drinking fountain on the northern aspect.

IN THE VICINITY

Istanbul University Botanical Gardens: This was the first botanical garden in the Turkish Republic. It is located behind the Süleymaniye mosque, on the northern side of the complex, on the hills overlooking the Golden Horn. The garden is shared by the Istanbul Directorate of Religious Affairs. The foundation was laid in 1933. Three Jewish professors Alfred Heilbronn, Leo Brauner and Andre Naville, who fled from Hitler's Germany, were invited by Atatürk to give botany and zoology courses. They established the botanical garden within a year. It is one of the two botanical gardens in the world to be acknowledged by the World Botanical Association and the seed catalogues of the gardens are published. It occupies a large piece of land measuring 20,000 square meters. There are between 5,000 and 6,000 different species from 127 different families.

Tour Note: *An appointment is necessary for group visits. The gardens are open from 9 am to 4.30 pm. It takes at least one hour to complete the visit, but on average at least 3 hours should be allowed.*

CAFÉ / RESTAURANT

Tarihî Süleymaniye Kurufasulyecisi Süleymaniye Mosque Complex, Darüzziyafe (212) 511 8414– 512 1100

ŞEHZADE MOSQUE

Amount of time recommended for visit: **30 minutes**

BOZDOĞAN
SU KEMERİ

ŞEHZADE
CAMİİ

This mosque is located across from the Head Office of the Istanbul Metropolitan Municipality. The Şehzade Mosque was commissioned by Sultan Süleyman I between 1544 and 1548, in memory of his eldest son, Prince Mehmet, who died from smallpox. It consists of a complex, as most other Ottoman imperial mosques; there is a *madrasa*, primary school, sultan's gallery, and a tomb. The *madrasa* and the primary school, which have been converted into a restaurant, are located in the western part of the mosque. The inn is close to this restaurant.

At the time of construction the mosque cost 15 million *akçe*s. In the courtyard, there are 16 domes supported on 12 columns. In the middle of the courtyard is a fountain that was constructed during the reign of Murad IV. The interior is 38 x 38

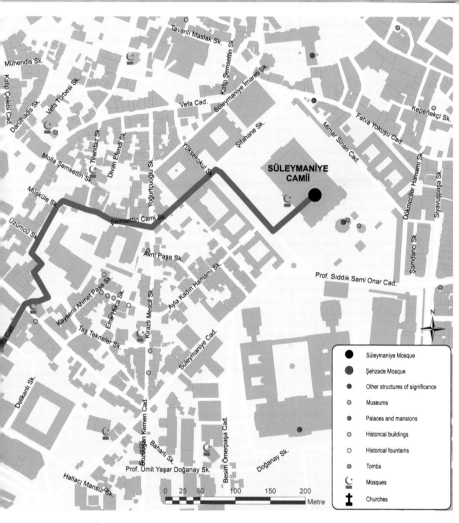

SÜLEYMANIYE
CAMİİ

● Süleymaniye Mosque
● Şehzade Mosque
● Other structures of significance
◉ Museums
● Palaces and mansions
◉ Historical buildings
○ Historical fountains
◉ Tombs
☾ Mosques
✝ Churches

0 25 50   100   150   200
Metre

meters. The center and the exterior are almost equal in size. Four semidomes support the central dome, which has a diameter of 18.5 meters and twenty-four windows. The design of the dome is the first of its kind, and makes it appear larger.

The exterior is very decorative, in contrast to the interior which is relatively plain. The exterior is faced with red marble. The two minarets, measuring 41.5 meters, are placed on both sides of the mosque and have elaborate tear-drop designs, representing the suffering of Sultan Süleyman I after his son Şehzade Mehmed died. The niche and pulpit of the mosque are made of marble. The acoustics in the mosque are extremely well designed. The mosque is protected by the walls which envelop it. In the tomb, Şehzade Mehmed and other princes lie. The tomb is inlaid with colorful stonework and tiles, and the door with ivory. The tombs of Prince Cihangir, the son of Mehmed III, Prince Mahmud and also Hatice Sultan are located here.

IN THE VICINITY

Tomb of Ali Tabli:
Between the Şehzade Mosque and the restaurant is a great plane tree under which lies one of the Companions of Prophet Muhammad, Ali Tabli. It appears lonely and sad; Ali Tabli was martyred in a battle while playing a drum called a *tabl* to encourage the soldiers.

Valens Aqueduct (*Bozdoğan Kemeri*):
The aqueduct, left from the late Roman or early Byzantine period, is known as either Hadrian or Valens Aqueduct. The exact date of construction is not known. The aqueduct, which was built to solve the problem of bringing water to the city, fell into ruin over time. After the conquest of the city by the Ottomans, Mehmed II repaired the aqueduct so that it could be used. It is not known how the aqueduct came to be known as Bozdoğan. Additions were made to the aqueduct by Sultan Mehmed II, Sultan Bayezid II and Sultan Süleyman the Magnificent.

The aqueduct used to be 1 kilometer long and is thought to have originally been longer. The missing part of the aqueduct is located on what is now Saraçhâne Atatürk Avenue. The aqueduct, which underwent renovation in 1988, has traces of Roman, Byzantine and Ottoman influences. This ancient aqueduct has been one of the most important water supplies to the city for 15 centuries.

CAFÉ / RESTAURANT

Şehzade Mehmed Sofrası,
Şehzade Camii Külliyesi,
(212) 526 2668

FATİH MOSQUE

Amount of time recommended for visit: **40 minutes**

Fatih mosque was constructed on the fourth of the seven hills in Istanbul. It was built on the site of the former Byzantine Church of the Holy Apostles, the ruins of which served as a quarry for supplying building materials for the new mosque. It was one of the first mosque complexes in Istanbul, a city which was quickly Islamized after the conquest. Our knowledge of the original architecture of the mosque, constructed by the Sultan Mehmed II between 1461 and 1470,

is limited, as it was almost completely destroyed by an earthquake in 1766.

The mosque as we know it today was built during the reign of Sultan Mustafa III, after being completely destroyed in 1766. It was restored by

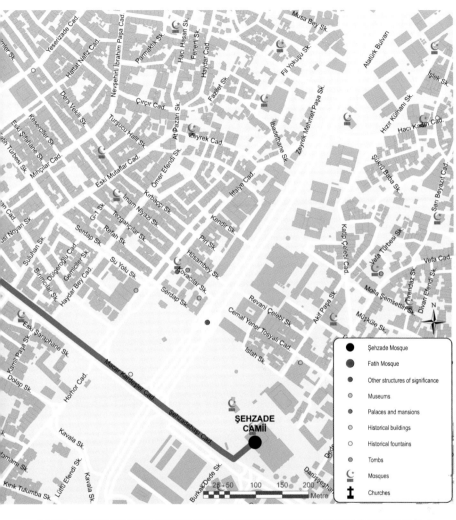

Şehzade Mosque
Fatih Mosque
Other structures of significance
Museums
Palaces and mansions
Historical buildings
Historical fountains
Tombs
Mosques
Churches

ŞEHZADE
CAMİİ

Fatih Mosque, the rear wall:
In the name of God, the Most-Merciful, the Most-Compassionate.

the famous architect Mehmed Tahir Agha in the Baroque style.

The complex is located on a large area. The complex used to consist of a *madrasa*, primary school, library, inn, public kitchen, hospital, caravanserai, and public baths; most of these buildings have not survived. The entrance to the courtyard is through two tall gates. In the center is a fountain with eight columns and marble corners. On the entrance wall is an inscription by the calligrapher Ali bin Safi that contains the *basmala* (in the name of God, the Merciful, the Compassionate in Arabic) and Surah al-Fatiha, the initial chapter of the Qur'an. The main dome, resting on four grand marble pillars of a 26-meter diameter, is supported by four semi-domes. The mosque has two minarets with two balconies each.

There are eight well-known *madrasa*s in the complex. During the Ottoman era, it was a great privilege to be able to study here. There are two groups of *madrasa*s, called the Mediterranean and the Black Sea *madrasa*s. The Mediterranean *madrasa*s, which are located in the southern part of the complex, are called the Akdeniz *madrasa*, the Başkurşunlu *madrasa*, the Çiftekurşunlu *madrasa*, and the Ayakkurşunlu *madrasa*. The Tehime and Semaniye *madrasa*s no longer exist. The entrance to the block of *madrasa*s is through two gates at the front of the complex. The *madrasa*s surround the courtyard from three directions. The tiles on the last part of the sultan's gallery

in the mosque are priceless, as the colors that were used in these tiles cannot be reproduced today. There is also a small fountain in the interior of the mosque; it is not known when or why it was constructed. The sultan's gallery in the northwestern part of the mosque was built during the reign of Mustafa III. The tombs are just like those in other mosques. The tomb of Sultan Mehmed II lies alone. The tombs of Gülbahar Sultan, the wife of Sultan Süleyman the Magnificent and that of Nakşidil Sultan, the wife of Sultan Abdülhamid I are also located here. The tombs of the hero of Plevna, Gazi Osman Pasha, and the last Ottoman ministers are also located here.

IN THE VICINITY OF FATİH MOSQUE

Amount of time recommended for visit: **10 minutes**

Kıztaşı / The Column of Marcian: The Column of Marcian is located right below Fevzi Pasha Street. It was erected and dedicated to Emperor Marcian in 452. It is a plain monument not built on a large scale. Due to the figures carved around its base, it was also called the Kıztaşı (girl's stone) after the conquest of Istanbul.

CAFÉ / RESTAURANT

Ziya Şark Sofrası,
(212) 531 3003
Bizim Köfte,
(212) 531 6850

YAVUZ SELİM MOSQUE

Amount of time recommended for visit: **40 minutes**

Yavuz Selim Mosque is an Ottoman imperial mosque located on top of the fifth hill of Istanbul, overlooking beautiful scenery. The Cistern of Aspar, which dates back to Byzantium, is located near the mosque. The mosque was constructed on the ruins of a Roman palace. Apart from its historical beauty, the mosque affords a picturesque view of the Golden Horn. The courtyard of the mosque is the best place to observe the Golden Horn and its surroundings. The location of the mosque was chosen by Sultan Selim I (Yavuz Selim), who also laid the foundation. His son Sultan Süleyman I opened the mosque in 1522. The architect was Acem Ali. The large courtyard has a colonnaded portico and a fountain in the center. The stairs of the Kırk Merdiven gate descend toward the Golden Horn. There are two more gates, one leads

to the tombs and the other one out to the street. The mosque is very imposing, standing under the cypress trees. The simplicity and modesty of Yavuz Selim are reflected in this mosque. The mosque itself is decorated with very early examples of İznik tiles. These tiles have mostly been placed above the windows. The dome was

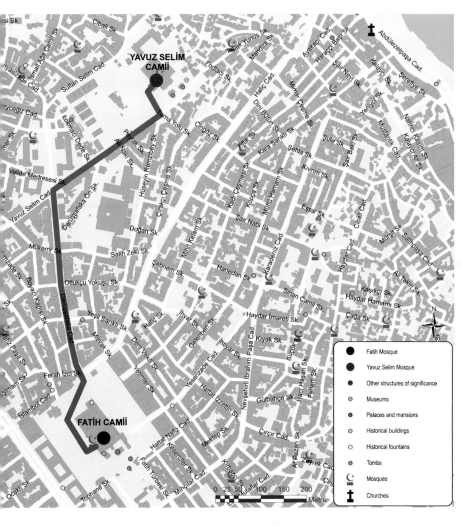

Map legend:
- Fatih Mosque
- Yavuz Selim Mosque
- Other structures of significance
- Museums
- Palaces and mansions
- Historical buildings
- Historical fountains
- Tombs
- Mosques
- Churches

constructed over an area with a 24.5-meter diameter, and there are no semi-domes. The mother-of-pearl inlay is an exquisite example of the art of this period. The niche, which displays a cover brought from the Ka'ba, is made of high quality marble.

The mosque sits in a complex with different sections including a school. The tombs are located in the garden behind the mosque. The architectural style of the tomb of Yavuz Selim is octagonal and there are panels of tiles with different designs. Yavuz Selim lies alone in this tomb. There are also the tombs of princes and Sultan Abdülmecid in the garden.

THE MUSEUM OF KARİYE MOSQUE CHORA CHURCH

Amount of time recommended for visit: **30 minutes**

This ancient structure is located on the sixth hill of Istanbul. Near Edirnekapi in Fatih, Chora Church was built inside the city walls. The name Chora, which means "countryside" was given to this church because of the great distance from the city center. This name was probably originally given to a small church built in the area in the 5th century, before the construction of the city walls; the same name was also given to churches built afterwards on the same location. The current structure is known to date back to either the 11th or the 14th century. The interior mosaic and fresco designs are examples of Byzantine and Renaissance art. Chora Church was converted into a mosque in 1511 by the Otto-man grand vizier Atik Ali Pasha. The building has one large and three small domes. The diameter of the large dome is 7 meters. The building is remarkable for its mosaic panels and frescos. The interior of the building was constructed in the shape of a cross. The mosque was converted into a museum in 1935. It is open to the public everyday except Wednesday.

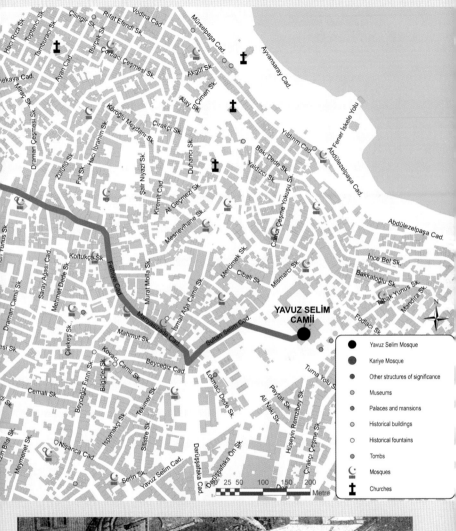

Yavuz Selim Mosque

Kariye Mosque

Other structures of significance

Museums

Palaces and mansions

Historical buildings

Historical fountains

Tombs

Mosques

Churches

YAVUZ SELİM CAMİİ

MİHRİMAH MOSQUE

Amount of time recommended
for visit: **30 minutes**

The Mihrimah Mosque is located on the 7th hill of Istanbul, inside the city halls in Edirnekapı. The mosque was built between 1562 and 1565 by the architect Sinan and it was dedicated to the beloved daughter of Sultan Süleyman the Magnificent, Mihrimah Sultan (who died in 1566). There are many legends about the construction of the mosque. The mosque is built on an elevated base to which one ascends via 9 steps. This magnificent masterpiece can be seen from every part of Istanbul. It stands majestically alone because no other building that can equal its splendor is located nearby. The mosque is based on a square plan topped by a dome and surrounded by a portico. The mosque is glorious with its great number of windows. The architectur-

al style is characteristic of the 16th century. On the front right corner there is a minaret with one balcony; this was rebuilt after having collapsed. In the center of the mosque, which is built within a small complex, is a fountain. Along the sides of the courtyard there are small rooms that were used as a

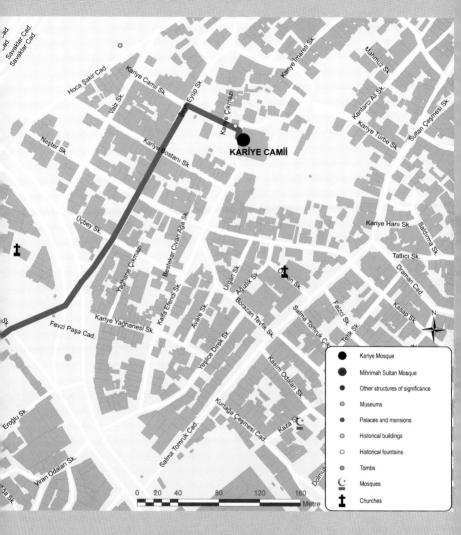

KARİYE CAMİİ

●	Kariye Mosque
●	Mihrimah Sultan Mosque
●	Other structures of significance
○	Museums
●	Palaces and mansions
○	Historical buildings
○	Historical fountains
●	Tombs
☾	Mosques
✝	Churches

madrasa. The dome, which appears to cover the entire mosque, has a diameter of 9 meters and is 27 meters high.

A vast area of the walls is covered by windows, making this one of the lightest mosques. Some parts of the complex were changed during the restoration process. The fountain that is attached to the hamam was built at a different time period. Among the tombs are those of Mihrimah Sultan, as well as that of her husband, Güzel Ahmet Pasha. This mosque is also known as Edirnekapı Mosque.

LALELİ MOSQUE

Amount of time recommended
for visit: **30 minutes**

Laleli Mosque was built by the architect Mehmed Tahir Agha in 1764 on the orders of Sultan Mustafa III. The mosque is an example of Ottoman Baroque style; its unusual architectural design is a symbol of the first Western influence on the empire. Unlike the traditional Ottoman mosques, the height of the mosque is given importance. The minarets are tall and thin. The imperial entrance leading to the sultan's gallery which seems to be seperate from the mosque is highly decorated. This was the last complex to be restored in Istanbul, and it consists of a mosque, main center, shops, guesthouse, fountain, inn, and a tomb. The dome rests on a portico with eight columns. The small domes that surround the main dome also support it. The niche appears to protrude from the building. The mosque takes its name from Laleli Dede who cured Sultan Mustafa III of an illness; he requested that the mosque be named after him.

●	Mihrimah Sultan Mosque
●	Laleli Mosque
●	Other structures of significance
○	Museums
●	Palaces and mansions
●	Historical buildings
○	Historical fountains
●	Tombs
☾	Mosques
✝	Churches

LALELİ CAMİİ

0 100 200 400 800
Metre

PERTEVNİYAL VALİDE SULTAN MOSQUE

Amount of time recommended for visit: **30 minutes**

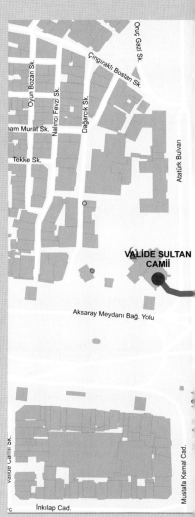

Oruç Gazi Sk.

Çıngıraklı Bostan Sk.

Oyun Bozan Sk.

Nalinci Fevzi Sk.

Dağarcık Sk.

am Murat Sk.

Atatürk Bulvarı

Tekke Sk.

VALİDE SULTAN CAMİİ

Aksaray Meydanı Bağ. Yolu

Valide Camii Sk.

Mustafa Kemal Cad.

İnkılap Cad.

This mosque was built on the orders of Pertevniyal Valide Sultan, the wife of Sultan Mahmud II and mother to Sultan Abdulaziz, in 1871. The architect was the Armenian architect Serkis Balyan. It is located in the northern part of Aksaray. The exterior is different from the classical Turkish architectural style. It is neo-Gothic in style with intricate stonework. The mosque sits on a square plan and has two minarets that have grooves running their length. The dome looks more like the dome of a church, being high but narrow. The interior of the mosque is decorated with calligraphic inscriptions from the Qur'an, executed by the calligrapher Mehmed Efendi. The shutters of the mosque are rather impressive, as well as the main entrance gate that faces the center. This is a rare example of Turkish stone carving. Shutters made of stone complete the door.

The mosque has no distinct style because the intention was a cultural synthesis. The interior decoration is very attractive. The niche and the pulpit are both made of marble. It is recorded that the opening ceremony of the mosque was magnificent. The mosque rests in a small complex consisting of the mosque, a fountain, a library, and the tomb of Pertevniyal Valide Sultan.

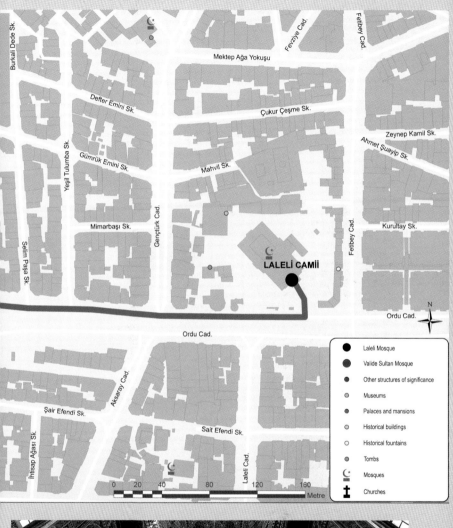

Burkali Dede Sk.

Mektep Ağa Yokuşu

Fevziye Cad.

Fetibey Cad.

Defter Emini Sk.

Çukur Çeşme Sk.

Yeşil Tulumba Sk.

Gümrük Emini Sk.

Zeynep Kamil Sk.

Ahmet Şuayip Sk.

Mahvil Sk.

Selim Paşa Sk.

Mimarbaşı Sk.

Gençtürk Cad.

Kurultay Sk.

Fetibey Cad.

LALELİ CAMİİ

N

Ordu Cad.

Ordu Cad.

Aksaray Cad.

Şair Efendi Sk.

Sait Efendi Sk.

İhtisap Ağası Sk.

Laleli Cad.

●	Laleli Mosque
●	Valide Sultan Mosque
●	Other structures of significance
◐	Museums
◑	Palaces and mansions
○	Historical buildings
○	Historical fountains
◉	Tombs
☪	Mosques
✝	Churches

0   20   40   80   120   160
Metre

MURAT PAŞA MOSQUE

Amount of time recommended
for visit: **15 minutes**

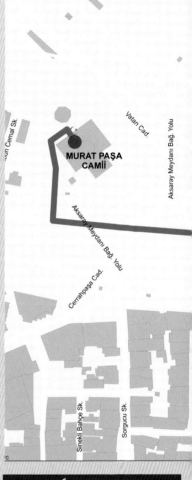

Murat Pasha Mosque was built in 1465–1471 by Has Murat Pasha, who was the governor of Rumeli—the Ottoman lands on the European side of the Bosphorus. The two domes have a diameter of 10.5 meters and are 20 meters off the ground. The architectural style of Murat Pasha Mosque has elements of early Ottoman architecture. The walls are made of cut stones and bricks. The courtyard is relatively wide. There is a fountain in the center. The interior of the mosque is simple and the mosque has one minaret. The *madrasa* and public baths of the complex were demolished at a later date. The portico at the back has six columns. The mosque is located at the point where Vatan Avenue and Millet Street intersect, on Aksaray Square.

CAFÉ / RESTAURANT

Ziya Şark Sofrası, Aksaray Şubesi, (212) 529 8836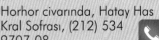

Horhor civarında, Hatay Has Kral Sofrası, (212) 534 9707-08

Halil İbrahim Şark Sofrası (212) 621 7732

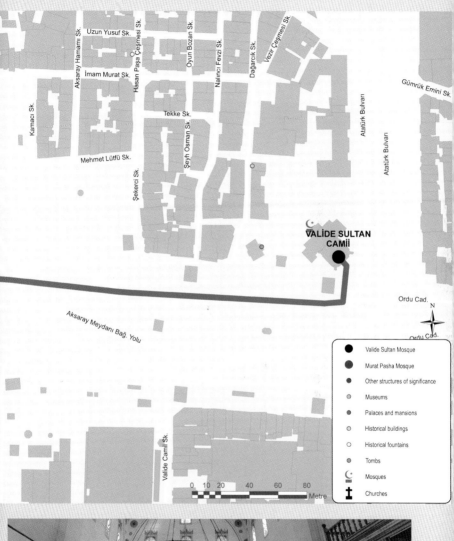

Kamacı Sk.

Aksaray Hamamı Sk.

Uzun Yusuf Sk.

İmam Murat Sk.

Hasan Paşa Çeşmesi Sk.

Oyun Bozan Sk.

Nalıncı Fevzi Sk.

Dağarcık Sk.

Vezir Çeşmesi Sk.

Gümrük Emini Sk.

Tekke Sk.

Şeyh Osman Sk.

Mehmet Lütfü Sk.

Şekerci Sk.

Atatürk Bulvarı

Atatürk Bulvarı

VALİDE SULTAN CAMİİ

Ordu Cad.

N

Aksaray Meydanı Bağ. Yolu

Ordu Cad.

Valide Camii Sk.

●	Valide Sultan Mosque
●	Murat Pasha Mosque
●	Other structures of significance
◎	Museums
●	Palaces and mansions
◎	Historical buildings
○	Historical fountains
●	Tombs
☾	Mosques
✝	Churches

0 10 20   40   60   80

Metre

THE MOSQUE OF MOLLA FENARİ İSA

Amount of time recommended for visit: **30 minutes**

Located in the Fatih district of Istanbul, on Vatan Avenue, this building was constructed on a former early Roman graveyard; it was built in 907 during the reign of Emperor Leon VI on the orders of the Byzantine Admiral Konstantinos Lips. The building therefore is also known as Lips Monastery. One important architectural feature is that the dome is surrounded by four chapels. Because of its unique architectural style, many prestigious architectural schools offer courses about the plan of the building and its structural characteristics. Lips Monastery is unlike other Byzantine churches that were converted into mosques after the conquest of Istanbul. The Christians left the church around 1481–1512, under the reign of Beyazıd II. It is known to have been converted into a mosque under the regulations of "rejuvenation of the unused Byzantine churches." It is known that at this time Fenari Ali Efendi of the *ule-ma* (religious scholars) converted it into a dervish lodge. In the reign of Sultan Murad IV, Sheikh İsa al Mahvi initiated the use of the monastery rooms for secluded worship, a characteristic of the Khalwati Sufi order. Thus, the current name of the mosque is a combination of the names Fenari and İsa.

This edifice has five apses. The reason why the cells were construct-

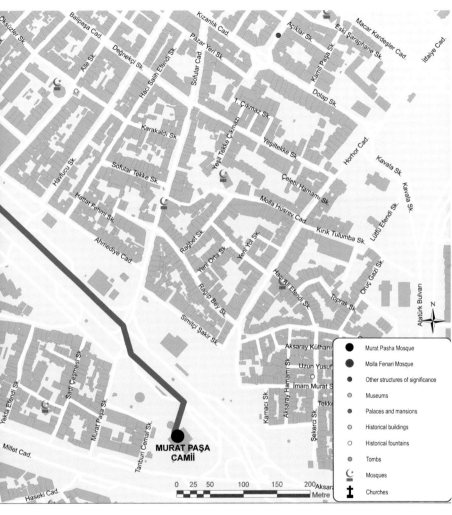

Murat Pasha Mosque
Molla Fenari Mosque
Other structures of significance
Museums
Palaces and mansions
Historical buildings
Historical fountains
Tombs
Mosques
Churches

ed close to one another, according to archeological evidence discovered during restoration, was to prepare this place as the imperial graveyard. Some prominent figures from the Ottoman Era were buried here, such as the wife of Sultan Murad III, Shah-ı Hatun.

Inside the apses along the walls that have windows there are marble works, geometric designs and figures of peacocks. The original structure was built as a complex, but most of this has collapsed. The east part of the mosque was used as a *madrasa* during the time of Yavuz Sultan Selim. The current Şadiye Hatun Medical Clinic is in the annex. The mosque is still open for public worship.

HIRKA-İ ŞERİF MOSQUE

Amount of time recommended
for visit: **20 minutes**

This is one of the most beautiful structures in the Karagümrük district of Fatih. The mosque was built by Sultan Abdülmecid on an elevated parcel of land in 1851. Our knowledge about the architect is limited, even though the mosque was not built very long ago. It is reported that it could have been the work of the Balyan family. The mantle which Prophet Muhammad gave to Uways al-Qarani as a present is kept here. The Honored Mantle (*Hırka-i Şerif*), which gives its name to the mosque, can be seen during the month of Ramadan. The mantle was taken from Uways al-Qarani's grandsons, who were its guardians (the Uways Family), and brought to Istanbul in the 17th century on the order of Sultan Ahmed I. After being protected in various locations, it was brought to this mosque which had been constructed for its safekeeping. The top floor of the mosque is the imperial apartment, which is adjacent to the section dedicated to the Uways family, as a sign of respect. The mosque has a single minaret with two balconies. The top of each minaret resembles the capital of a column. There are three entrances to the courtyard via three wooden gates. The niche, pulpit and podium reflect the Rococo style. The carvings and engraving were designed by the famous calligrapher Mustafa İzzet. The handwritten plaques on the niche are the work of Sultan Abdülmecid himself. This is one the most frequently visited mosques.

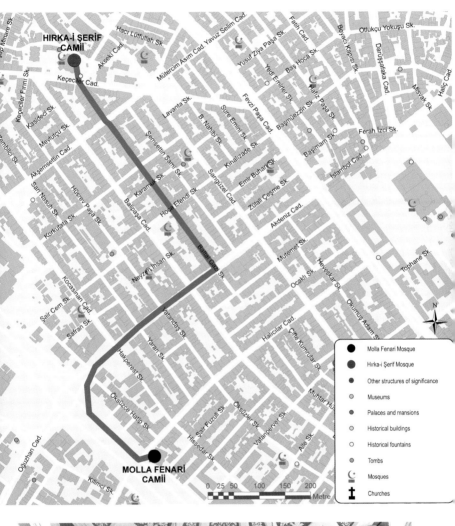

HIRKA-İ ŞERİF CAMİİ

MOLLA FENARİ CAMİİ

- ● Molla Fenari Mosque
- ● Hırka-i Şerif Mosque
- ● Other structures of significance
- ○ Museums
- ○ Palaces and mansions
- ○ Historical buildings
- ○ Historical fountains
- ○ Tombs
- ☾ Mosques
- ✝ Churches

0 25 50   100   150   200
Metre

YEDİKULE

Amount of time recommended for visit: **20 minutes**

Yedikule is important because of the area it occupies and the historical events that took place here. This fort served as an indispensable stronghold not only for Byzantium, but also for the Ottoman Empire and afterwards. The Golden Gate, the main state entrance into the capital which was used for triumphal returns by victorious emperors from battle, is located here. The gate is extremely high and glorious. Inside, there is a relief of the two-headed Byzantine eagle. The gate was built by Theodosius I.

During the Ottoman era, this location served as the treasury for some time, but later the treasury was relocated in the palace for security reasons. The original single tower that existed during the Byzantine era was joined by six more towers in the Ottoman era. Later, this fort was used as a dungeon. Political criminals, including very famous politicians, were held in the cells, which can still be visited, and executed here. A famous historical figure who was executed here was Sultan Osman II (Young Osman), who was killed by rebels. Also foreign messengers or spies were held here. The writings on the walls left from this period can still be read. Today, the whole district is named after the towers, which are now used as a museum.

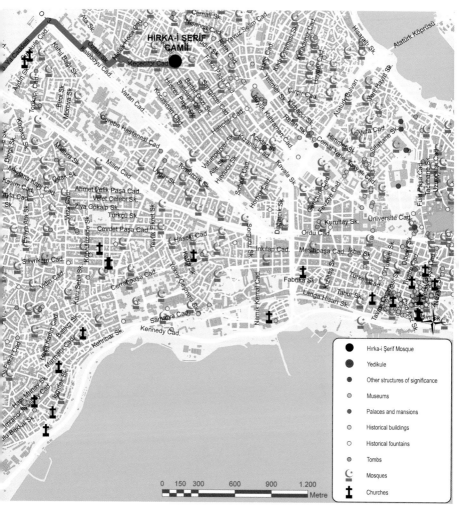

●	Hırka-i Şerif Mosque
●	Yedikule
●	Other structures of significance
○	Museums
●	Palaces and mansions
○	Historical buildings
○	Historical fountains
◐	Tombs
☾	Mosques
✝	Churches

CHAPTER 2

HALİÇ / THE GOLDEN HORN

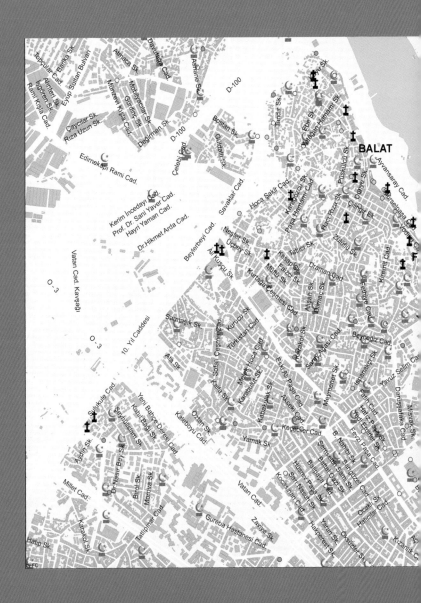

BALAT

Amount of time recommended for visit the Golden Horn: Minimum 2 hours should be allowed to visit Unkapani, Fener and the Balat region.

UNKAPANI

○	Museums
●	Palaces and mansions
○	Historical buildings
○	Historical fountains
●	Tombs
☪	Mosques
✝	Churches

The four buildings of commerce which controlled and distributed staple foods such as flour, butter, honey and silk to the city, used to be located here. These were known as *kapan*, which comes from the Arabic word *qabban* meaning "large scale." So the name implies that this is where goods were measured and inspected. In this district, there was an *unkapanı* (flour scale) and mules. Thus, the area was later called after the building of commerce, that is, *unkapanı*. The sacks of flour that were imported from other cities were checked and weighed at Unkapanı before they could be distributed to different cities. The Valens Aqueduct is close to the entrance gate of Unkapanı.

VALENS AQUEDUCT
(Bozdoğan Su Kemeri)

Amount of time recommended
for visit: **2 minutes**

The Valens Aqueduct is located in the Saraçhane district of Istanbul. It was first built during the reign of Constantine I and was completed in 378 during the reign of Emperor Valens, whose name it bears. The aqueduct carried drinking water from Alibeyköy to the city and it consists of double-tiered arches. Even though it was originally 1 kilometer long, now the aqueduct measures 800 meters. The aqueduct, which dates back to the East Roman and early Byzantine Period, was also known as the Aqueduct of Hadrian. It was built to solve the problem of obtaining water, but over time fell into disrepair. After the conquest of the city by the Ottomans, Mehmed II had the aqueduct repaired so that it could be used again. New additions were made to it under the reign of Sultan Mehmed I, Sultan Bayezid II and Sultan Süleyman I. The aqueduct has been one of the most important water supplies for the city for 15 centuries. Next to the Valens Aqueduct is the Gazanfer Agha Complex.

GAZANFER AGHA COMPLEX
(The Caricature and Cartoons Museum)

Amount of time recommended
for visit: **45 minutes**

The complex, which consists of a *madrasa*, a tomb and a fountain, is located on Kırkçeşme Street, Atatürk Avenue in Saraçhanebaşı, attached to the Valens Aqueduct. It was constructed in the 16th century by Gazanfer Agha, one of the Black Eunuchs in Darüssaade. The architect was possibly Davud Agha. The complex was renovated in 1950 and was used as the Head Offices of the Istanbul Municipality until 1945. After 1989, it was reopened as the Caricature and Cartoon Museum. The northern part of the area, in the direction of the Valens Aqueduct, was allocated

to the *madrasa*, while the northeastern section was given over to the fountain, and the northwestern part was allocated to the tomb. The architectural style of the Gazanfer Agha Complex reflects architecturally the stagnation and decline of the Ottoman Empire in the 17th and 18th centuries. Going down from Unkapanı towards the Golden Horn, Molla Zeyrek Mosque is located on the left.

MOLLA ZEYREK MOSQUE

Amount of time recommended for visit: **30 minutes**

The Pantokrator, also known as Molla Zeyrek Mosque, is one of the Byzantine churches. The building, which was converted into a mosque during the reign of Sultan Mehmed II, dates back to the first quarter of the 12th century. Molla Zeyrek Mosque in its current desolate state is made up of three Byzantine churches. The building has two domes. After the con-

quest of Istanbul and until its conversion into a mosque, the surviving buildings of the Pantokrator were first converted into a *madrasa*. Sultan Mehmed I assigned Zeyrek Mehmet Efendi as the chief scholar, and it is his name that was given to this edifice and the district. The opening date of the *madrasa* in 1453 is accepted as the opening date of Istanbul University. Currently, the building is open for worship as a mosque, but this forms only a part of the entire building. The mosque and its complex are in a dilapidated state today.

ZEYREKHANE

Amount of time recommended for visit: **30 minutes**

The Zeyrekhane is part of the Divan chain of restaurants located in Unkapanı in the direction of Aksaray, next to Molla Zeyrek Mosque. This is a foundation established by the Fatih Municipality and Rahmi Koç Museum and Culture Foundation. It was opened under the name of Zeyrekhane (House of Wisdom) after the restoration of the church of the Pantocrator (Molla Zeyrek Mosque), which was damaged by fires and earthquakes. The Zeyrekhane has a wonderful view of

the Molla Zeyrek Mosque behind it, with Süleymaniye in the front, and the Golden Horn, Karaköy port, the Maiden's Tower and Kadıköy. The interior design of the mosque, which was restored by remaining faithful to the historical position, consists of traditional Turkish motifs. The restaurant offers the specialties of classic Turkish cuisine. Out of respect for the nearby mosque, no alcoholic beverages are served. The expense of the meal is balanced by the picturesque view as well as the wonderful ambience of the location. Now let us continue the tour by turning towards Eyüp before walking across the Unkapanı Bridge. After passing Cibali, the Fener District lies ahead of us.

CAFÉ / RESTAURANT

Unkapanı- Zeyrekhâne (212) 532 2778, Zeyrek Cafe.

FENER

Amount of time recommended for visit: **20 minutes**

Fener District is located in the northeastern part of Fatih, overlooking the Golden Horn, in the region known as First Istanbul or Suriçi (within the ramparts) Istanbul. To the east of the district is the Cibali district and the northwestern part forms Balat. These districts have survived since the first establishment of the city. It seems as if time has come to a halt here; one moment we see an Armenian church and the next a mosque, a synagogue, or a Greek church. The non-Muslim citizens of

the Ottoman Empire lived side by side with the Muslim citizens after the conquest. Fener continued to be a Greek city after the conquest, much as it was in the Byzantine Era. The first name of the city was *Porta Phari* or *Porta del Pharo*. The street next to the gate was known as *Fanari* during the Byzantine Era, as we can see from a document dated 1351. There was a *fener* (lighthouse/beacon) on this part of the wharf. This lighthouse was destroyed either by a great earthquake or during attacks on the city. The name of this area is more ancient than Istanbul itself.

The history of the district started with the foundation of Constantinople. According to the Armenian writer Lazar of Farb (5th century), when Emperor Constantine arrived in the city called Byzantium, he saw that this beautiful location was appropriate for settlement. He invested all he could in the city on the peninsula, even after comprehending the difficulty of the work required. The city was surrounded by the sea on three sides, except for a small piece of land to the west. Constantine started work from within the city and upon the hills. He designed the plan of the city

walls. The money lender Hovhannesyan says that the houses of wealthy Greeks, Moldavian and Wallachian rulers used to be here, in the region between Ayakapı and Fener. Near the sea was a Janissary center. Further ahead, were Jewish houses and a Jewish neighborhood. Here, Greeks and Jews lived together. In his *Seyahatname*, Evliya Çelebi mentions that the Greeks had moved inside the gate of Fener. He says that at the time, Fener was famous for its fishermen and pubs.

GREEK ORTHODOX PATRIARCHATE (Fener Rum Patrikhanesi)

Amount of time recommended for visit: **15 minutes**

The Ecumenical Patriarchate of Constantinople is considered to be a sacred place located on Sadrazam Ali Pasha Street. The Patriarchate was originally built in 1602, and was restored to its current state in 1800.

There are three entrances to the Patriarchate. There is a staircase that leads to the main gate. The main gate is closed in remembrance of Patriarch Gregory and three other metropolitan bishops who were executed in 1821 for supporting the Greek Revolution. This is why the left gate is used as an entrance. This is also the entrance to

Aya Yorgi (Haghia Yorgi), the Patriarchate Church.

The Aya Yorgi Church is the historical place of worship in the Patriarchate. In the era of Patriarch Timoteos II, the convent was completely renovated, and began to function as the Church of the Orthodox Rum Patriarchate in 1614.

According to two conflicting stories, the building housing the patriarchate was torn down either in 1701, during the reign of Sultan Mustafa I, or in 1704, during the reign of Sultan Ahmed III, on the order of the chief vizier. The present church was built in 1720 on a traditional basilica plan and was restored again in 1798.

Three mosaic icons, which were designed so that they can be moved between different churches, are also located here. There are only ten or fifteen of this type of icon in the entire world. Rumor has it that two master artisans labored for over forty years in order to complete the impressive icons.

On the right corner are three coffins (one of them is silver) of three female saints, St. Euphemia, St. Theophano, and St. Solomone. It is thought that the silver coffin was a gift from Russia. There are some priceless sacred relics from the Russian Orthodox Congregation in the Patriarchate. The Patriarchate, acting as the center of an orthodox congregation consisting of 450 million people, is important. For instance, the baptism of the Greek King Constantine's granddaughter, Princess Maria Olympia was realized here.

The history of the Patriarchate stretches back to the 12th century. The Aya Yorgi Church, which is the historical place of worship in the Patriarchate, was used as a nunnery until 1601. The church's central hall of worship was constructed with twelve columns, which offer descriptions and depictions of the twelve apostles. The library in the Patriarchate is one of the most important archives in the world. Manuscripts, *firman* from the sultans, paintings, miniatures, engravings, and photographs are all carefully kept here.

Old Gates around the Neighborhood of Fener

Fener Gate: This is a gate in the city walls that stands between the Golden Horn, Balat and Petrikapı. It was originally called Porta Phari.

Petrikapı Gate (Iron Gate): This gate in the city walls used to stand between the Golden Horn, Fener, and Ayakapı. It no longer exists today. It used to stand at the point where Abdülezzel Pasha Street and Mürsel Pasha Street intersect. Troops entered through this gate during the Latin invasion and the conquest of Constantinople.

The Gate of Theodosia: This is the entrance that stands between Petri on the Golden Horn and Ayakapı. It is the gate to Gül Mosque (Aya Thedosia Church).

ABDİ SUBAŞI MOSQUE

Amount of time recommended for visit: **15 minutes**

This mosque is located on Abdi Subaşı Street behind the Fener Rum Patriarchate. It was built by Abdi Subaşı during the reign of Fatih Sultan Mehmed. Due to its falling into disrepair over time, it was later rebuilt by Mimar Sinan, on the orders of Mehmet Agha, during the reign of Sultan Süleyman. Rebuilding of the mosque, which was damaged in a fire in 1941, started due to charitable donations, in 1989 and it opened for worship in the month of Ramadan in 1996. The minaret, which is detached from the building, is on the left side of the mosque. The Golden Horn can be seen from here. It is thought that Abdi Subaşı was a descendant of Rumi, and he is buried near the mosque.

SÜZGEÇÇİ YUSUF MOSQUE

Amount of time recommended for visit: **15 minutes**

This mosque is located on the coastal road that goes to Fener. It was constructed during the reign of Sultan Mehmed II. After being destroyed in a fire, the mosque was rebuilt by Süzgeççi Yusuf and Hacı Reşit in 1890–1891. The mosque is made of stone and is roofed. There are shops under the mosque. The sultan's gallery has been separated for women, while the ceiling and the niche are made of wood. The minaret is brick, with a lead cone. The entrance to the minaret is from inside the mosque. Sultan Mehmed II had the mosque built for the soldiers on duty; the sultan also prayed here.

DARÜL-MESNEVİ (Mesnevihane Şeyh Murad) MOSQUE

Amount of time recommended for visit: **15 minutes**

This is located in Fener on Mesnevihâne Street, behind the Rum Lisesi (Greek high school). It was founded by Sheikh Murad Nakşibendi and built in 1844. The large cistern in the courtyard was built on the orders of Nevfidan Hatun in 1852. The vaulted mosque has a rectangular plan. It is made of bricks and stone. The pulpit is made of wood. In the first courtyard, there is a six-cornered fountain with a con-

crete dome. The mosque is called *Darülmesnevi* because of its purpose, which was to give instruction in the *Mathnawi*, Sufism, and Persian. Sultan Abdülmecid is known to have attended the graduation ceremony of the first students and he gave rewards to all those who received their diplomas. He encouraged learning Persian and the teachings of the *Mathnawi*.

MESNEVİHANE / MATHNAWI TALKS LODGE

Amount of time recommended for visit: **15 minutes**

The Mesnevihane is located on Tevkii Cafer Street. This foundation, also known as the *Darülmesnevi Tekke*, was built by Sheikh el-Hac in 1844, the third *postniş* of the Murad

Molla Lodge, which is affiliated with the Naqshbandis. Mehmed Murad Efendi built the lodge as a place to instruct in the *Mathnawi*. The Mesnevihane originally consisted of a masjid that is also used as a classroom, an independent *tevhidhane*, dervish cells, a library, fountain, water reservoir, and probably a kitchen. Later, a minaret was added to the classroom, and the tomb of Mehmed Murad Efendi was added to the complex in 1848. Nevfidan Kadin Efendi, who was the chief concubine during the reign of Mahmud II, donated money for building the well. After the closure of the dervish lodges in 1925, this building started to lose its purpose, and fell into disrepair. During this period, the other elements of the complex, such as the dervish cells, the library and the kitchen were destroyed. In the empty location an apartment for the *imam* was built. The masjid and classroom were renovated in 1968 to be used as a mosque. The original parts left from the masjid were removed in 2000. The lodge, which held religious services on Fridays, remained under the supervision of the Naqshbandi Sufi order and functioned as a Mathnawi School according to its original purpose until 1925.

HOUSE OF DIMITRI KANDEMİR

Amount of time recommended for visit: **15 minutes**

D imitri Kantemir was a prominent leader from Moldavia in the Ottoman Empire. He wrote books on the history of the Ottoman Empire, and about classical Turkish music. The garden in which the house is located used to belong to one of the largest Greek families, the Kantakouzenos.

HAGHI GEORGIOS CHURCH
(Ayios Yeoryios Jerusalem Metakhion Church)

Amount of time recommended for visit: **10 minutes**

T he church is located on Vodina Street. The building dates back to 1132, during the Byzantine era. After burning down in 1640, it was repaired by money collected from the furriers' guild. It has been a branch of the Ayios Yeoryios Metakhion Church since the mid-17th century. The church is still connected to the Patriarchate in Jerusalem. In 1708, it was rebuilt during the time of the Patriarch of Jerusalem Chrisanthos by the master Pavlos. The church burned down again in 1728 and was rebuilt during the 1730s. It underwent renovations in 1913. Some resources suggest that until the end of the 18th century, the Patriarch of Jerusalem lived here and put up church members who came from Jerusalem. The vaulted church is made of rough-hewn stones. It is laid out as a basilica and is decorated with silver icons and oil paintings.

THE LIBRARY OF WOMEN'S WORKS

Amount of time recommended for visit: **30 minutes**

The library is located on Fener Square across from the Fener Wharf. Information about the history of the building is limited. It is thought to be a structure left from the Byzantine era. The Istanbul Metropolitan Municipality Head Office started to repair the building, which was derelict, in 1989 and opened it as a library on 14 April, 1990. The most important feature of the library is that it houses publications that were written by or are related to women. It is possible to find here all kinds of publications about women from the Ottoman Empire. The library is open to the public from Monday to Friday, 10:00 a.m.–5:30 p.m.

FENER WHARF

Amount of time recommended for visit: **30 minutes**

Similar to the Fener District, the Fener wharf challenges history. Next door is the Fener police station, a two-storied wooden building. It is possible to travel to Üsküdar, Eyüp, Kasımpaşa, Balat, Sütlüce or Ayvansaray by the two ferries that leave from this port.

CAFÉ / RESTAURANT

Fener- Tarihi Haliç İşkembecisi (212) 534 9414,
Nev-i Cafe (Közde Çay ve Kahve Keyfi (212) 531 8602

BALAT

The district takes its name from the Greek word *palation*, meaning palace. The name *Balat Kapusu*, used after the conquest, is thought to have derived from this word. The history of Balat dates back to the Byzantine period, when it was a Jewish district. This was also one of the leading Jewish districts in Istanbul in the Ottoman Empire, with unique architecture, churches, synagogues, trade guilds, public baths, and social life. the contemporary Balat may rathe appeal to those specially interested.

The Balat district is of historic importance for the Jews of Istanbul. The reason for this is that all the Jews who immigrated to Istanbul or who were exiled to the city moved to this region and settled here. Thus, after the conquest of Istanbul, the Jews who immigrated from Macedonia and Spain all resided here.

According to the deed of trust kept in Fatih, the first arrivals in Balat were around 100 poor Jewish families from Kastoria, Macedonia. These families built the Kastoria Synagogue and started living around it. After this, Istanbul continued to attract Jewish immigrants. The Jews who fled the Inquisition in Spain in 1492 and from Portugal and Italy in 1497 came to Balat and built the Geruş, Neve Şalom, Messina and Montias Synagogues. Also, some Jews who came from Rhodes in 1599 moved to Balat. After the great fire in 1660, the Jews who had been living in Bahçekapı, Tahtakale and Yemiş wharf in the Eminönü district also moved to Balat.

After the second half of the 19th century, most of the residents of Balat emigrated to the Galata district. The income tax law in 1842 and the foundation of Israel in 1948 were important factors in their departure from Balat.

SVETİ STEFAN CHURCH (Demir Kilise)

Amount of time recommended for visit: **15 minutes**

This church is between Balat Vapur İskelesi Street and Mürsel Pasha Street, on the right side of the road going along the Golden Horn as one goes from Fener to Balat. The Bulgarian word *sveti* means saint.

Sveti Stefan is an interesting building because it is made entirely out of iron. For this reason, it is also known as the Iron Church. Initially, the frame was made of steel. The façade of the building is also made of steel. All the doors, windows and shutters are made only of iron. In the interior of the building, the walls, staircases, all the columns and capitals are also made of iron. Only the entrance columns and the capitals have been faced with marble to increase the impressive appearance of the building.

The church was built in eight months in 1896 and opened for worship in 1898. It was produced in its entirety in Vienna and transported by train to Istanbul. The church was then erected on land that had been prepared. It is the first cast iron church in the world. The architect was Hovsep Aznavur.

The most important feature of the church is that it broke away from the Greek Orthodox Patriarchate and became an independent Bulgarian church in 1870. It is thus an arena of competition and religious struggle between the Bulgarian Orthodox Christians and the Fener Patriarchate.

TAHTAMİNARE (Wooden Minaret) MOSQUE

Amount of time recommended for visit: **15 minutes**

This mosque is located on Vodina Street. It was constructed on the orders of Sultan Mehmed II in 1458. In 1865, when the mosque was in a derelict state, it was renovated by Halil Agha of Sivas, who was in charge of the Tahtaminare public baths. It was renovated again through donations from the congregation in 1957. The mosque is vaulted and sits on a square plan. The sultan's gallery is reserved for women. The ceiling is wooden. Verses from the Qur'an written on Kütahya tiles cover the altar. The wooden minaret which gave its name to the mosque was rebuilt out of concrete and its cone was made of metal. The minaret has only one balcony. The fountain next to the mosque was built during the reign of Sultan Süleyman the Magnificent. In front of the wall behind the altar is the tomb of Hüseyin Efendi, who took part in the conquest of Istanbul.

AHİRDA SYNAGOGUE

Amount of time recommended for visit: **15 minutes**

This synagogue is located on Kürkçü Çeşme Street. It was constructed in the 15th century and the name derives from the city of Ohri, which is where the congregation immigrated from to Istanbul. The synagogue, which was destroyed by a fire in 1693, was ordered to be rebuilt by

the sultan. It underwent renovations in 1709, 1823 and 1881. The *teva* (prayer desk) at the synagogue resembles the bow of a ship. According to legend, the shape brings to mind the storms that the Jews who came from Spain to the Ottoman Empire underwent, or Noah's Ark. Sabetay Sevi, who declared himself a prophet in the 17th century, gave a sermon here.

SURP HRESHDOGABEN CHURCH

Amount of time recommended for visit: **15 minutes**

This church is located on a street 500 meters from Balatkapı. The well-known church, located in the old Bulgarian street, was originally a Russian Orthodox church, called Haghi Eustratios in the 16th century; this was given to the Armenians in 1627. The church was blessed by Isdeponos of Bursa in the same year. The epigraph on the wall behind the main altar reveals that the church was renovated in 1628.

BALAT (Ferruh Kethüda) MOSQUE

Amount of time recommended for visit: **15 minutes**

This mosque is located in the Molla Aski region, on Mahkemealti Street, of the Balat district. It is thought that it was designed by the architect Sinan. The mosque was used as a dervish lodge and is the center of a small complex.

BALAT İSKELE (Yusuf Şücaaddin) MOSQUE

Amount of time recommended for visit: **15 minutes**

This stone building is located outside the Balatkapısı, in Karabaş Mahallesi and Vapur İskelesi Street. It was constructed in the time of Sultan Mehmed I the Conqueror. It was destroyed by the fire in 1892 and it underwent repairs which gave it its current structure. The walls of the building are made of stone. The entrance to the mosque is through its south face. There is a fountain at the left side and a storeroom at the right side.

BALAT WHARF

Amount of time recommended for visit: **10 minutes**

In Balat there used to be wharfs that connected the Golden Horn to other districts in Istanbul. These were the Yemiş Wharf, which was connected to the stores in Eminönü and used for the transportation of dried fruits, the Odun Wharf, the wharf that connected Eyüp to Galata, and the Kayık Wharf, which served the dense Hasköy-Balat traffic.

Until 1838, the coasts of the Golden Horn served as protected and safe wharfs for the residents. They were actively used for either fishing or sea transportation. However, after the 1840s, sea trade significantly altered. These old, wooden trade wharfs, extending from Sirkeci to Balat, and the warehouses in the region lost their importance.

BALAT HOSPITAL

Amount of time recommended for visit: **5 minutes**

Or-Ahayim Hospital was constructed in 1858. The hospital building was closed in 1883, when it consisted of a small house. In its place the Or-Ahayim Foundation was established to provide healthcare. The foundations of the current Or-Ahayim Hospital were laid in 1886 and it started providing services in 1898. Later, a synagogue was built inside the hospital.

CAFÉ / RESTAURANT

Meşhur Balat İşkembe Salonu-Kebap, Izgara, Dürüm
(212 631 7683

CHAPTER 3
EYÜP

THE FESHANE

The Feshane was founded in 1839 on the order of Sultan Abdülmecid. It was thought that with this factory the demand for fez and felt cloth could be met. This first industrial foundation of the country in real terms was one of the very first steel structures built in the world; the columns were imported from Belgium and installed here. The Feshane was renewed in 1866 as one the most advanced textile

factories of its time with textile machines imported from abroad. The fabrics woven in the Feshane won countless gold medals in the 1855 Paris Exhibition, the 1863 Istanbul exhibition *Sergi-i Umum-i Osmanî* and the 1893 Chicago International Exhibition. The Feshane was closed in 1939 and reopened as Sümerbank Defterdar Factory. The factory was emptied in 1986 due to environmental improvements that were happening in the Golden Horn. It was then renovated, remaining faithful to the original design of a weaving hall measuring eight thousand square meters.

EYÜP MOSQUE AND THE TOMB OF ABU AYYUB AL-ANSARİ

Amount of time recommended
for visit: **1 hour**

The name of the famous companion of Prophet Muhammad was Abu Ayyub al-Ansari (Khalid ibn Zayd). He embraced Islam along with his wife in 621, two years before the Hijra (migration from Mecca to Medina). When Prophet Muhammad came to Medina, everyone wanted to put him up in their own house. The Prophet asked for his camel to be released, so that he could make the decision according to where the camel stopped and not break anyone's heart. The camel stopped in front of the house of Abu Ayyub al-Ansari, thus honoring him. The second floor of the house was prepared for the Prophet and Prophet Muhammad

stayed there for seven months. For this reason, Abu Ayyub Al-Ansari is also known as the *Mihmandar-i Nebi* (Host of the Prophet). Abu Ayyub's house in Medina was later used as a school to teach Islam. The Prophet continued to visit this family, even after he moved to his own house. Abu Ayyub participated in all the battles with the Prophet, most importantly in the battles of Badr, Uhud, Handaq, Khaybar, in the conquest of Mecca and the Battle of Hunayn, all of which are of great importance to Islam. Abu Ayyub did not abandon the Prophet in the wars, always looking to protect him from those who wished him harm. Sometimes, Abu Ayyub would spend all night on guard duty near the Prophet's tent. During the conquest of Khaybar, Abu Ayyub was on duty all night to prevent anyone from trying to assassinate the Prophet. The Prophet was

pleased when he saw that Abu Ayyub was on duty, and he prayed God to protect Abu Ayyub in this world and the next, who stayed awake all night to protect him. Abu Ayyub helped to record the Revelation and he helped gather all the Qur'anic verses during the lifetime of the Prophet.

Abu Ayyub al-Ansari joined many battles. The last one he participated in was the first Muslim siege of Constantinople. Despite his age, he was hopeful of the glad tidings that Prophet Muhammad had mentioned in one of his hadith concerning the conquest of the city: "Constantinople will be conquered. Blessed is the commander who will conquer it, and blessed are his troops" (Ibn Hanbal, Musnad, 4:335). Abu Ayyub was in

his eighties when he joined the army and came to Constantinople in 669. He took his place in the front row during the siege and the attacks on the city ramparts. He fell ill during the siege. The commander in chief of the army, Caliph Yazid, visited him and asked his last wishes. He answered, "I desire nothing from this world. I only wish that you bury me at the farthest point you can go in enemy territory, near to the city ramparts because I have heard from the Prophet that a good Muslim would be buried under the city walls of Constantinople. It is my hope that I be that person."

Abu Ayyub al-Ansari died in 669, while the siege was continuing. After his funeral, he was buried where he had asked. The Byzantines watched this burial in astonishment from behind the city walls. After learning that the person buried in Constantinople was an important person for the Muslims and Prophet Muhammad, the Byzantine emperor remarked that the Muslims should be aware that the emperor would exhume the body and feed the corpse to wild animals. The Muslims replied that the Christians would suffer greater losses if they were to do this. The Byzantine emperor then assured them that the grave would be protected. The Byzantines erected a structure over the tomb, which they respected and visited. After the conquest of the city, at the time of Sultan Mehmed II, the first desire of the sultan was to find the grave. His mentor Akşemseddin discovered it. After finding the grave, Sultan Mehmed II built a shrine over it. He also constructed a mosque and a *madrasa* around the tomb, as well as establishing a charitable foundation. The mosque and the other structures within the complex were completed in 1459. The mosque is the very first imperial mosque built by the Ottoman emperors in Istanbul. The importance of Abu Ayyub is reflected in the fact that the girding of the sword ceremony took place here. The girding of the sword was one of the most important symbols of the Ottoman sultanate and was carried out at the time of the enthronement of a new sultan. After the conquest of Con-

stantinople, Sultan Mehmed II started the girding of the sword ceremony in front of the tomb of Abu Ayyub al-Ansari. This tradition continued until the last Ottoman sultan.

THE TOMB OF ABU'D-DERDA

Amount of time recommended for visit: **15 minutes**

Walking parallel to the seashore from the south of Eyüp Mosque one can see Zalpaşa Street next to Kızılmescid Mosque. The tomb of Abu'd-Derda (Abu al-Darda) is located here, next to Zal Mahmud Paşa Mosque.

This mosque is 15 minutes from the tomb of Abu Ayyub. Abu'd Derda was another of the Companions of the Prophet. In addition to the honor of being praised by the Prophet, Abu'd Derda had the honor of reciting the Qur'an in his presence. Abu'd Derda was one of the Companions who had memorized the entire Qur'an. In the

last years of the caliphate of Abu Bakr was appointed as a military judge. He was sent to Damascus so that he could teach the basics of Islam to the people there and he was appointed to the position of judge of Damascus, a position he maintained through the caliphate of Uthman ibn Affan.

There are two other tombs that carry the name of Abu'd Derda, one in the Karacaahmet Cemetery and the other in Eyüp. The one in Eyüp is located in Nişanca, on Zalmahmud Pasha Street, between Zalmahmud Paşa Mosque and Cezeri Kasım Paşa Mosque. We do not know when or why this was built. Muslims in particular acknowledge this place as a mausoleum in the name of this Companion of the Prophet according to our limited knowledge and visit it out of respect for his memory. According to the inscriptions on the gate to the tomb, it was renovated on the orders of Sultan Mahmud II in 1835. The text on the tomb was composed by Sahaflar Şeyhizâde Es'ad Efendi and written by the famous Ottoman calligrapher Yesarizade Mustafa İzzet Efendi in the *ta'liq* style.

PIERRE LOTI

Amount of time recommended for visit: **45 minutes**

There is a cemetery to the north of the Eyüp Mosque which takes about a ten-minute walk. Some of the students of the great

Muslim thinker Bediüzzaman Said Nursi are buried on the side of Eyüp Sultan Hill facing away from the Golden Horn: Zübeyir Gündüzalp, Mustafa Nezihi Polat, Tahiri Mutlu, Sadullah Nutku, and Bekir Berk. After walking 3–4 minutes up the

slope, there is the grave of the famous poet Necip Fazıl Kısakürek. To enjoy the view, continue up the hill a little. Here is Pierre Loti, where you can enjoy a cup of tea accompanied by a magnificent view of Istanbul.

This area known as Pierre Loti is named after a French novelist who lived here from 1850 till 1923. Pierre Loti, whose real name was Louis Marie Julien Viaud, was a naval officer. While serving in the navy, Pierre Loti had the opportunity to see Middle Eastern and Asian countries, and become acquainted with their cultures. He used his knowledge of such places in the memoirs and novels he wrote. When visiting Istanbul, the city and the Ottoman culture had a great effect on him. Subsequently, Pierre Loti visited the city many times and lived here for a long time.

The Pierre Loti Café House, which rests on the back of Eyüp, is a calm and serene place. Pierre Loti, who admired Ottoman style and lifestyle, often visited the coffee house here.

MİNİATÜRK

Amount of time recommended for visit: **2 hours**

Miniatürk was opened by the Istanbul Metropolitan Munici-

pality Head Office in 2003. The park contains 105 models of famous buildings. New models are constantly being added the park. Visiting Miniatürk is like a quick journey around Turkey. A minimum of 2 hours should be allowed.

KOÇ MUSEUM

Amount of time recommended for visit: **1 hour**

The Golden Horn and its coastline have been brought back to life, and the Golden Horn is now lined with parks and gardens. One of the most popular places here is the Rahmi Koç Industrial Museum. The museum is well worth see-

ing during a tour of the Golden Horn. The museum displays industrial development and gives us an opportunity to see machinery, both old and modern.

People with private vehicles can reach Hasköy by the coastal road at the side of the hospital Kasımpaşa Deniz Hastanesi.

(212) 297 6639 / 40

AYNALIKAVAK PAVILION

Amount of time recommended for visit: **1 hour**

The Aynalıkavak Pavilion is the only remaining structure from the Tersane or Aynalıkavak palace, which was situated on the coastline and among the woody hills for three centuries. According to historical sources including Evliya Celebi, a fa-

mous traveler and writer, it is thought that the area on which the pavilion was constructed was an imperial retreat during the Byzantine Empire. After the conquest, starting with Sultan Mehmed II, all the Ottoman emperors were fond of the great grove and vineyard that stretched along the coastline of the Golden Horn, reaching the hills of Okmeydanı and Kasımpaşa. After the construction and development of the imperial shipyards here, this area became known as Tersane Has Bahçesi (the Royal Shipyard Gardens).

The beginning of settlements around the region dates back to the reign of Sultan Ahmed I (1603–1617). The Aynalıkavak Pavilion is thought to have been constructed in this period under the reign of Sultan Ahmed III (1703–1730). It was later renovated under the reign of Sultan Selim III (1789–1807), in the form we find it today. The pavilion, with its divanhane (reception room) and beste odası (composition room) forms a graceful whole; there is an inscription in *taliq* script executed by the famous calligrapher Yesarizade Mustafa İzzet Efendi. This praises the pavilion and Sultan Selim III, as well as the poems by Enderunlu Fazıl Efendi and Sheikh Galib. The pavilion occupies a special place in 18th century architecture.

The pavilion, with one story on the landward side and two stories on the seaward side, is one of the last

and the most interesting examples of classic Ottoman architecture. Its decorations reflect the taste of the era; there are many elements that reflect the era of Sultan Selim III, which is known as the Tulip Era. The rooms are decorated with cultural symbols of this era, such as a divan that stretches along the walls and bay windows, and braziers and lanterns, the elements of an extinct lifestyle. It should not be forgotten that Selim III was also a composer. Today, the pavilion is a palace-museum and houses the Turkish Music Research Center and the Museum of Instruments in its basement.

The center was founded with various musical instruments that had been presented as gifts and the visual material that had previously been kept in Topkapı Palace Museum. The pavilion is the only example left of the palaces on the Golden Horn. It is open every day except Mondays and Thursdays.

Address: T.B.M.M. Millî Saraylar Dairesi Başkanlığı Aynalı Kavak Kasrı Aynalı Kavak Caddesi, Hasköy

Phone: (212) 227 3441

Fax: (212) 250 4094

CHAPTER 4
GALATA-BEYOGLU
TAKSIM-TOPHANE

SİRKECİBAŞI CAMİİ

Livi... Sk.
Oda... Sk.
Siraselviler Cad.
Bakraç Sk.
Cihangir Cad.
Güneşli Sk.
Emanetçi Sk.
Başkurt Sk.
Tavuk Uçmaz Sk.
Mebusan Yokuşu
yriye Cad.
Bostanbaşı Cad.
Çukur Cuma Cad.
Ağa Hamamı Sk.
Hayrat Sk.
Susam Sk.
Defterdar Yokuşu
Kadirler Yokuşu
Tunusgücü Cad.
Salih Sk.
Kumrulu Sk.
Cihangir Yokuşu
Set Sk.
aptan Sk.
Meclis-i Mebusan Cad.
Karabaş Deresi Sk.
Boğazkesen Cad.
alti Cad.
athbey Cad.
aşa Değirmen Sk.
Dericiler Sk.
Yuva Sk.
es Cad.

N

● Structures of significance
◉ Museums
● Palaces and mansions
◉ Historical buildings
○ Historical fountains
● Tombs
☪ Mosques
† Churches

0 50 100   200   300   400
                              Metre

GALATA

The original name for Galata is said to be a plural form of "milk" in Greek; it is thought that formerly dairies were here. These lines from Evliya Çelebi also record this story: "Because Galata was a nice, green, fertile land, they used to bring all the

sheep and cows to graze in Galata. Then, they would milk the animals and offer the milk to the kings. Because of the good quality of the milk produced on this fertile land, they called it Galata."

The History of Galata

Galata was surrounded by walls during the time of Constantine I (324–337); there were four hundred thirty-one houses here, a wharf, church, forum, public baths, and a theater. The limits of the original town are not known. Emperor Justinian I constructed important buildings inside Galata in 538. The city walls of Galata, built by Constantine, surrounded the city along the coastlines of the Golden Horn and Bosphorus. As protection against potential attacks

from the land, the walls surrounding Azapkapı, Şişhane and Tophane were connected to the walls along the coastlines. Deep moats surrounded the base of the city walls on the land. The gates on this side were connected by wooden bridges that stretched over the moats. The city walls of Galata were about 2 meters thick. The walls were nearly two thousand eight hundred meters long and surrounded an area of thirty-seven hectares.

Galata Tower was in place when the Muslim army and navy arrived in front of Constantinople in 717. When the Fourth Crusade came to Constantinople on 6 and 7 July 1203, the Latins succeeded in capturing the tower. So they were able to remove the chain that prevented ships entering the Golden Horn and thus seized the city. When the Byzantines retook the city in 1261, they took back the tower that controlled the entrance to the Golden Horn and protected it from the Latin colonies in the region.

The Genoese expanded the boundaries of the neighborhood and

carried it beyond the city walls. They protected the city first from the Venetians and later from the Ottomans. The Genoese built the Christea Turris, the Tower of Christ, which is the current Galata Tower.

The boundaries of the Genoese colony start from Tophane and go as far as Azapkapı along the city walls. The boundaries continue up Şişhane Hill and down to the coastline from the east of Galata Tower to the south of Yüksekkaldırım. The Galata region ends at the sea in the Topkapı District.

Depicted on the city walls of Galata was a Genoese coat of arms, in the shape of a B in the middle of a cross, representing the sovereignty of the Byzantines, the official rulers of Galata. An example of the coat of arms, with *Basileus Basileon Basileuon Basileousi* (the ruler of the rulers who rule the rulers) survived until the 20th century. This plaque, which dates back to 1335, was decorated with three crosses, arranged side by side. The cross in the middle represents Genoa, while the ones at the sides symbolize the Byzantine Empire.

The most important structure built by the Genoese was Galata Tower; it is thought that this was constructed in 1349. The Genoese Palace, built after 1316, served the Genoese colony. The churches and monasteries built by the Genoese, such as San Paola, San Francisco, San Domenico, San Giorgio, San Benedetto (St. Benoit), San Sebastian, San Nikola and Santa Maria, were a reflection of their religious lives.

As the Ottomans grew stronger, the Genoese started to form relationships with them, and a trade agreement was signed in 1387. The Genoese stayed neutral during the conquests of 1394 and 1396. Despite the French-Genoa agreement to stop the Turks, the Genoese preferred to remain close to the Ottomans. In 1403, Süleyman, the son of Sultan Beyazid I signed an agreement with Genoa, Venice, Rhodes, and the Byzantine Empire.

During the conquest of Istanbul in 1453 by the Ottomans, the Genoese from Galata did not take sides, even though they had provided the Byzantines with 5 ships.

Sultan Mehmed II assigned a *subaşı* (or *voyvoda*) and a judge to Galata after the surrender of the city and placed it directly under Ottoman administration. The Sultan demolished parts of the city walls in order to protect the city, afraid that the Christian majority could surrender the tower to Crusaders arriving from the sea.

In time, two different nations, the Florentines and Umayyad Arabs were added to the cosmopolitan structure of the population. The Florentines were mainly occupied with trade from 1463 to 1520. However, they could not continue to live in the city and left their places to the Venetians after the 16th century.

The settlement of the Umayyad Arabs continued. The Ottoman administration wanted to increase the Muslim population for reasons of security. After 1533, Barbaros Hayreddin Pasha continued to bring Moorish naval officers and refugees from Andalusia. The Umayyad Arabs immigrated en masse in 1610. The bankers in Galata turned the city of Galata into a unique money market.

GALATA BRIDGES

> Amount of time recommended for visit: **45 minutes**

Increasing commercial relations and the transfer of the Ottoman palace from the historical peninsula to Dolmabahçe in Beşiktaş in the 19th century resulted in heavier traffic between Eminönü and Karaköy.

At this time, horse carriages imported from Europe became more common, and there was a need for a second bridge to cross the Golden Horn. A wooden bridge between Karaköy and Eminönü was built in a shipyard as an alternative to the Hayratiye Bridge. This new bridge would constitute a model for three other bridges to be built over the Golden Horn later. Even though it had general similarities with Hayratiye Bridge which was built on rafts, the new bridge had pontoons.

In the place of the first bridge, which was renovated in 1853, another bridge was constructed from wooden materials in the shipyard on the orders of the Kaptan Pasha, Ateş Mehmed Pasha, in 1863. This bridge measured approximately five hundred and four meters long and was fourteen meters wide. In order for small ships to be able to pass under the bridge, there was a passage measuring five meters high.

This bridge did not last long. An agreement, known as the "Forges et Chantiers de la Mediterranée," was signed with a French firm on 24 September 1869 to construct a stronger iron bridge. The bridge was opened with a formal ceremony in 1872. As the bridge quickly became worn by the increased speeds of the trolleys in the city in the 19th century, another agreement was signed with the German firm MAN on 18 February 1907 for the construction of a new bridge.

The bridge was built out of steel, having to be strong enough to allow travel on rails. It was opened on 27 April, 1912. This was the longest lasting of all the bridges built over the Golden Horn to date. However, the narrow space between the pontoons prevented the natural flow of water to and from the Golden Horn, thus increasing the problem of pollution. The New Bridge was opened in 1992. Today, in addition to its use for transportation, this bridge, with its lower level consisting of restaurants, is a place where one can dine across from a picturesque view of Istanbul. The bridge also offers an excellent location for amateur fishing from the upper level.

ARAB MOSQUE

Amount of time recommended for visit: **15 minutes**

This mosque is located at the intersection of Tersane Street and Galata Mahkemesi Avenue. This is the largest mosque on the Galata side of the Golden Horn. When Istanbul was conquered a church stood here.

CAFÉ / RESTAURANT

Sucuk Evi
Rıhtım Cad. No 41.
(Across from the wharf) Karaköy
Phone: (212) 245 4076
        (212) 244 9515

The church was turned into a mosque in 1475 on the order of Sultan Mehmed II and became the Galata Mosque. After Arabs who emigrated here from Andalusia in 1492 took up residence around this mosque, it became known as the Arab Mosque. Over time, it has had repairs carried out and there have been some changes in its appearance. During maintenance carried out in 1913 the epigraph and tombstones of the Genoese that were located under the floor were transferred to the Archeology Museum. The mosque is a rectangular-planned Gothic building. The belfry of the old church was turned into a minaret. This minaret resembles the minarets of Andalusia.

GALATA TOWER

Amount of time recommended for visit: **45 minutes**

The Genoese, who had gradually enlarged the boundaries of the

Galata district, took over the Galata Tower area only in 1349. It was at this time that they built the tower here.

The Byzantine resources refer to this tower as the "Great Tower" (Megolas Purgos), while the Genoese sources refer to it as the Tower of Christ (Christea Turris). It was constructed during a turbulent time in the Byzantine Empire by Genoese men and women of all ages, who worked day and night to complete it.

The Byzantines were not happy with this *fait accompli*, but there was nothing they could do about it. In 1445 or 1446, there was an attempt to enlarge the tower. The Genoese wanted to maintain good relationships with the Turks to oppose their rivals in Middle Eastern trade. They asked the Ottoman ruler Murad II (1421–1451) for a loan, in order to buy construction materials to add to the height of this tower, which they had built during the fortifications of Galata. In return, they agreed to inscribe Murad II's name on the tower. When the central administration in Italy heard of this Genoese enterprise, they sent an angry letter, stating that they were rich enough to finance the fortification and enlargement of the tower.

After the Ottoman conquest of Constantinople, the tower was damaged by an earthquake which razed the city. It was repaired by the architect Murad bin Hayrettin. In the 16th century, Galata Tower was used as a

prison for war prisoners and was part of the shipyard. It is known that in the 17th century the Ottoman inventor Hezarfen (thousand-science) Ahmet Çelebi flew from Galata Tower to Üsküdar, on the other side of the Bosphorus. It is reported that he used 2000 eagle feathers in the artificial wings he invented.

In 1717, a Janissary band was placed here to let the people know when it was midnight. A fire-watch station was also set up in the tower. The fire brigade would use large drums to inform the locals of a fire.

Today, this wonderful tower dating back to the Middle Ages provides tourists with an irresistible view of Istanbul.

GALATA MEVLEVİHANESİ WHIRLING DERVISHES' LODGE

Amount of time recommended for visit: **25 minutes**

The hall is located on Galib Dede Street in the Şahkulu Neighborhood. Galata Mevlevihanesi is also known as the Kulekapı Mevlevihânesi, later becoming the Galib Dede Dergâhı, and was the first great Mevlevi establishment. It was built in 1491 on the orders of Vizier İskender Pasha during the reign of

CAFÉ / RESTAURANT

Yunus Balık, Yeni Galata Köprüsü
E-H No:16 Eminönü- Istanbul
Phone: (212) 519 8591

Sultan Bayezid II (1481–1512) on a hunting estate. The dervish lodge, constructed on the orders of Semai Mehmed Dede, one of the grandsons of Jalaladdin Rumi, was subsequent-

ly converted into a Khalwati Order lodge. It was only repaired and restored as a Mevlevi lodge at the beginning of the 18th century by Sırrı Abdi Dede. The lodge was renewed after a fire in 1765 and underwent repairs during the reign of Sultan Selim III and Abdülmecid. The Galata Mevlevihanesi was an establishment in its time, and the complex contains structures that fulfill various functions. These are Halet Efendi Library, the Halet Efendi Fountain, the Halet Efendi Shrine, the Hadikat-ül-Ervah (the Garden of Spirits, where the dervishes gathered to meditate), the *hamuşhâne* (house of silence, namely the cemetery), the kitchen, the Hasan Agha Fountain, the *semahâne*

(dervish hall), the Harem section and the Laundry room.

Many musicians were trained in music here, including Ottoman sultans. Some of these musicians were Nayi Osman Dede, Sırrı Abdülbaki Dede, Sheikh Galip Dede, Ataullah Dede, Neyzen Şeyda Veli Dede, and Leyla Hanım. The tombs of İbrahim Müteferrika, İsmail Ankaravi, and Sheikh Galip can also be seen here. In 1925, a law was passed that closed all the dervish lodges and the Hall was altered; one section is now the Beyoğlu General Registry Office.

The main artworks that remain in the museum are musical instruments, dervish garments, Banaluka prayer rugs that were embroidered in the 18th and 19th centuries using different techniques, silver chandeliers, and lecterns. In addition to these, the museum has a rich collection of poetry books, consisting of one hundred ninety-four pieces. The museum is open to the public and whirling dervish demonstrations are given

set (Apollon) and Zulfaris Synagogues could not meet the demands of the rapidly increasing Jewish population in Galata and Beyoğlu. The Jewish community then decided to renovate the primary school on Büyük Hendek Street and convert it into a synagogue. The Synagogue was opened after the requirements were met, on September 26, 1938 on the Jewish holiday Rosh Hashanah. The Synagogue was renovated by Elyo Ventura and Bernar Motola in 1946 in keeping with a decision by the Galata Jewish Congregation.

THE OTTOMAN BANK BUILDING

Amount of time recommended for visit: **35 minutes**

on the first and last Saturdays of every month.

NEVE SHALOM SYNAGOGUE

Amount of time recommended for visit: **15 minutes**

The synagogue is located on Büyük Hendek Street in the Kuledibi District. The Neve Shalom (meaning "Peace Oasis") Synagogue is the former gymnasium of a Jewish school. This area was rented out to be used as a place of worship, particularly on religious holidays during the 1930s when the Kene-

The bank is on Bankalar Street. Until very recently, parts of the building were used by the Ottoman Bank, Department of the Treasury. The name has been changed with the merger of the Ottoman Bank and Garanti Bank. The rest of the building is used by the Central Bank. In 1890, the Ottoman Bank building was built, along with the Reji Administration of Tobacco, by the renowned French-Turkish architect Alexander Vallaury. The part of the building that belonged to the bank opened in 1892.

BEYOĞLU

The Beyoğlu district encompasses the area from Taksim to the Tünel, and consists of the main street İstiklal Caddesi, which lies between the Tünel and Taksim, and all the side streets branching off from here.

The district formerly known as Pera is separated from the part of the city that is surrounded by the city walls. Until the 16th century, when the Ottomans started to establish foreign embassies, Pera was in the countryside and part of the Galata district, a crowded Latin Settlement which was host to summerhouses.

Today, the most important structures here are the Galatasarayı Ocağı, also known as the Acemi Oğlanlar Barracks, the Galata Mevlevihanesi, the Şahkulu Mosque, Asmalımescit Street and Agha Mosque. Süleyman the Magnificent was the sultan who literally changed the face of this area. As a result of support he gave to the French and the commercial treaties (known as capitulations) he granted them, the Franco-Ottoman relationship improved. The foundation of a French embassy here played a great role in the conversion of this rural area into a district that housed embassies.

After the French embassy (known as the French Palace), the Venetian embassy was built here, and then an English embassy, Polish embassy, and Dutch embassy were built. In the 17th and 18th centuries, other embassies and consuls were established here.

Only in the 19th century did the legendary city of Pera start to form. According to Çelik Gülersoy, until the 19th century, the foreigners here lived like the Turks. They did not

use luxurious furniture, or glamor-
ous porcelain plates. Instead, they ate
on sini (large trays) and heated their
food in tandoors.

With the fire of 1831, this rural
location started to become more urban. The liberties given as a result
of earlier treaties and the legal and
commercial security given to foreigners, as well as the right to own
private property with the start of the
Tanzimat Era, provided a legal environment for Europeans to start con-
verting the region into a miniature
European city. While being renewed
and renovated as a regulated settlement, it started to turn into a center
for entertainment and luxury con-
sumption.

As a result, İstiklal Avenue and
the streets that run off here were the
locations of Italian and French theaters, luxurious residences, hotels,
bars, high-class retail stores, entertainment centers, and passages full

of exotic items next to the embassies.
As a result there are not many Turkish structures in Pera. With the arriv-
al of the electric tram in 1913, con-
necting Beyoğlu to the Şişli District,
a cosmopolitan ambiance was created, also attracting Turks.

With an increase in the Mus-
lim population in the region, the city
started to change. With World War
I, social life somewhat stagnated and
then entered a phase of change with
the foundation of the Turkish Republic. With the fall-off in the non-Muslim population after 1914, the attraction of the district decreased. Even
though the new era seemed to start
with the old ambiance, brought by the
refugees from the 1917 Russian Revolution, Beyoğlu continued to change
as a result of the relocation of embassies in Ankara in 1929, the Wealth
Tax law, passed in 1942, World War
II, Jewish emigration with the foundation of the State of Israel, and the

Greek emigration after the events of 6–7 September 1955.

The Name

The Beyoğlu district, an extension of the Galata district across Sarayburnu, was known as Pera before the Ottoman Empire. The name Beyoğlu started to be used after the conquest of Istanbul. The name, which literally means the son of a *Bey* (Beg, governor or lord) indicates from where the name of the area derived. There are two hypotheses as to who this *Bey* was. The first one of them proposes that the *Bey* was the prince of Pontus, Alexios Comnenus, who converted to Islam during the reign of Sultan Mehmed II and who began to live in a mansion he owned in the district. The other hypothesis is that the name referred to the son of the Venetian ambassador A. Gritti, Luigi Gritti, who had a mansion in the area.

İSTİKLAL CADDESİ (Avenue)

Amount of time recommended for visit: **1 hour**

İstiklal Avenue is one of the most lively and crowded places in Istanbul with its shops and movies. This street is what keeps the district alive; historically it has been the main entertainment center. The street, which runs between Taksim and the Tünel, is the most cosmopolitan street in Istanbul.

The development of İstiklal Avenue happened in parallel with the development of the Beyoğlu district. The initial heart of the street encompassed the area, starting from the feet of the Galata tower up until Galatasarayı. This place remained the heart of the street until the 19th century. The development of the street, which was a dirt road until the 18th century, started with the rising number of foreigners. The street was called "Grande Rue" by the foreigners and "Cadde-i Kebir" by the Ottomans, both meaning "Grand Avenue."

During the second half of the 19th century the Grand Rue adopted its current structure. The heart of Pera, which was the residential area for foreigners from the West, attachés, and non-Muslim minorities, beat here. The Grande Rue was lined with shop windows reflecting luxury and glamour, hotels, an ever-growing number of restaurants, bars and entertainment centers, movie theaters, opera, ballet and circus performances; this was the location in Istanbul where Western entertainment was at its most lavish.

FRENCH CULTURAL CENTER

Amount of time recommended for visit: **5 minutes**

The French Cultural Center is located at the beginning of İstiklal Avenue when coming from the direction of Taksim Square, the starting point of the Beyoğlu district. The center offers cultural activities reflecting the Franco–Turkish relationship as well as language courses. It was built at the same time as the first foreign embassy building in Istanbul, the French embassy or the French Palace, in the 17th century. It was originally constructed as a hospital. This wooden building underwent several repairs in the 19th century. It was rebuilt as a stone building in 1898 and started serving as the French Embassy in 1920.

AGHA MOSQUE

Amount of time recommended for visit: **15 minutes**

This is on İstiklal Avenue in the Beyoğlu district. The mosque overlooks Sakızağacı Street to the west and Maliyeci Street to the north. The mosque was built in 1594 by the Agha of Galatasaray, Sheikh-ul Islam Hüseyin, and was later renovated during the reign of Mahmud II in 1894. The mosque is attached to the Rumeli Han from the east and it is completely surrounded by a courtyard wall.

GALATASARAY TURKISH BATHS

Amount of time recommended for visit: **15 minutes**

The *hamam* (Turkish baths) is on the left side of Galatasaray High School, at the crossroads between the Turnacıbaşı Street and Çapanoğlu Street. It was originally constructed on the order of Sultan Beyazid II in 1481 in the complex of the Galatasaray School, which gave its name to the district. The *hamam* was affiliated with the Enderun School until the Republican Period. Later, the gate that overlooks the rear garden of Galatasaray High School was blocked and the *hamam* was made completely independent. Upon being separated from the school, it became a public bath. The *hamam* was last repaired and renovated in 1965.

GALATASARAY HIGH SCHOOL

Amount of time recommended for visit: **15 minutes**

This school was originally known as the *Galata Sarayı Mekteb-i Sultanisi*, or the *Mekteb-i Sultani*— School of the Sultan, signifying that it was founded by the sultan. It was opened as an educational institution on September 1 in 1868. The school was a symbol of education from the *Tanzimat* era with a Turkish and French curriculum. Galatasaray High School was established on the foundations of the Galata Palace Guild (*Galata Sarayı Ocağı*), which had been constructed on the order of the sultan to educate the Enderuns. Sultan Abdulaziz, the grand vizier of the era, the foreign affairs minister Keçecizade Fuad Pasha, and the minister of education Saffet Pasha's trip to Europe in 1867, together with the efforts of the French ambassador M. Bourée all played an important role in the opening of Galatasaray High School.

The original purpose for opening the *Mekteb-i Sultani* was to train people to meet the need for highly skilled individuals for important positions in the government. There was a need for staff members to implement the fundamental practices of the reforms that were part of the move to Westernize the country. The *Mekteb-i Sultani*, with its new regulations and Franco–Turkish curriculum became the source of such people. From 1885, the director of the institute, who had been brought from France, organized preparatory courses in French and Turkish. The school accepted pupils between 9 and 12 years of age. Afterwards, students who graduated from the Turkish program were awarded an *ehli-*

yetname, while those who graduated from the Franco–Turkish program were awarded a *şahadetname*. The *Mekteb-i Sultani* was renamed Galatasaray High School in 1924 and still maintains its unique status as an educational institution, offering education in Turkish and French.

SAINT ANTOINE CHURCH

Amount of time recommended for visit: **5 minutes**

Saint Antoine Church is on İstiklal Avenue in Beyoğlu, on the left-hand side as one goes from Galatasaray to the Tünel. The church, and the buildings that surround it are the work of the architect Giulio Mongeri. The priests of Saint Antoine Church are mostly Italian. In the area where St. Antoine Church was built the *Concordia Theater an Garde* used to stand. However, the original building was demolished and the foundation of the church was laid in 1906, being completed in 1912. Even though the church is a recent addition to the street, its history dates back to earlier times.

The church was originally in Azapkapı (the location of the Perşembe Pazarı), and had been built by monks of the Franciscan order in 1272. The wooden church was destroyed by fire in 1699. Attempts were made to rebuild the church, but the sultan, Mustafa II, did not give permission for its reconstruction due to some political reasons. He built a mosque known as the New Mosque (Yeni Camii) in this area. In 1762 the Catholic Franciscan church was built on the land of the French Embassy, but it was later demolished because it stood in the way of the tramlines that were going to be built. The church was then built in its current location. However, the church took six years to complete, as the construction of the apartments had to be completed first; this was a precondition imposed by the Ottoman Empire for the building of the church. This church has the largest Catholic congregation in Istanbul.

ANADOLU PASSAGE

Amount of time recommended for visit: **25 minutes**

Anadolu Passage is on İstiklal Avenue, next to the Atlas Cinema. It leads up to Alyon Street, one of the famous old streets in Beyoğlu. The passage was opened to public in the 20th century. Before this, Anado-

lu Passage and two other passages in the region, Rumeli Passage and Africa Passage, belonged to one of the chamberlains of Sultan Abdülhamid II, Ragıp Pasha. Ragıp Pasha built the passages with his private income to contribute to the future commercial development of the city. The building on İstiklal Avenue reflects typical Beyoğlu architecture.

RUMELİ PASSAGE

Amount of time recommended for visit: **25 minutes**

Rumeli Passage is located between Sakız Ağacı Sokak and İmam Adnan Sokak, on the right side of İstiklal Avenue as one goes from Taksim towards Galatasaray. The passage was built by Ragıp Pasha. This is the second passage of three that he owned in Beyoğlu. Ragıp Pasha had all the passages built in order to remind the people of Beyoğlu of the Ottoman Empire and he gave them the names of the three large land masses that bring to mind the Ottoman Empire. This passage, like the other two, is constructed of stone. The construction of the building was started in the second half of the 19th century.

AFRICA PASSAGE

Amount of time recommended for visit: **15 minutes**

This is located between Büyük (Big) and Küçük (Small) Parmakkapı Streets in Beyoğlu. Africa Passage belonged to Ragıp Pasha, like the two other passages in Beyoğlu. This is the newest of all three, being constructed last. The final floor of the six-story building was an apartment in which Levantines lived.

HACI ABDULLAH RESTAURANT

Amount of time recommended for visit: **35 minutes**

The history of Hacı Abdullah starts in the Ottoman era; in the final years of the Ottoman era a restaurant called Abdullah Efendi opened at Karaköy Wharf. The license for the restaurant was granted by Sultan Abdülhamid II himself. Envoys and ambassadors would be entertained at this restaurant. In 1915, the Hacı Abdullah Restaurant was transferred from Karaköy Wharf

to the Beyoğlu district. It continues to serve the public on the ground floor of Rumeli Passage.

İNCİ PATISSERIE

Amount of time recommended for visit: **25 minutes**

This pastry shop on İstiklal Avenue, near the Atlas Cinema is famous for its profiteroles. The patisserie was established in the 1930s, although the foundation of the building was laid in 1910.

At first, it was opened to public service next to the Rekor Patisserie in a partnership between Luka Zigoris and Lefter İlyadis, and later it was run inside a big delicatessen store under the name of Balkan Tereyağları administered by Aleko Pilarinos. The patisserie has been famous for its profiterole since the first day of its exis-

CAFÉ / RESTAURANT

Beyoğlu-Barcelona Cafe & Patisserie (212) 292 4321
Beyoğlu MADO (212) 244 1781
Bereket Döner (212) 251 4221

tence. The İnci Patisserie has always maintained very high quality over the years and is renowned for its sweets.

TAKSİM

The Taksim district can be considered one of the relatively new districts in Istanbul. Centuries ago, an Armenian cemetery in a huge meadow and a Muslim cemetery with cypress trees were located here. Taksim Square and its surroundings had the best view of the Golden Horn and the Bosphorus and were used as imperial gardens. The Taksim district was used for Levantine, Russian, Armenian and Muslim cemeteries for a long time. The Ayazpaşa side was where the Muslim cemetery was located, while the Harbiye side, namely the Talimhane district, was for graveyards for minority subjects. In subsequent years, the artillery barracks of the Ottoman Empire were built here. After the 1870s, gardens in the English style were built around the barracks. Over time, the barracks fell out of use and the area

became a resort. Today, Taksim is one of the most central, lively, and crowded places.

The name Taksim literally means division, and the name comes from the water distribution reservoir that is found here. This classical stone structure with a grooved dome is located at the corner of Taksim Square; it was constructed during the reign of Sultan Mahmud I. This is where the water arrived from the northern mountains to be distributed to the city.

TAKSİM SQUARE

Amount of time recommended for visit: **30 minutes**

The meadow that lay between the Taksim Maksemi (reservoir) and the Artillery Barracks started to

serve the function of a town square after the Republican era when the Republican Monument was erected there, and with better transportation. Taksim Square became a symbol of the Republic in the early years of its establishment. In recent years, the square has been the meeting point of the Taksim tram, subway, buses and cars and it is very crowded most of the time.

THE REPUBLICAN MONUMENT

Amount of time recommended
for visit: **5 minutes**

The monument, which has become the symbol of Taksim Square, was a commissioned work by the Italian sculptor Pietro Canonica. It was erected in 1928. It took 2½ years to make the statue out of stone and bronze. The expenses for the statue were collected from the people.

ATATÜRK CULTURAL CENTER

Amount of time recommended
for visit: **25 minutes**

When there was a need to construct a building to host cultural activities, naturally Taksim was the first place that came to mind. After the demolition of the Ayazpaşa cemetery in the 1920s, it was the location chosen for building apartment buildings; while in the 1930s it was the location chosen for the Great Opera Hall. Although the construction plans for the Great Opera Hall were accepted, the project was not realized, due

to the start of World War II. In 1946, the foundations of the Opera Building were finally laid. The building was to be composed of three main structures. The middle part of the building consisted of the entrance, foyer, lounge, theater, and concert hall. However, the project was left half finished. The new engineer who took on the task changed the project and transformed the building into a sophisticated and multifaceted cultural center. He added a concert hall with the capacity to accommodate an audience of five hundred people, a theater that held two hundred people, a cinema that held two hundred and fifty people and an art gallery. Today, this is still the most popular culture and art center in Istanbul.

KAZANCI MOSQUE

Amount of time recommended
for visit: **15 minutes**

The mosque is located on Kazanci hill in Taksim. It was constructed in the 17th century in the Ottoman style. The mosque is constructed on a square plan and has a brick minaret.

SİRKECİBAŞI MOSQUE

Amount of time recommended for visit: **15 minutes**

This mosque is located across from the Taksim Sıraselviler İlkyardım Hospital. It is built of brick and stone on a square plan, and was constructed in the 18th century. The pulpits are made of wood.

HAGHIA (AYA) TRIADA GREEK ORTHODOX CHURCH

Amount of time recommended for visit: **15 minutes**

Situated on Meselik Street in Taksim, this church was built on land surrounded by İstiklal Avenue and Sıraselviler. The façade of the historical church overlooks Sıraselviler Street houses and shops owned by the church foundation.

TEPEBAŞI AND TAKSİM TURKISH BATHS

Amount of time recommended for visit: **15 minutes**

Hygiene and cleanliness is an important element in Turkish culture. The concept of hygiene existed even when the Turks were leading nomadic lives. This understanding developed further with the introduction of Islam and it acquired a special place in the Ottoman era. This understanding of hygiene led to the creation of the *hamam* (Turkish bath) culture. *Hamam*s were constructed in the streets, town centers and mosque complexes in order to serve the local people. In the registry of *hamam* proprietors from the year 1734, there is a *hamam* registered under the name of Tepebaşı Hamamı. However, the location of the *hamam* is not known. What used to be the Taksim Hamamı, however, is currently being used as a retail shop on İstiklal Avenue and its upper floor operates as commercial premises.

Taksim Maksemi (reservoir/distribution point)

This structure is located at the meeting points of İstiklal Avenue and Taksim Street. Its construction started under the rule of Sultan Ahmed III to resolve a problem in supplying water to the city. The construction process continued during the reign of Mahmud I and was completed in 1731 along with Taksim Waterworks. The Taksim Maksemi is literally the water distribution center of the city. It has a body made of limestone and an octagonal pyramidal roof. Over the vaulted gate of the *maksem*, there is an epigraph dated 1732, consisting of three couplets. There is a window with a bowed arch and bird houses, made in the classical Turkish style, on both sides. While going from the Maksem in the Harbiye direction there is a wall, which is the "Taksim Treasury," that is a water reservoir, which supplied water to the *maksem* in case the water was cut off.

TAKSİM WATERWORKS

The water infrastructure, that is the water network and reservoirs that supplied water to the city, were designed in such a way that water first came to the *hamam*s, fountains, and cisterns, and then to important private homes. Starting from the 18th century, the northern part of the Golden Horn started becoming very populated and the shores of the Bosphorus were becoming new settlement sites with construction of *yalı* (waterside residences). With this increasing settlement, the city started to have problems in supplying everyone with enough water. Taksim Waterworks measures twenty-five meters in length. Through this system water can be delivered to all regions from Maslak to Taksim, as well as surrounding areas of Taksim. This is the most developed water system that was inherited from the Ottoman era and is still currently in use.

THE FOUNTAINS OF MAKSEM

Amount of time recommended for visit: **5 minutes**

On the right of the Maksem gate stands the Mahmud I Fountain, which reflects the style of its time. The fountain was not functioning at the time of writing and has been neglected. The fountain that is inside the archway has also been badly neglected.

HAFIZ AHMED PASHA FOUNTAIN

Amount of time recommended for visit: **5 minutes**

Immediately across from Taksim is the Hafız Ahmed Pasha Fountain, at the intersection of Kazancıbaşı Mosque Street and Başkurt Street. The fountain was built by Hafız Ahmed Pasha. The epigraph of the mosque, which dates back to 1732,

consists of thirteen couplets. The fountain has a classic design and is made from hewn stone. This is one of the most beautiful fountains in Istanbul that have a water reservoir included. The fountain takes its water from the Taksim water that comes from the Kazancı Hills. After renovations the water supply was cut off.

TAKSİM TOPÇU KIŞLASI ARTILLERY BARRACKS

After a period of stagnation in the Ottoman Empire, the decision to reform the empire was taken in the 17th century. After these reforms, new schools quickly started to open, one of which was the Taksim Artillery Barracks. The barracks were constructed in the 19th century, during the reign of Sultan Abdülmecid (1839–1861), under the supervision of Halil Pasha. However, the barracks gradually lost their importance between 1860 and 1870. The barracks were used as lodges of imperialist powers' troops, which consisted of the soldiers—some of whom were Muslims—they brought from their colonies. during the occupation

of Istanbul. After 1939, the barracks were completely destroyed with the Taksim area being turned into a promenade and excursion spot.

HARBİYE MILITARY MUSEUM

Amount of time recommended for visit: **1 hour**

The military museum and the cultural complex are located in the Harbiye district of Istanbul.

The history of the Military Museum

The foundation of the museum dates back to the 15th century. After the conquest of Constantinople by the Turks in 1453, Haghia Irene Church was used as an arsenal where all the valuable weapons and war materials were collected.

In 1726, all the objects in the arsenal were arranged under a new organization known as the *Dar-ül Esliha* (House of Weapons). The foundation of the museum in modern terms was established by Damat Ahmet Fethi Pasha in 1846. The establishment of this museum was the first real museum in the history of Turkish museology. The spaces between the porticos of Haghia Irene were covered with display windows and turned into exhibition areas. In some parts of these areas exhibitions of ancient war weapons, tools and materials are displayed, while in others there are collections of archeological art works. The collection in Haghia Irene was first called the *Müze-i Hümayun* (Imperial Museum). Over time the building became inadequate for the collection. The restored old building in Harbiye was chosen as the Military Museum, and the new museum was opened in 1993.

Military Museum Exhibition Halls

Here only five thousand pieces from the collection of the Military Museum, which numbers of forty-five thousand, are exhibited. The rich collection, which is classified according to different themes, dates, or eras, is composed of various weapons, military uniforms, tents, flags, and other similar examples of militaria. Among these can be found weapons, which are elegantly engraved or inscribed, armor, shields and helmets, and other equipment signifying the majesty of the Ottoman army, as well as precious examples of Ottoman royal tents and pavilions.

Public Mehter Concerts

Concerts by *Mehter* (traditional Janissary bands) are given in two sessions, 20 minutes long, with a history of the Janissary band being given in Turkish and English. The concerts are open to the public every day (except Monday and Tuesday) from 15:00 until 16:00 inside Atatürk Hall. The repertoire of the *Mehter* includes pieces of music from the Ottoman Empire and works composed in the twentieth century.

NİŞANTAŞI

Amount of time recommended for visit: **1 hour**

At the intersection of Teşvikiye, Osmanbey, Valikonağı and Harbiye there is a stone that is the symbol of Nişantaşı; this stone gave the district its name. On the stone is written: "This work of art was made by Sultan Mecid for no compensation." This stone commemorates the donation of this land to the public by the sultan; in the Ottoman Empire all the land belonged to the sultan. The district, once composed of vast orchids and strawberry fields, starts from the hill behind Dolmabahçe Palace and extends from Maçka through Teşvikiye, Rumeli Street and the Governor's Mansion.

In the Ottoman Empire there were archery competitions; the furthest point where an arrow was shot would be marked by stone column. The name of the Nişantaşı (meaning marker stone) district is derived from these columns. Moreover, such columns have been used since the Roman era to mark distances. The stones erected on the order of Sultan Abdülmecid were placed to mark Teşvikiye. This

region was the area where target practice was carried out during the early years of the *Nizam-ı Cedid* (New Order, the first attempt at Westernization in the 18th century) in the Ottoman Empire. A small wooden mosque was built as a resting place and a place for the sultan to pray during the displays of skill, and acted as the foundation for the current Teşvikiye Mosque, the first building to be erected in Nişantaşı. A primary school was built on the order of the sultan in the current location of the Sait Çiftçi Primary School.

With the move of the royal residence to Dolmabahçe Palace the district became a popular area for members of the royal family and leading statesmen, thus gaining importance. Abdülmecid had two inscribed stones erected in the region indicating his intention that it was to be a residential area. Nişantaşı is close to Pera and due to the fact that Pera was a trade center this new settlement developed rapidly. Nişantaşı—with its rich history and socio-cultural mosaic—is one of the more important districts of Istanbul. Here there are a large number of coffee houses, restaurants and retail stores The old structures of westernized Nişantaşı reflect its history.

TEŞVİKİYE MOSQUE

Amount of time recommended for visit: **15 minutes**

This was the first building to be constructed in Nişantaşı, which previously had been empty and uninhabited land. The original mosque was very small and became run down, and unable to meet the needs of the local people. According to the inscription on the gate of the sultan's gallery, which praises the city, the mosque was constructed on the orders of Sultan Abdülmecid. There are two target stones (*nişantaşı*) in the courtyard of the mosque. The inscription on one of the target stones tells us that Sultan Selim III shot an arrow a distance of 1,260 *gez* (a measuring unit equivalent to the length of an arrow). The other inscription provides us with the same information about Sultan Mahmud II.

CAFÉ / RESTAURANT

Saray Muhallebicisi
(212) 292 3434

CİHANGİR MOSQUE

Amount of time recommended for visit: **15 minutes**

Cihangir Mosque is the pearl of the Cihangir district and its unequaled view enchants the people who visit here. The four-hundred-year-old magnificence of this mosque is complemented by the beauty of Istanbul and the Bosphorus, which we can see from the courtyard. Cihangir is an enchanting, proud, and intellectual district of Istanbul, well aware of its beauty. The Cihangir Mosque is placed in the most beautiful spot where the land meets the sea. Although it is in the center of Istanbul, people who live outside the district are unaware of this mosque, and thus it gives the impression of a serendipitous jewel. The fame of the mosque is spread by those who have visited it and beheld the picturesque view. Once having entered the courtyard of the mosque, which resembles an imperial garden, it is difficult to leave without getting one's fill of the Bosphorus. The mosque and its courtyard are open from the morning

TAKSİM

Acara Sk.
Yeni Çarşı Cad.
allavi Sk.
Nuri Ziya Sk.
Gül Baba Sk.
İstiklal Cad.
Tomtom Kaptan Sk.
Bostanbaşı Cad.
Çukur Cuma Cad.
Faik Paşa Sk.
Kadirler Yokuşu
Türkgücü Cad.
Defterdar Yokuşu
Salih Sk.
Ağa Hamamı Sk.
Sıraselviler Cad.
Matara Yokuşu
Havyar Sk.
Coşkun Sk.
Akarsu Yokuşu
Ağa İş Sk.
Simsirci Sk.
Liva Sk.
Soğancı Sk.
Bakraç Sk.
Oba Sk.
Cihangir Cad.
Güneşli Sk.
Kumrulu Yokuşu
Başkurt Sk.
Tavuk Uçmaz Sk.
Hardal Sk.
Emanetçi Sk.
Mebusan Yokuşu
Özoğul Sk.
Susam Sk.
Kumrulu Sk.
CİHANGİR CAMİİ
Cihangir Yokuşu

Tombaz Sk.
Borazan Sk.
Batarya Sk.
Bostan İçi Sk.
Ortme Altı Sk.
ostan Sk.
Kumbaracı Yokuşu
Karabaş Cad.
Boğazkesen Cad.
I. Set Sk.
Lüleciler Cad.
Sanatkarlar Cad.
Sanatkarlar Mektebi Sk.
Meclis-i Mebusan Cad.

TOPHANE KASRI
NUSRETİYE CAMİİ

TOPHANE

Dibek Sk.
Ali Hoca Cad.
Lüleci Hendek Cad.
KILIÇ ALİ PAŞA TÜRBESİ

Alişan Sk.
Kemeralti Cad.
Çeşme Sk.
Arapoğlan Sk.
Vekilharç Sk.
Ali Paşa Değirmeni Sk.
Mumhane Cad.
Murakıp Sk.
Denizciler Sk.
Yuva Sk.

Arşın Sk.
Necatibey Cad.
Demirciler Sk.
Maliye Cad.
Kemankeş Cad.
tük Sk.
YERALTI CAMİİ
ıhtım Cad.

N

●	Structures of significance
◉	Museums
●	Palaces and mansions
◎	Historical buildings
○	Historical fountains
●	Tombs
☪	Mosques
✝	Churches

0 50 100   200   300   400
Metre

prayer at the break of dawn until the last prayer at night. The mosque, like all mosques in Istanbul, has a unique history; it was constructed between 1559 and 1560, and was rebuilt on the orders of Sultan Abdülhamid II after being damaged by fire. The niche, pulpit and the sultan's gallery are made of wood and are pleasing to the eye. The thirty-nine plaques which embellish the interior of the mosque date back to between 1868 and 1890. They were made by the most renowned Ottoman calligraphers, such as Hafız, Sami, Rakım, Şevki, Hasan Rıza, Sabri Şefik, Muhammed Fehmi, Mehmed Tahir, Arif, and Seyyid Ali. The architectural style of the mosque is similar to that of Mihrimah Sultan Mosque in Edirnekapı, which was built by Mimar Sinan. In the tomb of the mosque there are twenty-eight graves, one of which is that of Sheikh Hasan Burhaneddin Cihangir of the Khalwati Order.

YERALTI (Underground) MOSQUE

Amount of time recommended for visit: **30 minutes**

A staircase leads us down a few steps into the mosque. The interior of the mosque is unique. This is not surprising as the original building was not constructed as a mosque. The Yeraltı Mosque, also known by the name of *Kurşunlu Mahzen* (Lead Cellar), was actually a prison during the Byzantine period. Tradition has it that the colossal chain used to blockade ships from entering the Golden Horn was anchored here. The Umayyad Empire laid siege to the Byzantines several times with no success. On one of these occasions after seven days of fighting, the Umayyad troops returned to Damascus. Before doing this, the commander in chief, Maslama, put some weapons into this dungeon and closed all the doors by covering them with molten lead. The dungeon was turned into a mosque by one of the leading officials under Sultan Ahmed III, Mustafa Bahir Pasha of Çorlu, in 1725. The graves of the Companions of the Prophet that are inside the dungeon were a very important factor in the decision to turn this structure into a mosque.

TOPHANE

Amount of time recommended for visit: **15 minutes**

The Tophane-i Amire (cannon foundry) was one of the first buildings to be established by the Ottomans to create weapons for war. Sultan Mehmed II, who used cannons greatly in the conquest of Constantinople, established the Tophane outside of the city walls of Galata and at the entrance to the Bosphorus. Even though we have limited knowledge about the details of the original construction of this building, it is known that it was much used until the reign of Sultan Abdülaziz due to the need for weapons and related technology. Over the years, there have been additions made to the building and it has undergone several renovations after fires.

After 1958 the main building was restored and converted into a series of shops. It was kept empty for 40 years, as it could not be decided how to put the building to use. In 1998, Tophane started to serve as the Cultural and Art Center for Mimar Sinan University.

TOPHANE PAVILION

Amount of time recommended for visit: **15 minutes**

This is located on Necatibey Street in Tophane, next to Nusretiye Mosque. This building was one of the most important elements of the old Tophane Square. It was commissioned by Sultan Abdülmecid to be built by the English architect James Smith and completed in 1852. The pavilion was used as accommodation for the sultans who were visiting the army in Tophane or as a reception place for foreign government representatives arriving in the city. Moreover, the pavilion hosted very important historical events. The pavilion was built on the orders of Sultan Mahmud II in 1823–26 in the Baroque style out of hewn stones and marble. The brother of the tsar,

Grand Duke Constantine, was put up here by Sultan Abdülmecid. The international conference which ended the Ottoman–Greek War in 1897 and the Commission des Détroits (International Straits Commission) were summoned here after the Treaty of Lausanne. The pavilion is rectangular and consists of two floors, and it is located parallel to the sea. Among the most attractive features of the pavilion are its exterior carvings, the Baroque--style balcony supported by columns, the ceiling decorations and the marble fireplace.

NUSRETİYE MOSQUE

Amount of time recommended for visit: **15 minutes**

This mosque has two elegant minarets. The sultan's gallery, the pasha apartment of the mosque, which also has fountain, and the *muvakkithane* (a pavilion where prayer

times are calculated) all have architectural styles that are well worth seeing. The interior is magnificent with, gold-foiled wooden ornamentation adorning the dome. The niche and pulpit are made of marble and delicately engraved. The calligraphy in the mosque was written by the most famous and important calligraphers of the Ottoman Empire.

KILIÇ ALİ PASHA COMPLEX

Amount of time recommended for visit: **25 minutes**

This complex is located on Tophane Square. It is a small complex composed of a *madrasa*, shrine, fountain and Turkish baths. It was commissioned by the *kaptan pasha* Kılıç Ali Pasha in 1581 and built by Sinan. It is one of the last works of Sinan. It is said that when Kılıç Ali Pasha asked Sultan Murad III for land in order to build a mosque, he was told that he should build the mosque on the sea, as he was the *kaptan pasha*. Thus, Kılıç Ali Pasha had the mosque built on reclaimed land. There is a fountain in the courtyard, the dome of which rests on eight marble columns. The mosque is seen to be a smaller version of Haghia Sophia, and is in a rectangular shape. The hurricane lamp that used to hang from the dome here from the 16th century on was transferred to the Naval Museum in 1948. On the right of the mosque there is a single minaret with a single balcony. The tomb of Kılıç Ali Pasha is in the courtyard, lying in the direction of the Ka'ba. There is a fountain by the garden wall that faces the street. The Turkish baths are on the right side of the mosque and are still used today. The *madrasa* is located on the side of the mosque that faces the sea.

CAFÉ / RESTAURANT

Cihangir-Kahvedan
(212) 292 4030
Tophane-Erzurum Çay Evi
(212) 252 2469

by FC

Amount of time recommended for visit: On average half a day. However, if one wants to see all the sights here, a whole day should be allowed.

BEŞİKTAŞ

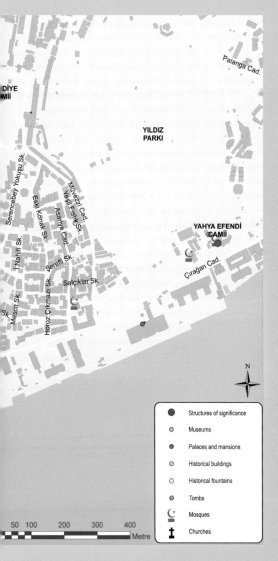

Structures of significance
Museums
Palaces and mansions
Historical buildings
Historical fountains
Tombs
Mosques
Churches

50   100   200   300   400
Metre

B eşiktaş is one of the oldest districts built outside the city walls of Istanbul. It is on the European (Rumeli) side of the Bosphorus, lying between Tophane and Ortaköy. To the west is Şişli, with Beyoğlu and Sarıyer to the north. Beşiktaş used to be a part of Beyoğlu till 1930. The name used to be *Kune Petro*, or "stone cradle." The famous Ottoman traveler Evliya Çelebi tells us about a stone basin in which Jesus had been bathed as a child that was brought from Jerusalem; a priest called Yashla established a large church at this location. However, there are some historians who support the idea that the city was named "Beştaş"

(5 Stones) because of the 5 columns that were erected in the sea by Barbaros Hayrettin Pasha to anchor ships; the name altered over time and became Beşiktaş.

According to Dr. Cavit Baysun, this area of the city was closely connected with the Ottoman navy and there used to be a dry dock among the stone columns on the seashore. This is why the locals may have called the place "Beşiktaşı" which turned into "Beşiktaş" over time.

Beşiktaş was one of the important residential areas on the Bosphorus during the Byzantine era; from the 4th century until the 15th century, the city of Beşiktaş was famous for three important structures: Haghios Mikhail Church at Auaplus (meaning against the current), the Haghios Mamas Palace complex, which was the summer residence for the emperors, and the Fokas Monastery.

Haghios Mikhail Church was constructed by the founder of Constantinople, Constantine, emperor between 305 and 337. It was an important place for pilgrimage and attracted many Christian pilgrims. A mosaic icon of Archangel Mikhail was kept in this church.

Beşiktaş became a residential area in the Ottoman Empire. This was an important place for maritime and naval affairs, particularly due to the fact that the navy commander Barbaros Hayreddin took a great interest in the

region. He had a *yalı* (waterside residence) in Beşiktaş. Barbaros Hayreddin Pasha had a mosque, *madrasa* and primary school built here and he was buried here.

According to the city plan, during the reign of Süleyman the Magnificent, Beşiktaş came back to life and the area was important in the reign of Sultan Selim II.

The area surrounding the tomb of Barbaros is known to have operated as a slave market, is known as the *Deve Meydanı* (camel square). This was the origin of the route for caravans, the means of transportation between Anatolia and Rumeli. Later, Beşiktaş became the gateway to Üsküdar for soldiers who were being sent from Anatolia to Rumeli or from Rumeli to Anatolia.

THE HISTORICAL DISTRICTS OF BEŞİKTAŞ

Arnavutköy: This area is located between Bebek and Kuruçeşme. It was formerly known as Hestai or Promo-

tu or Anaplus in the Byzantine era. Information about how or when Arnavutköy got its present name is very limited. According to one story, the name dates from when Sultan Mehmed the Conqueror brought Albanians to live here.

Aşiyan: This region is situated between Bebek and the Rumeli Fortress, on the hills of the cemetery. It was known in Greek as Lomekopi and in Turkish as Boğazkesen, meaning "the Bosphorus Breaker," as this bit of land narrows the Bosphorus. The area today takes its name from the house of the poet Tevfik Fikret, which is on the hill, overlooking the sea; the word *aşiyan* means "bird's nest" in Persian.

Balmumcu: This street is situated on the crossroads between Yıldız and Zincirlikuyu on Barbaros Avenue. There used to be a farm at the current location of Balmumcu Street during the reign of Sultan Mahmud II (1808–1839). The mansion, known as Balmumcu Kasrı was built during the reign of Sultan Abdülaziz.

Bebek:

Information about the origin of the name Bebek dates back before the conquest of Istanbul. According to one theory, Bebek is named after Bebek Çelebi (which is most likely a nickname, as *bebek* means "baby" in Turkish), a lieutenant of Sultan Mehmet II; he was sent here to build the Rumeli Fortress and thus establish control of the Bosphorus. Bebek Çelebi built himself a mansion and garden here, giving this area his name. From the end of the 18th century until the middle of the 19th century the shore extends from Bostancıbaşı Defterleri to the Arnavutköy Wharf and to the Rumeli Fortress. There were about 40 waterside palaces belonging to Ottoman statesmen, such as the Sheikh-ul Islam (the chief religious official in the Ottoman Empire), the *kazasker* (military judge) of Rumeli, the *reisülküttab* (foreign minister), and the chief physician.

Kuruçeşme:

This area is situated on the coast and the steep hill that rises behind it; the region stretches from the little point in Ortaköy known as Defterdarburnu up to the beginning of Arnavutköy at Sarrafburnu and Çorlulu Ali Pasha Mansion (the current entrance to Robert College). The green groves of Kuruçeşme have been depicted in engravings throughout history. It is mentioned as being one of 28 gardens in the Başvekâlet archives in the early 1800s. The coastal and mansion gardens

Kumpir

that were given to members of the imperial family and high-ranking officials were very important; in fact, often gardeners from Europe were hired to plan and care for the gardens.

Ortaköy:

In the past this was a cosmopolitan area with Turkish, Greek, Armenian and Jewish communities. People of different races and beliefs lived together in peace and this characteristic of the area has survived until today. Ortaköy can be easily identified from the Bosphorus because of it ornate mosque on the pier.

Yıldız:

This area near the Bosphorus is not far from the bridge. Yıldız Palace and Yıldız Park are located here. The residential area lies between Yıldız Street and Yıldız Posta Street on the west side of Barbaros Avenue. The palace and the district are situated on the forest-covered hills that descend to Beşiktaş and Ortaköy.

DOLMABAHÇE PALACE

Amount of time recommended
for visit: **1.5 hours**

The location of Dolmabahçe Palace is believed to be the spot where the Argonaut anchored while Jason was on his quest for the Golden Fleece. This is also the spot where Sultan Mehmet II is believed to have brought his fleet to land during the conquest of Constantinople; from here he was able to reach the Golden Horn. This bay, which acted as a natural harbor, is where the *kaptan pasha*s anchored and where naval ceremonies took place. The land on which Dolmabahçe stands was reclaimed from the sea starting from the 17th century and was used first as gardens for the sultan's palace.

Throughout history, this area was full of villas and pavilions built by various sultans; over time, these buildings took on the appearance of a palace and were known as the "Beşiktaş Waterside Palace." During the reign of Sultan Abdülmecid, the Beşiktaş Waterside Palace was demolished, as it was built of timber and had fallen into disrepair, and starting in 1843 the foundations of today's Dolmabahçe Palace began to be laid in its place.

Dolmabahçe Palace stands on an area that measures fifteen thousand square meters, and is based on oak pillars and wooden mats.

The construction, including the perimeter walls, was completed in 1856. Dolmabahçe Palace is made up of sixteen separate sections in addition to the main structure. These sections include buildings with different functions, such as the palace stables, mills, pharmacies, kitchens, aviaries, glassblowing workshop, foundry and patisserie shop. During the reign of Sultan Abdülhamid II (1876–1909), the clock tower and the lodges in the rear garden of the Heir's Apartments were added.

The main structure of the building was erected by the Ottoman architects Karabet and Nikogos Balyan; this building consists of three main sections: the *Mabeyn-i Hümayun* (traditional reception chamber for men), the *Muayede Salon* (Celebration Reception Hall), and the *Harem-i Humayun* (the Imperial Harem – the family quarters of the sultan). The *Mabeyn-i Humayun* was used as administrative offices, while the *Harem-i Humayun* was used by the sultan and his family. The *Muayede Salon*, which lies between the other two sections, was used as a reception or ceremonial hall where the sultan greeted high-ranking officials and where ceremonies were held. From 1910–12 electricity was brought to the palace and a central heating system was added to the main heating system. The three-storied palace, covering an area of 110,000 square meters, has 285 rooms, 46 reception rooms, 6 balconies, 68 toilets, and 6 Turkish baths. The floors of the entire building are covered by the most precious carpets in the world, Hereke carpets, covering a total area of 4,454 square meters. The *Mabeyn* section of the palace, where the Sul-

tan kept an eye on government administration, is the most important part of Dolmabahçe Palace.

The *Medhal* Salon, at the entrance, welcomes visitors, and the Crystal Stairs connect the lower floor to the upper floor; here is the Süfera Salon where the ambassadors were entertained and the Red Room where they were admitted into the sultan's presence. These sections are decorated in a way that reflects the magnificence of the Ottoman State.

The *Zülvecheyn* (facing two sides) Hall on the upper floor is a room that was private for the sultan. In this special room,

there is a splendid Turkish bath for the sultan; the marble was brought from Egypt. There is also a study and reception rooms.

In the *Muayede* Hall, between the *Harem* and the *Mabeyn*, there is the room that has the highest ceiling in Dolmabahçe Palace. This reception hall, measuring over two thousand square meters in area, has fifty-six columns, a dome that is thirty-six meters high, and English chandeliers, weighing between four and five tons, hanging from the ceiling.

The hall is heated by the air coming up through the columns from the ground floor. In this way, ceremonies could be held in cold seasons as well. Other principal sections of the palace are the suite of the Valide Sultan (mother of the sultan), the Blue and Pink Halls, the bedrooms of Sultan Abdülmecid, Abdülaziz and Mehmed Reşad, the section that housed the lower ranking palace women, known as the *Cariyeler Dairesi* (Concubine Rooms), the rooms of the *kadınefendi* (the sultan's wives), and the study and bedroom used by Atatürk; in the Harem section there are countless priceless goods, carpets, vases, and chandeliers. The palace is open to visitors.

CAFÉ / RESTAURANT

Dolmabahçe Tea Garden (next to Dolmabahçe Palace)

ISTANBUL PAINTING AND SCULPTURE MUSEUM

Amount of time recommended for visit: **45 minutes**

The museum is located in the Heir's Apartments of Dolmabahçe Palace. The museum was established as part of the Istanbul Academy of Fine Arts (today Mimar Sinan University) on 10 September 1937 on the order of Atatürk. The entrance is facing the Beşiktaş Wharf. This is a three-story building consisting of many rooms and halls. There are small structures known as *Hareket Pavyon* where special exhibitions are held. The Istanbul Painting and Sculpture Museum has examples from several famous Turkish artists, such as Osman Hamdi Bey, Şeker Ahmet Paşa, İbrahim Çallı, Bedri Rahmi, Abidin Dino, and Sabri Berkel. There are four hundred and ninety-five

sculptures and seven thousand two hundred and thirteen drawings in the museum. The museum is open on Wednesdays, Thursdays, and Fridays between 9:00–17:00. There is no entrance fee for the museum. Telephone: (212) 261 4298

YAHYA EFENDİ DERVISH LODGE

Amount of time recommended for visit: **30 minutes**

This is next to Yıldız Park in Beşiktaş on Yahya Efendi Cul-de-sac on the right corner. The Dervish Lodge was established by Sheikh Yahya Efendi in 1538. It is in a complex consisting of a masjid, *tevhidhane*, *madrasa*, Turkish baths, cemetery and various houses. New buildings were later added to the lodge, making the structure very complex. Another characteristic of the lodge is the special relationship of the architectural structures with the natural environment.

Yahya Efendi Lodge became affiliated with the Uwaysi Sufi order. It then joined the Qadiri and Naqshbandi orders. However, the Uwaysi influence continued. The lodge was constructed by the architect Sinan on a square plan with a single dome. Among the tombs, in addition to that of Yahya Efendi, there are the tombs of his wife Şerife, his mother Afife Hatun, his son Ali, and some other sheikhs and sultans.

The shrine was repaired by Sultan Mahmud II, and by Pertevniyal Sultan, the mother of Sultan Abdülaziz and by Sultan Abdülhamid II. The epigraph over the door leading to the tombs reveals that it was repaired by Pertevniyal Sultan in 1873. It is also said that Yahya Efendi of Beşiktaş used to see off the Ottoman navy as it sailed off to war from the hill where his lodge is situated.

BARBAROS HAYRETTİN PASHA MONUMENT

Amount of time recommended for visit: **5 minutes**

The statue is a work of Ali Hadi Bara and Zühtü Müridoğlu. The height of the bronze monument is 11.5 meters. It was revealed to the public on 25 March, 1944.

TOMB OF BARBAROS HAYRETTİN PASHA

Amount of time recommended for visit: **5 minutes**

Barbaros Hayrettin Pasha was appointed commander of the Ottoman navy by Sultan Süleyman the Magnificent in 1534. When he died in 1546, Barbaros Hayrettin Pasha was buried in the tomb constructed for him next to a *madrasa* in Beşiktaş as he had requested in his will. The tomb, which lies across from the Sinan Pasha Mosque, was built by the architect Sinan.

The tomb was built near the mansion of Sinan; this mansion was pulled down to make room for the tomb of this most important Ottoman naval officer in 1541–1542. The tomb was

constructed in the classical Ottoman architectural style of the 16th century with hewn stones on an octagonal plan; the dome rests on an octagonal frame. Inside are also found the tombs of the captain Cafer Pasha, and Barbaros' son and wife. Over the casket is a banner made out of green silk on which a depiction of Zulfikar, the famous sword of the Caliph Ali ibn Abi Talib, has been worked.

NAVAL MUSEUM

Amount of time recommended for visit: **1 hour**

This is the largest museum in Turkey as far as square footage is concerned. As for the diversity of the collection kept here, this is one of the leading museums in the world. There are twenty thousand different works of art in the collection. The Naval Museum is a subsidiary of the Turkish Naval Forces and was the first military museum in Turkey.

On the orders of the commander in chief of the navy, Hasan Hüsnü Pasha of Bozcaada, and with the support of the commander of the Imperial Naval Arsenal, Admiral Hikmet Bey, the Naval Museum was established in 1897 by Commander Süleyman Nutki in the Imperial Naval Arsenal (now the Taşkızak Shipyard in Hasköy, Istanbul), as the Museum and Library Administrative Office.

When the museum first opened its doors it acted for the most part as a repository of unclassified objects. However, in 1914 the Minister of the Navy, Cemal Pasha, carried out reforms here much as he did in all other aspects of the navy, restoring both the museum and its administration. Ali Sami Boyar was appointed director; a maritime artist, Boyar subsequently reorganized the collections of the museum scientifically, establishing a ship-model workshop for building models and half-models of Turkish ships, and a workshop to manufacture human figures for the museum displays; all of these were integral steps in the development of the museum as we see it today.

Finally, in 1961 the museum was transferred to its current location near the monument and tomb of the Ottoman Navy Commander Barbaros Hayrettin, in İskele Square in the Beşiktaş district. Some of the peerless royal *caiques* are exhibited in the museum in their original forms. The most valuable work of art is the excursion galley which belonged to Sultan Mehmed IV from 1648 to 1687. Measuring forty meters in length and 5.90 meters wide, this boat weighs 140 tons; every oar was pulled by three men (with a to-

tal of 144 oarsmen). There were 24 double oars, with room for the oarsmen to sit down. The pavilion part of the boat is an elegant example of Turkish workmanship. This boat is on display in the museum garden. Also exhibited in the garden is a mosaic reproduction of the Piri Reis map and three wall maps showing the limits of Ottoman rule, as well as busts of famous Turkish seamen and other objects that are weatherproof, such as original mines, torpedoes, sea cannons and ancient books connected to maritime matters. The Naval Museum still owns 3,742 works. There are more than 20,000 books in the library, including some manuscripts. There are approximately 25 million manuscript documents in the Historical Naval Archives. The museum is closed on Mondays, Tuesdays, official holidays, and during the lunchbreak between 12:30–13:30.

SİNAN PASHA MOSQUE

Amount of time recommended for visit: **15 minutes**

This is across from Beşiktaş Wharf. The mosque was built on the orders of Vizier Sinan Pasha who served as *kaptan pasha* from 1548 to 1550 and who died in 1553. The mosque, a work by the architect Sinan, sits on a rectangular plan. The central dome is supported by vaults and six-cornered columns, and there are two domes on the sides. The portico at the back of the mosque was surrounded by a *madrasa*. The royal lodge has been destroyed. The mosque has a single minaret.

ÇIRAĞAN PALACE

Amount of time recommended for visit: **5 minutes**

The area where Çırağan Palace now stands was known as Kazancıoğlu Gardens in the 17th century. In the second half of the 16th century, commander of the navy Kılıç Ali Pasha had a waterfront residence here, and in 1648 Sultan Murad IV gave the imperial garden to his daughter Kaya Sultan and her husband Grand Vizier Melek Ahmed Pasha. They had a small wooden mansion built here, where they would spend the summer months. At the beginning of the 18th century, Ahmed III presented the house and grounds to his son-in-law Grand Vizier İbrahim Pasha of Nevşehir; here he organized torchlight fetes, known as Çırağan Festivals with his wife, Fatma Sultan. This was when the area became known as Çırağan.

The most beautiful locations on the Bosphorus were dedicated to the pavilions and mansions of the sultans and high-ranking officials. Over time most of these have disappeared. Çırağan, which used to be a grand palace, burned down in 1910. The Çırağan Palace, built on the same location as the previous wooden palace, was constructed in 1871 by the royal architect Serkis Balyan on the orders of Sultan Abdülaziz. The four-year-long construction cost 4 million *akçe*. The rich decoration was completed with columns that displayed superior craftsmanship in stonework. The rooms were decorated with expensive carpets and furniture detailed in gold and mother-of-pearl. Like the other Bosphorus palaces, Çırağan has been the site of many important meetings.

The exterior of the palace was faced with marble and there were monumental gates; an overpass linked this palace to the grounds of Yıldız Palace, which was high on the ridge. The side facing the public road was surrounded by high walls.

Lady Mary Wortley Montagu, the wife of the English ambassador Edward Wortley Montagu, lived in Istanbul between 1717 and 1718; in her letters she mentions the original Çırağan Palace: "It is situated on one of the most delightful parts of the canal, with a fine wood on the side of a hill behind it. The extent of it is prodigious; the guardian assured me there were eight hundred rooms in it. I will not, however, answer for that number since I did not count them; but 'tis certain the number is very large, and the whole adorned with a profusion of marble, gilding and the most exquisite painting of fruit and flowers. The windows are all sashed with the finest crystalline glass brought from England, and here is all the expensive magnificence that you can suppose in a palace founded by a young man, with the wealth of a vast empire at his command."

After the rebellion of 1730, which brought the great Tulip Era to an end, the palace was left empty and it fell into disrepair. It was finally taken over by Sultan Mahmud I to be used as a banqueting hall for foreign ambassadors. The grand vizier of Selim III, Yusuf Ziya Pasha, bought the palace, knocked it down, and commissioned Kirkor Balyan to build a new palace in marble, which he presented to the sultan in 1805. Selim III then presented the palace to his sister, Beyhan Sultan, but she turned it down.

This palace was used as a summerhouse during the reign of Mahmud II; it was then again demolished and rebuilt on a larger scale by Garabed Balyan from 1835 to 1843. Although great quantities of wood were used,

Çırağan Palace

the main section was made from marble and stone, and there were forty classical columns.

When Sultan Abdülmecid decided to move the official residence to Dolmabahçe Palace in 1855, Çırağan Palace was again torn down, to be replaced by an imposing stone edifice designed by Nikogos Balyan, and the foundations of the present palace were laid. However, due to financial problems and the "Kuleli Event," a conspiracy to assassinate the sultan, the construction of the palace was left half finished. It was only completed in 1874, after Sultan Abdülaziz succeeded to the throne. Sultan Abdülaziz demanded that this palace be built in the Arab style as a memorial to his reign. Artists were sent to Spain and North Africa to make drawings of famous buildings there. It is said that the sultan interfered with the design so much that the plans were redrawn twenty times before he was satisfied. The palace doors, each worth one thousand gold *akçe*, were so admired by Kaiser Wilhelm that some were presented to him as a gift; these can be found in the Berlin Museum today. The finest marble and mother-of-pearl were brought from all over the world for the new Çırağan Palace;

construction was completed at a total cost of five million Ottoman gold liras. But Sultan Abdülaziz only lived here for a few months before pronouncing it too damp to live in.

When Sultan Abdülhamid acceded to the throne in 1876, Sultan Murad V whose mental health was impaired was held prisoner here, with his family until his death in 1905. After this, the palace became the new location for parliament and was opened on November 14, 1909. Parliament convened here for just two months before a fire broke out in the central heating vents and destroyed the entire palace in just under five hours, leaving only a stone shell. Priceless antiques, paintings and books were lost, along with many vital documents.

In 1946, Parliament gave the palace, its outbuildings and grounds, to the Istanbul Municipality; it was used as a dumping ground for sand and other construction materials. It was also used as a swimming pool and a football ground for the local team. It seemed only a matter of time before the last remnants of the former palace would be torn down once and for all. However, the palace has now been restored and is a luxurious hotel.

ORTAKÖY MOSQUE

Amount of time recommended
for visit: **1 hour**

O rtaköy Mosque is situated on
the Rumeli side of the Bosphorus, in the Beşiktaş district, next
to Ortaköy Pier Square. It is surrounded by the sea to the west and
south and is located on a small point
of land. This mosque is also known

as the Grand Imperial Mosque. It is
one of the structures that were built
to symbolize the opening of the Bosphorus as the new historical center of Istanbul during the construction of Dolmabahçe Palace. Prior
to the construction of the mosque,
there was a smaller mosque, built by

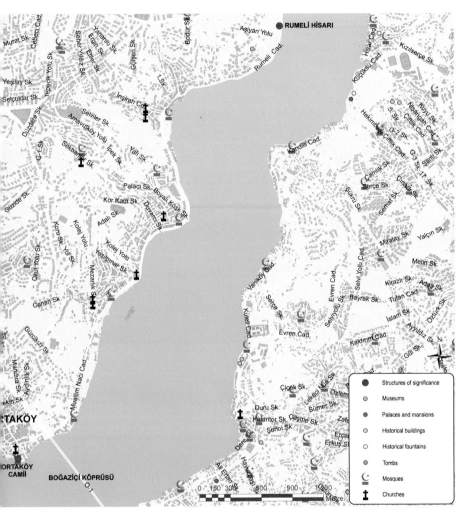

●	Structures of significance
◉	Museums
●	Palaces and mansions
◎	Historical buildings
○	Historical fountains
◉	Tombs
☾	Mosques
✝	Churches

Mahmud Agha, the son-in-law to Vizier İbrahim Pasha, on this spot. The small mosque dated back to the
beginning of the 18th century and it is said that it was
demolished after the death of Mahmud Agha during
the Patrona Halil uprising.

The current mosque was constructed during the reign of Sultan Abdülmecid in 1853. The inscrip-

tion on the entrance gate bears the imperial signature of Abdülmecid and the date that indicates the completion of the construction of the mosque. The architect was Nikogos Balyan. As with all royal mosques in the 19th century, the mosque consists of two parts, the main worship hall and the sultan's section in front of the entrance.

RUMELİ FORTRESS

Amount of time recommended for visit: **1 hour**

The fortress is located within the borders of the Sarıyer district and has given its name to the location; it covers an area of 30,000 m². The fortress was built at the narrowest section of the Bosphorus, just opposite Anadolu Hisarı (Anatolian Fortress); when looked from above, the shape of the fortress resembles the name of the Prophet, "Muhammad" in Arabic. The fortress was completed in a very short period of time, only one hundred and thirty-nine days, and consists of three large towers, which have the largest bastions in the world.

The construction of the fortress started on April 15, 1452 and was built so rapidly thanks to a division of labor. Each part of the construction was supervised by a different general. Sultan Mehmed II supervised the side of the fortress that overlooks the sea himself. The tower on the right side, when seen from the

sea, was overseen by Saruca Pasha, the one on the left by Zağanos Paşa, and the one at the quay by Halil Pasha. These towers are named after the pashas. The construction of the fortress was completed by August 31, 1452.

The wood used in building the fortress came from İzmit and the Black Sea, while the stone was brought from various places in Anatolia and from the derelict buildings around. E. H. Ayverdi states that approximately 300 master workmen, 800 workers and 200 porters were used, in addition to a large number of boats, vehicles and other types of workers.

The amount of mortar used in the building which covers 60,000 m² area is about 57,700 m³. The outer wall that connects the large towers of the fortress measures 250 meters from the north to the south, and from east to west 125 meters. There are four main gates in the fortress, while there is also a secondary gate known as Mezarlik Gate. Near the southern tower, at the end of the passage that leads to the ammunition and food stores, are two secret doors. Here there were two water ducts, one of which is blocked, and three fountains. Two of the fountains no longer exist. Of the mosque that was built here only the ruins of one minaret remain.

Rumeli Fortress is now a museum and an open-air theatre. In the garden are exhibited the cannons, cannonballs and chains that were used (so it is claimed) to block the Golden Horn. Every year summer concerts are held here.

CAFÉ / RESTAURANT

Antik Cafe
Phone: (212) 265 5089
Kale Tea Gardens
Phone: (212) 257 5578
Kale Café and Patisserie
Phone: (212) 265 0097

YILDIZ PALACE

Amount of time recommended for visit: **1 hour**

IHLAMUR KASRI

Yıldız Palace is a complex of mansions and gardens scattered over a large hilly area that overlooks the Bosphorus and which is surrounded by high walls. Yıldız, the second largest palace in Istanbul, has now been separated into various sections, each serving a different purpose. The five-hundred-thousand m^2 grove was reserved for the sultan; after the first mansion was built here in the early 19th century, the others quickly followed. When Sultan Abdülhamid II decided that this palace offered better security than Dolmabahçe, the complex quickly developed into its present form.

During his thirty-three-year reign, Abdülhamid used this well-protected palace, which resembled a city within a city, as his official quarters and home. The different courtyards with pavilions, pools, greenhouses, aviaries, workshops and servants' quar-

ters, were connected with one another by passageways and gates. Outside the two main entrances are two small and charming mosques. The buildings that were allocated to the military academy have been vacated over time. The facilities to the north are still used for military purposes, but the other sections have been given over to Yıldız Technical University, the Municipality, the Department of National Palaces, and the Institute for Research in the History of Islamic Arts and Cultures.

In Yıldız Park a large part of the palace gardens, some old pavilions and the famous porcelain workshops are open to the public. The park is

connected to Çırağan Palace by a bridge. The best-known building in the complex is the Şale (chalet) Pavilion. The pavilion is an important museum with its well-kept gardens, its exterior architecture that echoes Alpine hunting lodges, its rich decorations, valuable furniture, carpets, and large ceramic stoves.

The main entrance to Yıldız Palace is up the hill from Beşiktaş. The Muayede Pavilion to the left of the entrance is now being renovated as a museum. On the left side is the sin- gle-storied Çit Pavilion, where the guests of the sultan were accommodated, as well as the entrance to the harem. On the opposite side were the offices of the military officers, known as the Yaveran chambers. The greenhouse and theater of the harem section are attractive buildings.

The staff dining room to the right of the entrance is currently dedicated to exhibitions and concerts. Yıldız Palace Museum and the Municipal Museum of Istanbul are also located in this complex. The palace mu-

seum was established in 1994 and it occupies the former carpentry workshops. Carved and painted wooden artifacts, thrones, porcelain produced in the palace workshops, and other objects from the palace are exhibited here, while in the Municipal Museum next door are glass and porcelain, silverware, paintings depicting Istanbul and a rare 16th century oil lamp.

The group of buildings that comprise Yıldız Palace constitute an example of Turkish Ottoman imperial architecture. This area where the palace stands and which is recorded as *Hazine-i Hassa* (Treasury Land) was used as hunting grounds by the sultans from the time of Süleyman the Magnificent. Sultan Ahmed I (1603–1617) built the first mansion on this land. Sultan Murad IV (1617–1640) lived and rested in this mansion when he used to go hunting. At the end of the 18th century, Sultan Selim III (1789–1807) built a mansion here for Mihrişah Sultan, his mother; this is when the area became known as Yıldız. Sultan Selim also ordered a fountain built here in the Rococo style; this is situated in the palace garden.

After Sultan Murad V was dethroned due to mental illness, the thirty-three-year reign of his brother, Sultan Abdülhamid II (1876–1909), began. The former sultans, Sultan Abdülaziz and Murad V had lived in Dolmabahçe Palace by the Bosphorus. However, Dolmabahçe Palace was vulnerable from the sea, and

therefore on April 7, 1877, Sultan Abdülhamid II moved to Yıldız Palace.

The main part of the palace was built during the reign of Sultan Abdülhamid and it was known as Yıldız Imperial Palace. The surrounding area was also purchased at this time, and the external garden, which is today Yıldız Park, was expanded, and large-scale renovations began. The palace and its gardens cover nearly 80,000 square meters.

Just outside the palace, there was the Guard's Corps of the first army.

Mehmed Reshad (1909–1918), who became sultan following Sultan Abdülhamid II, underwent an operation at the "Four Season Hall" in the pavilion called the "Special Apartments." When he died in 1918, Mehmed Vahideddin VI (1918–1922) became sultan.

Sultan Vahideddin resided for the most part at Dolmabahçe Palace, but on occasion he stayed at Yıldız Palace. In the Republican Era, the palace, which had been used as a Military Academy for many years, came under the supervision of the Ministry of Culture in 1978 and the Yıldız Palace Directorate was opened. Initial efforts to convert the palace into a museum began in 1994. On January 6, 1994, the Palace Theatre and the restored Stage Arts Museum were opened. On April 8, 1994, Yıldız Palace Museum was opened to the public.

Visiting Hours and Days: Everyday between 9:30 and 16:00, except Monday.

YILDIZ CITY MUSEUM

Amount of time recommended for visit: **45 minutes**

Yıldız City Museum has been established since 1988. The collection is, in general, made up of ethnographic and historical works from the 18th and 19th centuries. Here one can find paintings, calligraphy, textiles, porcelains made in the imperial workshops of Yıldız Palace, various glasswork, calligraphy tools, objects and emblems belonging to Sufi orders, kitchen tools, censers, plates, jewels, scales and weights, stamps, binding blocks, ceramics and tiles, Tophane pipes and similar objects

from the Ottoman Empire. The calligraphers whose works are on display are Mustafa İzzet, Sultan Abdülmecid, Mehmed Raşid, Sami Efendi, Mehmed İzzet, Hamit Aytaç, İsmail Hakkı Altunbezer, Şefik, Mahmud Celaleddin. The museum is open every day between 9:00 and 16:00 except Sunday and Monday, free of charge. Phone: (212) 258 5844

MALTA PAVILION

Amount of time recommended for visit: **45 minutes**

M alta Pavilion is located in Yıldız Park on the east side of the wall that separates off Yıldız Pal-

known, but it is thought that during the Ottoman era certain parts of the palaces were called after the names of areas that had been conquered, so this name could have been given after the conquest of Malta.

ace. Here one can also find observation and resting pavilions in the grove that is the rear garden of Çırağan Palace; these date from the Abdülaziz I period. Malta Pavilion sits on a terrace that provides an expansive view to the north. The origin of the name is not

Sultan Abdülhamid connected the pavilion to Yıldız Palace and used it for resting and entertaining the palace residents. Like other pavilions at Yıldız Palace, Malta Pavilion has witnessed historic events.

In 1878, Ali Suavi tried to overthrow Abdülhamid II and bring Murad V to power with the "Çırağan Raid." When the attempt failed, Sultan Abdülhamid sent Murad V to this pavilion for security reasons, effectively keeping him here under house arrest.

IHLAMUR (LINDEN) PAVILION

Amount of time recommended
for visit: **45 minutes**

The pavilion, which is surrounded by high walls to protect it from the noise of the surroundings, consists of two mansions situated in an area known as *Ihlamur Mesiresi*. This area is composed of three sections: the Ihlamur Neighborhood with Pool, the Muhabbet Garden and Hacı Hüseyin Vineyards; this later became an imperial garden during the reign of Sultan Ahmed III (1703–1730). Particularly Sultan Abdülmecid liked this area. Here, he would frequently rest and entertain his guests, including the famous French poet Lamartine. Afterwards, in place of the simple and modest pavilion, the sultan had the present-day structures built here between 1849 and 1855.

The mansions were designed by the architect of Dolmabahçe Palace Nikogos Balyan. Merasim Mansion, another of the buildings, was intended to be used for official ceremonies, while the Maiyet Mansion was where the sultan's entourage and, on occasion, his family stayed. Both of these mansions were known as the Ihlamur Pavilion.

Today the Ihlamur Pavilion is connected to the Department of National Palaces. As with all the palaces and pavilions, any profit from the restaurants and cafes is directed into renovation and restoration.

CHAPTER 6
ÜSKÜDAR
KADIKÖY-BEYKOZ

BEYLERBEYİ CAMİİ

BEYLERBEYİ SARAYI

FETHİ PAŞA KORUSU

MİHRİMAH SULTAN CAMİİ

YENİ VALİDE KÜLLİYESİ

AYAZMA CAMİİ

KIZ KULESİ

AZİZ MAHMUD
HÜDAYİ TÜRBESİ

ÜSKÜDAR

CİNİLİ CAMİİ

HACI FAİK BEY
ÇEŞMESİ

NUHKUYUSU CAMİİ

KARACAAHMET
MEZARLIĞI

ZEYNEP KAMİL
HASTANESİ

İRANLILAR CAMİİ

SELİMİYE KIŞLASI

MARMARA ÜNİVERSİTESİ
TIP FAKÜLTESİ

●	Structures of significance
◉	Museums
●	Palaces and mansions
○	Historical buildings
○	Historical fountains
◉	Tombs
☪	Mosques
✝	Churches

ÜSKÜDAR

Ü sküdar is located on the Anatolian shore of the Bosphorus. The district of Üsküdar is surrounded by Ümraniye to the east, Kadıköy to the south, the Bosphorus to the west and northwest and Beykoz to the north. The district covers thirty-five kilometers. The district consists of fifty-two streets.

Üsküdar was founded in the 7th century BC by the inhab-

itants of the Greek colony of Chalde-on (Kadıköy) and was first known as Chrysopolis, meaning Golden City. The origin of this name has been interpreted in several ways. It is said that this name was given because of the gold collected as tributes from tribes in Anatolia and during the Persian invasion. Another interpretation is that Agamemnon's son Croesus fled and came to Anatolia, dying in Üsküdar, thus giving his name to the city. Some say that Üsküdar was called Gold-en City because at sunset the houses here appeared to be gilded from the opposite side. According to others, the name Üsküdar is derived from the Persian word *Eskudari*, meaning messenger.

After the conquest of Istanbul, Sultan Mehmed II encouraged Turks to settle in this former Greek area, which was now deserted as the Greeks had fled from the region. However, it is not possible to say to what degree the population increased over the centuries, as we have no documents from the time of the conquest with which to make comparisons. During the reign of Sultan Mehmed II, Üsküdar became one of the four legal centers after the sultan divided the residential areas in Istanbul to better administer the city.

One of the most important characteristics of Üsküdar in the Ottoman period was that the *Surre-i Hümayun* (caravan of royal gifts), which went to Mecca and Medina with pilgrims, started ceremoniously from here.

CAFÉ / RESTAURANT

Kanaat Lokantası
(216) 333 3791
Bafra Pide Salonu
(216) 391 5030

KIZ KULESİ / THE MAIDEN'S TOWER

Amount of time recommended
for visit: **1 hour**

This small and charming tower was built on an island at the entrance to the Bosphorus; it is recognized as one of the symbols of Istanbul. Used as a watchtower and a lighthouse in the past, the Maiden's Tower marks the entrance to the Bosphorus. The tower, which has maintained its attractive appearance over the centuries, serves as a tourist attraction with its restaurant and observation tower. The name Maiden's Tower comes from one of the legends connected to the tower. A soothsayer foretold that a king would lose his beloved daughter at the age of eighteen when she would be bitten by a

snake. So the king had the tower that stood in the middle of the sea repaired and kept his daughter here. However, fate cannot be escaped and a snake emerged from a basket of grapes that had been sent to the tower and bit the princess. The king had an iron coffin prepared for his daughter and had it placed above the gate of Haghia Sophia. Today, there are two holes in the vault, which has given rise to stories about how the snake did not leave the girl alone even after her death.

At the present time the Maiden's Tower is one of the symbols of Üsküdar and the Bosphorus. It is an important component of the silhouette of the Bosphorus. With restorations and repairs the appearance of this tower has been greatly improved. Today, the tower houses a restaurant that is open to the public.

MİHRİMAH SULTAN MOSQUE

Amount of time recommended for visit: **30 minutes**

Many mosque complexes have been built in the name of the female members of the Ottoman dynasty throughout history. One of these women was Sultan Mihrimah, the daughter of Sultan Süleyman the Magnificent. She ordered the architect Sinan to build the Mihrimah complex across the pier at Üsküdar; the complex consisted of a mosque, a *madrasa*, tomb, primary school, caravanserai, soup kitchen, and a small hospital, but only some of these buildings have survived until today. Mimar Sinan based the design of the mosque in the complex on a modern model of the Haghia Sophia Mosque. He did not use the semidome that is usual above mosque entrances. Thus, as soon as one enters the mosque the main dome dominates. The fountain at the entrance to the mosque is attractively designed. The window shutters and the podium have inlaid decoration in wood. The pulpit and the niche are made of marble with fine engraving. The *madrasa* is located to the north of the mosque. Between the mosque and the *madrasa* lie two tombs belonging to Mihrimah's sons and Grand Vizier İbrahim Ethem Pasha. The primary school is located on the *qibla* side of the mosque. The hospice, soup kitchen and caravanserai no longer exist. Sultan Mihrimah was not pleased with the lighting of the mosque and Sinan, when building another mosque in another complex on the order of Sultan Mihrimah in Edirne, many years later, created a brightly lit interior. Of the buildings that have survived today, the *madrasa* is now used as a polyclinic and the soup kitchen operates as a library.

THE TOMB OF AZİZ MAHMUD HÜDAYİ

Amount of time recommended for visit: **45 minutes**

One of the most frequently visited tombs in Üsküdar and Istanbul is the tomb of Aziz Mahmud Hüdayi. The tomb is located 15 minutes from the center of Üsküdar.

The main lodge of a Sufi order founded by Aziz Mahmud Hüdayi used to be at this location. Mahmud Hüdayi was one of the great Anatolian religious scholars. He was born in Şereflikoçhisar in 1572. Hüdayi moved to Istanbul to pursue his religious training and continued to pursue his education at the Small Haghia Sophia *madrasa*. In his early years, he mastered *tafsir* (exegesis of the Qur'an), *fiqh* (jurisprudence), and natural sciences. His master, Hazırzade Ramazan Efendi, accepted him as his assistant. At the age of 33, Mahmud Efendi came to Bursa with his master. Upon the death of Hazırzade Ramazan Efendi, he was promoted to be *qadi* (judge) in Bursa. Upon recieving a spiritual sign while working as the judge, he left this position and became a pupil of Sheikh Uftade.

After the death of his sheikh, Mahmud Hüdayi went to Rumeli upon receiving a spiritual sign. He later returned to Istanbul. During his time here, Hüdayi purchased the land where the tomb is presently located and he built a Sufi lodge here. He trained hundreds of students and his fame spread very quickly. His lodge hosted several administrators, from the poorest to the richest, as well as high-ranking officials. The sultans of the time respected him greatly, and he gave advice to Sultan Murad III, Mehmed III, Ahmed I, Osman II, and Murad IV. It was Hüdayi who girded the imperial sword of the sultans on Sultan Murad IV. Hüdayi died in 1628. Many people visit this tomb to seek guidance from his zeal and spirituality.

AYAZMA MOSQUE

Amount of time recommended for visit: **15 minutes**

This mosque is located in Üsküdar, between Salacak and Şemsipaşa, on a hill overlooking the Maiden's Tower. It was commissioned by Sultan Mustafa III in 1760–1761 for his mother Mihrişah Emine Sultan and his brother Şehzade Süleyman. It is the work of the architect Mehmet Tahir Agha. The name Ayazma derives from Ayazma Palace and Gardens which were once located here. This mosque clearly shows the influence of European style. One can reach the stairs to enter the mosque from a three-gated courtyard. The minaret has a single balcony. The pulpit is made of carved marble and the interior is of red porphyry. There are inscriptions by the calligraphers Seyyid Abdullah and Seyyid Mustafa inside the mosque. Many graves are housed here, and the fountain in the left corner is adorned with an epitaph by the poet Zihni.

SELİMİYE BARRACKS

Amount of time recommended for visit: **15 minutes**

The Selimiye Barracks were originally constructed in 1799 during the reign of Selim III for the *Nizam-i Cedid* (New Order) soldiers; originally the barracks consisted of a wooden building on a hewn stone base. When this wooden structure was burnt down by the Janissaries during a revolt, the barracks were rebuilt in stone during the reign of Sultan Mahmud II. During the reign of Sultan Abdülmecid, the barracks underwent important renovations twice. A seven-story tower was added to each of the four corners during the renovations. During the Crimean War (1853–6) the barracks were allocated to the British Army. Florence Nightingale arrived in the hospital to nurse wounded British soldiers in 1854. The room in which Florence Nightingale and her entourage stayed has been preserved as the Florence Nightingale Museum. The museum was first opened to the public in 1954.

Today the Selimiye Barracks hosts a branch of the Turkish Armed Forces. In the outer garden of the barracks stands the tallest flagpole in Turkey (eight meters high); this flagpole can be seen from several points in Istanbul. The pole weighs 12 tons and the flag that was hoisted on July 20, 2005 measures 15 x 10 meters.

BEYLERBEYİ MOSQUE

Amount of time recommended for visit: **25 minutes**

This mosque is on the Anatolian side of the Bosphorus, next to the Beylerbeyi wharf. It was commissioned by Sultan Abdülhamid I in 1778 in memory of his mother, Rabia Sultan. It is the work of the architect Tahir Agha. The mosque is Baroque in style and was built out of hewn stone. There are fifty-five windows in the mosque and two minarets. The mosque has one dome, while the

area before the mihrab is covered by a semi-dome. The interior is decorated with calligraphic artwork. There are lovely examples of Ottoman and European tiles inside. The mosque thus offers an exhibition of different cultures.

YENİ VALİDE COMPLEX

Amount of time recommended for visit: **25 minutes**

This complex stands on the crossroads of Hakimiyet-i Milliye Street and Üsküdar Square. It was constructed during the reign of Sultan Ahmed III in memory of his mother, Sultan Emetullah Gülnuş Valide, between 1708 and 1710. It was constructed by the architect Bekir. The complex consists of a mosque, a tomb, a fountain, a primary school, shops, a soup kitchen, and a fountain. The mosque is situated inside an outer courtyard. The mosque and the inner courtyard are higher than the outer courtyard.

Inside the inner courtyard, there is a fountain for making ablutions. The mosque is constructed in the classical style and has a main central dome supported by four semi-domes. The minarets of the mosque have two balconies and are built in the classical style as well. The mosque is decorated with tiles.

On the eastern side of the mosque, there is the imperial pavilion, which was built at a later date than the mosque. At the present time, this is quite derelict. On the southeastern corner of the outer courtyard, the shrine, fountains, and clock room are all located next to one another. The tomb is that of Queen Mother Emetullah Gülnuş. The primary school, soup kitchen and shops lie to the north of the outer courtyard.

KARACA AHMED

The district of Karaca Ahmed is an exceptional place lying amongst the oldest streets of Üsküdar such as Nuhkuyusu, İcadiye Tunusbağı, Çiçekçi, Talimhâne, Haydarpasha, and Harmanlık.

Karaca Ahmed was the son of Süleyman Bey of Khorasan. He came to Anatolia with the great Turkish nomadic groups which migrated to Anatolia in the 14th century to escape the Mongol raids. At this time, the Seljuk sultanate was in decline. Sultan Karaca Ahmed joined the forces that wanted to conquer the declining Byz-

antine Empire. Later, Sultan Karaca Ahmed, helped the people of Anatolia as a doctor.

Today, however, the name Karaca Ahmed generally reminds the people of Istanbul of death. The reason for this is that the Karaca Ahmed cemetery, the largest and oldest Muslim cemetery in Turkey, is in this district.

The establishment of the cemetery dates back many centuries. It is thought that the soldiers who were martyred during the sieges of Constantinople were buried here. The cemetery has never contained any Roman or Byzantine graves. The following are the most important historical relics in Karaca Ahmed:

Tombstones

The tombstones from the Ottoman era inside the Karaca Ahmed cemetery are works of art in their own right. These elegant structures give a very sedate and dignified air to the cemetery.

The tomb of Sultan Karaca Ahmed

This is located on the corner where Nuhkuyusu Street intersects with Gündoğumu. Across from the tomb is the Ahmed Agha Mosque. On the left of the tomb is the Sadeddin Efen-

di fountain, dated 1154AH/1741AD. Here also is a mosque and the tomb of Sadeddin Efendi. On the left is the tomb of Rum Mehmed Paşazade Nişancı Hamza Pasha, which at one time was thought to be the burial place of Karaca Ahmed's horse. The tomb has six columns and a dome.

The tomb was erected by a member of the staff of the imperial kitchen, Ziya Bey, in memory of his wife. The real tomb of Sultan Karaca Ahmed is actually in Horoz village, which is located 5 kilometers northwest of Manisa.

Sadeddin Efendi Tomb

This is located on the left of the grave that lies next to the tomb of Karaca Ahmed. The tomb is raised above the road and sits on a stone base. To the left of the tomb is the drinking fountain which Sadeddin Efendi built for charity in memory of his daughter who died in 1741. Here are the tombs of Sadeddin Efendi and his relatives; the headstones are wonderful examples of the art of stone carving.

Melek Baba Tomb

This tomb is located at the meeting point of the two roads that come from the cemetery administration building to the Yanık Ömer Gate. The tomb itself is enclosed with an iron grating. On the tombstone is an epigraph dated 1705. This is the tomb of a man called Melek Baba. There is no information about who this man was.

The tomb of Kaygusuz İbrahim Baba

This is located behind the Duvardibi Police Department on the 7th Island, against the cemetery wall. The tomb is enclosed with an iron grating. Kaygusuz İbrahim Baba was a sheikh of the Qadiri order and he had a lodge near Haghia Sophia Mosque. The wooden lodge still exists today.

The tomb of Hasan Efendi

This is located on the 9th island of the cemetery and is also surrounded with an iron grating. The date on the epigraph is 1877. The gravestone bears unique examples of the Naqshi, Badawi, and Mawlawi orders' emblems in relief. The calligraphy is distinctive and the epigraph next to the tomb of Hasan Efendi was done by Sheikh Osman Şems Efendi.

The Hacı Faik Bey Fountain

The fountain is located at the intersection of Tunusbağı Street with Ethem Pasha Street in Arakiyeci Hacı Cafer Mahallesi. This point marks the beginning of the Karaca Ahmed cemetery. According to the epigraph, composed of three lines, written in a beautiful *thuluth* style, the fountain was constructed in 1681. The fountain became greatly damaged over time. During the restoration of the fountain in 1907, the epigraph was replaced and a new epigraph was inscribed. Hacı Faik Bey was one of the people responsible for restoring the fountain, and due to a lack of knowledge about who originally built the fountain it is now known as the Faik Bey fountain.

İsa Agha Fountain

İsa Agha Fountain is located behind the street that connects Karaca Ahmed to İbrahim Agha and is adjacent to the cemetery. The fountain was constructed by the treasurer of Sultan Mahmud II, Hafız İsa Agha in 1811. The epigraph was composed by the poet Vasif and written by the calligrapher Mustafa Rakım.

Ahmed Agha (Karaca Ahmed) Mosque

Ahmed Agha (Karaca Ahmed) Mosque is situated across from the Karaca Ahmed Tomb and is part of the Karacaahmet Cemetery. The beautiful epigraphical monument, consisting of 14 lines, on the northwestern corner of the mosque between the imam's chamber and the window, is known to have been built as a wooden structure by one of the grooms of Hacı Hafız Ahmed Agha of Rhodes. It is also documented that the monument was rebuilt by his son Fethi Ahmed Pasha in 1857.

Cevriusta (Nuhkuyusu) Mosque

Amount of time recommended for visit: **1 hour**

This mosque is located on Nuhkuyusu Street. The mosque is thought to have been built in memory of Cevri Usta, who saved the life of Sultan Mahmud II. The mosque has no epigraph to tell us who the founder was. This mosque, also known as Nuhkuyusu Mosque, was restored and renovated in 1884.

İranlılar (Persians') Mosque

Amount of time recommended for visit: **15 minutes**

This mosque is located to the east of Karacaahmet Cemetery, inside İranlılar Cemetery at the end of Seyyid Ahmed Deresi Street. The mosque is also known as Seyyid Ahmed Deresi Mescidi. The original building was made out of wood, but it suffered in a major fire. This is why the original date of construction is not known. The oldest date found in the epigraphs of the current stone building is 1854. The mosque was designed in the neo-Classical architectural style. The congregation of the present mosque, which is extremely well maintained, consists mainly of Azeris from Iran.

Üsküdar in the Past

Miskinler Tekkesi (Cüzamhane) Leprosy Hospital

Amount of time recommended for visit: **15 minutes**

The first leprosy hospital, known as *Miskinler tekkesi* or *Miskinler Dergahı* in the Ottoman Empire was built by Sultan Murad II in Edirne; this remained open until 1627. The most important leprosy hospital was the *Miskinler Tekkesi* that was opened in 1514 in the Karaca Ahmed district of Istanbul. It contained nine cells, a masjid and a fountain. The hospital was surrounded by a garden, and the cell windows and doors opened onto a second garden that was used as an inner courtyard. In each room was a stove, in front of which was a portico. The hospital also had Turkish baths and a laundry.

The hospital was administered by a board of trustees who were appointed by a *qadi* (judge). The mother of the sultan would send forty loaves of bread, soup and rice from the soup kitchen daily. The meat for the lodge would come from the Kavak slaughterhouse. The other expenses of the lodge would be met with money donated by the public; this money would be left on the charity stones. The charity stones, which were hollowed out on top, providing a place to put the money, were located in front of the lodge. When the Gözcü Dede (supervisor) informed the patients that money had been left in the

stone, all the patients would pray in unison for the person who had left the money. Out of eight charity stones, none have survived until today.

The leprosy hospital, which treated patients with leprosy until 1927, suffered major fire damage. This structure remained in a derelict state until 1938, when it was completely torn down. The mosque, known as Dedeler Mosque, was also torn down during the construction of İbrahim Agha Road. The epigraph that was written for the Leprosy Hospital is at present stored in the Turkish and Islamic Arts Museum. Only the fountain is left from the hospital.

ZEYNEP KAMİL HOSPITAL

This hospital is located on Nuhkuyusu Street. It was constructed by Zeynep Hanım, who was the daughter of the governor of Egypt and the wife of Grand Vizier Yusuf Kamil Pasha, with her husband's support. The construction of the hospital started in 1860, and it was finished in two years. It was open for use in 1862. The hospital began admitting patients in 1895. After Haydarpaşa Numune Hospital was opened in 1936, Zeynep Kamil Hospital became a gynecology/obstetrics and pediatrics hospital.

ÇİNİLİ MOSQUE (TILED MOSQUE)

Amount of time recommended for visit: **15 minutes**

Çinili Mosque is located on the hills of Üsküdar, at the intersection of Allame and Çinçin Hamam streets. The mosque has gates that lead to the Çinili Mescit Street and Çinçinli Hamam Street. Ummi Ahmed Efendi lodge is situated only one hundred feet in front of the mosque. The lodge is located on the left side of the mosque. It was built in 1640 by Sultan Mahpeyker Kösem, the wife of Sultan Ahmed I and mother of sultans Murad IV and Ibrahim. The mosque was designed with a *madrasa*, school, fountain, Turkish bath and a fountain for making ablutions.

ÇAMLICA

Amount of time recommended for visit: **1 hour**

This place is known as Çamlıca because of the pine groves on the hills of Büyük (Grand) and

Küçük (Small) Çamlıca (*çam* means pine tree in Turkish). Today, only a few of the old pines exist, with most of the trees on Büyük Çamlıca having been planted in recent years. Küçük Çamlıca used to be called Yeni (New) Çamlıca, and was renovated in the era of Sultan Mehmed IV and transformed into a park. Murad IV constructed a mosque and a pavilion here. At that time, Büyük Çamlıca was considered to be a distant forest; there was a lodge here and a garden known as Bağ-ı Cihan. You can recognize both hills of Çamlıca from far away by the huge radio transmitters. There are many pavilions and gardens in both parks. The pavilion restaurants in both parks are run by the Istanbul Metropolitan Municipality.

Telephone numbers for the Çamlıca Municipality Establishments (0216) 443 21 98 (0216) 443 21 99

KUZGUNCUK

Amount of time recommended for visit: **1 hour**

Kuzguncuk was established in a valley between the Beylerbeyi and Üsküdar districts. According to some people, Kuzguncuk is another version of the former name of the district, "Kosnitza." According to Evliya Çelebi, the Ottoman traveler, the village here took its name from an individual called Kuzgun Baba who lived here. According to documents left from the 17th century, the village of Kuzguncuk was a Jewish settlement. At the time, the Jews who lived here considered the village to be a part of Jerusalem and gave great importance to it. Those who were unable to visit the Promised Land were buried in the Jewish cemetery at Kuzguncuk. It is also reported that Greeks lived here. After the 18th century Armenians began to settle here. In the middle of the 20th century, Turks started to settle in the area.

There are two Orthodox churches, one Armenian church, one synagogue, a mosque and a masjid as well as two Turkish baths. There is one Muslim, one Greek and one Jewish cemetery in Kuzguncuk. One reason why this place was thought to be an extension of the city of Jerusalem was because the three Abrahamic religions lived side by side here. This feature makes Kuzguncuk one of the areas that reflects the tolerance that has existed in Anatolia throughout the centuries.

This area has been used as a set in television programs and films due to its lovely atmosphere. The neighborhood offers a variety of options for dining. One popular place to eat is the Cinaralti Café or Ismet Baba Restaurant on the Bosphorus. Dilim Patisserie is another important location.

One of the places worth seeing is Fethi Pasha Woods. The park, which encompasses all the land on the hills starting from the north of Üsküdar until Kuzguncuk Hill, takes its

restaurants and cafes here operated by the Istanbul Metropolitan Municipality as well as by private companies. This park is also lovely for walking.

CAFÉ / RESTAURANT

(0216) 391 6560 - 391 0659

Beylerbeyi Palace

Amount of time recommended for visit: **1 hour**

name from Damat Fethi Ahmet Pasha, who served as the Tophane secretary during the reign of both Sultan Mahmud II (1808–1839) and Abdülmecid (1839–1861). There are

The settlements in the district of Beylerbeyi started to take form in the Byzantine era. According to the famous eighteenth-century traveler İnciciyan, the area was known as İstavroz Bahçeleri (Cross Gardens) because the great Emperor Constantine had erected a cross here. In the Ottoman era this was made into one of the imperial gardens. İnciciyan relates that the name Beylerbeyi was given to this area in the 16ᵗʰ century because Mehmet Pasha, who was the *beylerbeyi* (governor general) built a mansion here. The sultans built several mansions and pavilions on the

imperial estate here, and in 1829 Sultan Mahmud II built a wooden waterfront palace. Sultan Abdülaziz demolished this wooden palace and from 1861 to 1865 he built the present Beylerbeyi Palace, which is also known as the Summer Palace.

Designed by the famous Ottoman architect Sarkis Balyan, the palace was generally reserved for summer use by the sultans or to accommodate foreign heads of state who visited the Ottoman capital. The prince of Serbia, the king of Montenegro, the shah of Iran and Empress Eugenie of France are among the royal guests who stayed here.

Sultan Abdülhamid II spent the last six months of his life here, dying in 1918. The ground floor of the building contains a kitchen and storage rooms. The building consists of three floors and contains 26 rooms and six halls. The floors are covered with rush matting from Egypt which protects against damp in winter and heat in summer. Over this are laid

large carpets and rugs, mostly made in Hereke. The furnishings include exquisite Bohemian crystal chandeliers, French clocks, and Chinese, Japanese, French and Turkish Yıldız porcelain vases. The most interesting part of Beylerbeyi Palace, which was built during a time of good relations between the Ottomans and the West, is the historical tunnel which runs under the *Set Bahçeleri* (gardens). The epigraph on the fountain in the middle of the tunnel contains the name of Sultan Mahmud II, which gives us the necessary hint to date the structure. Similar to the Marble Pavilion, the large pool on the upper level garden was built during the reign of Mahmud II (1808–1839).

Kuleli Military High School

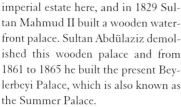

Amount of time recommended for visit: **15 minutes**

One of the important historical locations in the Üsküdar district, lying between Çengelköy and

Vaniköy, is the Kuleli Military High School. There has been a building here from the time of Sultan Mehmed II. When Sultan Mehmed II conquered Constantinople there was a wood here, known as *Papaz Korusu* (Priest Wood). In the wood there was a monastery and a tower. During the reign of Sultan Selim I (1512–1520), this monastery was converted into a Janissary barracks. The location of the barracks was originally called *Bostancıbaşı Odaları*. Later, after being transformed into a beautifully decorated garden, it began to be called *Kuleli Bahçesi* (Garden with Towers). Kuleli Garden was used for growing flowers and plants and Sultan Süleyman the Magnificent used to come here when he was a prince.

When Süleyman became sultan (1520–1577), he built a mansion in the garden; this consisted of nine floors. Each floor was furnished with a pool. This was used as the royal residence in the summer months. During the reign of Sultan Ahmed III (1703–1730), the tower and its surroundings were given to the sultan. In the era of Sultan Abdülmecid, a new stone building was built in place of the barracks (1843). After this period, the location was known as the Kuleli barracks because of the two towers located at the sides of the building.

During the reign of Abdülaziz (1861–1876), the main walls of the barracks were built out of concrete, while the interior and the floors and ceiling were made out of wood (1871). The newly built barracks consisted of two floors. Today these serve as barracks for the military school.

During World War I, the school was transferred for a semester to the Greek Orphanage in the island of Büyükada. At the end of World War I, the school building was evacuated in accord with the demands made by the English in the Armistice of Mudros. The building was then given to Armenian orphans and immigrants (November 5, 1920). After the victorious end of the "*Büyük Taarruz*" (Great Attack), which started on August 26, 1922 and with the Treaty of Lausanne, the British left Kuleli Barracks to Turkish officials. Thus, after an interval of three years, the school returned to its former building on September 6, 1923.

With the *Tevhid-i Tedrisat* (the unification of education) law, the school was turned into a civilian high school and its named was changed to Kuleli Military High School. At the end of the semester the same year the school was converted back into a military school. In 1925, Kuleli High School took on the structure it has today.

KADIKÖY

Around 1000 BC, a village was established by the Phoenicians in this area; this later was to become a Greek colony. The residential areas of this town extended to Moda. At this time, the name of the city was changed from Charcedon to Chalcedon (or from Harkedon into Halkedon).

Money was coined in the name of the city of Chalcedon, but it became a less popular place to live in the 7th century BC because of the quickly growing Greek town on the opposite side. This city was Byzantion, which would become Constantinople or New Rome 1000 years later. According to the historian Heredot, the Oracle of Delphi called Chalcedon "The Land of the Blind," referring the people living on the shore opposite Byzantion, as the position on the Historic Peninsula was so much more advantageous.

An important event in the history of Christianity took place in this area. It was the Ecumenical Council of Chalcedon in 451 AD, which made the decision to establish a patriarchate in Constantinople. The area was attacked by armies from the Umayyad, Abbasid, and Sassanid empires. It was captured by the Turks in 1080. The invaders, under the command of Kutalmışoğlu Süleyman Bey, who made the city of İznik their capital, added this area to the land of the Seljuk dynasty. Eventually, in the 14th century, Chalcedon met its new owners, the Ottomans. The glory of the Ottomans during the reign of Orhan Gazi in 1331 against the Byzantine Emperor transformed Chalcedon into Ottoman territory. Afterwards, some followers of Geyikli Baba in Bursa, Gözcü Baba in Göztepe, Eren Baba in Erenköy, Kartal Baba in Kartal, and Sarı Gazi in Sarıgazi moved to Kadıköy and settled here and started to conquer the hearts of the locals. The current name of Kadıköy was adopted after this conquest. After the conquest of Constantinople, Sultan Mehmed II appointed Hızır Bey Çelebi as the *qadi* (judge) of Istanbul and assigned him to this area and the surrounding areas. This was when the district began to be called "Kadı Köyü" (village of the judge). Later the name of the city became Kadıköy. In the 19th century, there was an increase in the density of the city's population and this region became a cosmopolitan city. The main turning point for Kadıköy started in the middle of the 19th century. From this period, ferry transportation started between Eminönü and Kadıköy. The opening of the Haydarpaşa-İzmit railway was another important development.

CAFÉ / RESTAURANT

EKO - Natural Çiğ Köfte (warning: çiğ köfte can be too spicy for some foreign visitors)
Food Order: (216) 545 0055

HAYDARPAŞA TRAIN STATION

Amount of time recommended for visit: **25 minutes**

This main terminal railway station was built in 1906 during the reign of Abdülhamid II by the architects Otto Ritter and Helmut Conu. Its construction took two years to complete. The Haydarpaşa terminal marked the beginning of the historical Hejaz Railway.

The station is designed in a U-shape and has five stories. On the façade overlooking the Bosphorus are towers. Only a few of the original hand-carved decorations on the ceilings have survived until today. Some of the stained glass windows were broken during a tanker accident in 1979.

MARMARA UNIVERSITY MEDICAL SCHOOL

Amount of time recommended for visit: **15 minutes**

Two monumental structures catch our attention on the seashore that connects Kadıköy to Üsküdar when looking from Eminönü. One of these is the Süleymaniye Barracks, mentioned in an earlier chapter, and the second is Marmara University Medical School. The transformation from *madrasa* education in the Ottoman era to modern medical education on March 14, 1827 was acknowledged with the opening of schools called the *Tıphane* and *Cerrahhane-i Amire*. It is for this reason that March 14 was declared and is still celebrated as the Medical Holiday in Turkey.

The first modern medical schools of the Turkish Republic, later to be called the *Mekteb-i Tıbbiye-i Adliye-i Şahane* existed in various parts of the country. The construction of the present Marmara University Haydarpaşa Campus, with its stunning architecture, began during the reign of Sultan Abdülhamid II in 1894. It was originally intended to be the Medical Faculty and was opened for education in 1903. With this institution all the medical schools, which were very scattered, from one district to the next, were collected under one roof in a modern campus. The building has been very important for the history of modern medical education because it has witnessed many important events in medical history.

İSKELE MOSQUE

Amount of time recommended for visit: **15 minutes**

This mosque was built during the reign of Sultan Mustafa III in 1760. It burned down completely in 1853. Eventually it was rebuilt in 1858 by Sultan Abdülmecid out of stone. The building reflects the influence of the Ottoman Baroque style. The primary school that was built next to the mosque no longer exists today. The architect of the mosque was the head architect of the time, Mehmed Tahir Agha. The mosque is called İskele (Wharf) Mosque because of the wharf that is near the mosque. However, due to land reclamation, the original relationship of the mosque to the sea has been lost. The area that was reclaimed from the sea carries a great deal of pedestrian and vehicle traffic in Kadıköy.

OSMAN AGHA MOSQUE

Amount of time recommended
for visit: **15 minutes**

This mosque is situated on the road that goes from Kadıköy to Söğütlüçeşme. It dates back to the reign of Sultan Mehmed II. The mosque of Hızır Çelebi Efendi, the *qadi* at the time of Mehmed II, used to stand here. In 1612, due to the dilapidated condition of the mosque, Osman Agha, built a new mosque here. By 1811 this new mosque was also in a very poor condition, and it was rebuilt during the reign of Mahmud II. In 1878 the mosque was damaged in a fire, but renovated in the same year. The magnificent plane tree in the garden is more than 130 years old.

BAHARİYE

Amount of time recommended
for visit: **15 minutes**

Walking from Kadıköy Wharf to the Söğütlüçeşme district,

we find a large bronze statue of a bull; this is located at an intersection known as Altıyol. This statue was presented as a gift by Kaiser Wilhelm II in 1917 to Enver Pasha. After being transported to various places, the statue was finally brought to Kadıköy in 1969. When approaching the statue, the pedestrian way on the right is Bahariye Street. This street resembles İstiklal Avenue in Beyoğlu district. This is a location that is often frequented by teenagers because of the large number of cafes, movie theaters and restaurants. Bahariye Street is busy and crowded every hour of the day.

An interesting building on Bahariye Street is Süreyya Pasha Cinema, constructed during the reign of Sultan Abdülhamid II. The building, with its interior design, boxes, ceiling decorations and statues, resembles old Baroque opera houses.

FENERBAHÇE PENINSULA

Amount of time recommended for visit: **1 hour**

One of the most pleasant characteristics of Kadıköy its long coastline. The great poet Istanbul poet Yahya Kemal Beyatlı describes the peninsula as "Most beloved and rambled place in the homeland." One of the most important locations of the peninsula is Fenerbahce Park. The park was used by Byzantine and Ottoman emperors as a summer retreat. The park was very popular when it was opened to the public in the 19th century. However, a result of this great interest was pollution. The peninsula was taken over by Turing company in 1990 and redesigned. The Fenerbahçe Peninsula provides a colorful harmony with its curving paths, large trees, variety of oleanders, and seasonal flowers.

Şükrü Saraçoğlu Stadium in Fenerbahçe is a modern stadium with a five-star UEFA rating that is used to host major cup finals and international matches. The stadium hosted the UEFA Cup Final in May 2009, when Shakhtar Donetsk defeated Werder Bremen.

BEYKOZ

Beykoz is one of the charming districts of Istanbul, where the green of the fields meets the blue of the sea. According to some, the history of this region dates back the 8th century BC. Our knowledge about the first settlers in Beykoz is limited, but it is known that during the Roman period there was a sacrificial area at Anadolu Kavağı where people who wanted to travel to the Black Sea would make a sacrifice to Zeus and Poseidon, hoping for favorable winds.

During the Byzantine period, Beykoz was a village for fishermen.

After the conquest of Constantinople, the Muslim population here increased. In the 18th century, Beykoz was a popular district and was an outing place and a holiday resort with its beautiful fields, natural spring waters, and seaside houses. Beykoz became the pearl of the Bosphorus, with the Kanlıca, Küçüksu and Göksu streams, and the Çubuklu and Tokat gardens. From the 19th century, Beykoz, adorned with groves, fountains, and palaces, maintained itself as an excursion place and played host to many travelers and many royal visitors.

Starting from the first quarter of the 19th century, industrialization started to come to Beykoz. The area is particularly famous for the glass ware produced here; there is also a factory in Paşabahçe.

CAFÉ / RESTAURANT

Hidiv Manor, Çubuklu Korusu Çubuklu Yolu No: 32 Beykoz (216) 413 9644; (216) 413 9664

Belediye Beykoz Tesisleri, Burunbahçe / Istanbul (216) 322 33 79 – 322 6769

ANADOLU HİSARI / ANATOLIA FORTRESS

Amount of time recommended for visit: **15 minutes**

The Anatolia Fortress is located where the Göksu Stream meets the Bosphorus. It was constructed in 1395 by Sultan Yıldırım Beyazıd. Sultan Mehmed II added external walls when he was having the Rumeli Fortress built. After the conquest of Istanbul, the Anatolia Fortress lost its military importance. The area around it slowly began to turn into a residential area. The fortress consists of the inner and outer areas and the walls surrounding them. When the fortress was first constructed, there was no entrance gate, but the fortress was entered via a suspension bridge that went over the inner walls. A wooden staircase led to the upper floors of the tower. The walls of the main castle measure 65 me-

ters from east to west and 80 meters from north to south, measuring 2.5 meters in width. There are strategically placed holes for cannons on the outer walls. Today, some parts of the fortress have been demolished and a road passes through the middle.

HİDİV MANOR

Amount of time recommended for visit: **1 hour**

One of the most important tourist areas in Beykoz is Hidiv Manor. It is located on the Çubuklu hills and has a picturesque view of Istanbul. During the reign of Sultan Mahmud II (1808–1839), the governors of Egypt were granted special status. According to this special status, the governorship became a dynasty and the governors of Egypt were known as *Hidiv* (Khedive). At the end of the 19th century, the governor of Egypt, Abbas Hilmi Pasha, sought Ottoman–German support against the British invasion of Egypt. The young pasha needed to stay in the Ottoman capital to get this support, and thus in 1903 he purchased two wooden manor houses in Çubuklu. Afterwards, the pasha purchased the hills behind the houses and the upper plateau, an area of two hundred and seventy thousand square meters. In 1907, the pasha commissioned the Italian architect Delfo Seminati to build the manor house in the Art Nouveau style.

The manor, a magnificent building, covers an area of one thousand square meters and has a view of the blue channel and the green forests

of the Bosphorus. Hidiv Manor is an excursion spot that takes the people of Istanbul away from the stress of the city. It is a common venue for wedding parties and other similar celebrations.

BEYKOZ MEADOW

Amount of time recommended for visit: **15 minutes**

Beykoz Meadow, also known as Yalıköy Meadow, is the place where students of both the military and civilian schools established by Sultan Mahmud II, a sultan greatly interested in modernization, would come on school excursions. The lamb feasts of Beykoz Meadow have been mentioned in many literary works. Students would be brought here before examinations or during holidays. Even today, Beykoz Meadow fulfills a similar function for Istanbul residents. Beykoz Municipality continues this tradition by arranging an International Beykoz Culture and Folklore Festival. Mecidiye Pavilion, also known as Beykoz Pavilion, stands next to Beykoz Meadow, between the sea and the hill. The coastline at the foot of this hill is known as the Hünkar İskelesi. This wharf is historically important as the

Ottomans and the Russians signed a treaty here in 1833.

KANLICA

Amount of time recommended for visit: **1 hour**

K anlıca is one of the charming regions on the Bosphorus, located at the Anatolian side feet of the Fatih Sultan Mehmed Bridge (also known as the second bridge). Kanlıca is best known for its yogurt. People from Istanbul come to Kanlıca just to eat the yogurt. Kanlıca yogurt is made of a mixture of milk from cows, sheep and buffalo and is traditionally eaten with powder sugar. The district is also a beautiful excursion spot.

KÜÇÜKSU PAVILION

Amount of time recommended for visit: **30 minutes**

O ne of the important monuments on the Istanbul Bosphorus is the Küçüksu Pavilion. Küçüksu attracted attention during the Ottoman period and became one of the royal gardens, known as *Kandil Bahçesi* (Lantern Garden). Sultan Murad IV (1623–1640) was particularly fond of Küçüksu and called it *Gümüş Selvi* (Silver Cypress); in several sources from the 17th century on, it is known as *Bahçe-i Göksu*. Starting from the 18th century the district became densely populated. Küçüksu Pavilion was designed by Nikogos Balyan, being completed and opened to the public in 1857. The

Küçüksu Pavilion was used as a government guesthouse after the establishment of the Republic as well. Today, it functions as a museum. Restoration began in 1994, and is still continuing today. The restored parts of the building are open to visitors.

YUŞA TEPESİ / JOSHUA'S HILL

Amount of time recommended for visit: **1 hour**

There are no documents indicating that Prophet Joshua died in Istanbul. Nevertheless, there is a great interest in this location. According to legend, Prophet Joshua's grave was discovered by Sheikh Yahya Efendi, who died in Beşiktaş. According to him: when Yavuz Sultan Selim I was a governor of Trabzon, his son, later to be Süleyman I, was born and a wet nurse was hired. Sheikh Yahya Efendi was the son of this wet nurse. After about forty years, when Süleyman became sultan, Yahya Efendi was a great scholar and an expert in Sufism. One day Yahya Efendi came to Istanbul to visit the sultan. Sultan Süleyman constructed two lodges for him, a winter house in Beşiktaş and a summerhouse in Anadolu Kavağı. Yahya Efendi had a dream when he was at the summerhouse. After this, Yahya Efendi and his friends climbed the hill and started their search. Eventually they asked a shepherd if he had seen anything extraordinary on the hills. The shepherd took Yahya Efendi to the location where the grave is and said, "Sir, do you see this place? Even though it is extremely green, the sheep do not

step on it, they do not eat the grass from here, and they go around it." Yahya Efendi then informed the sultan of this situation and constructed a tomb here.

Later, in 1755 Grand Vizier Mehmed Said Pasha constructed the mosque that is found here. Another characteristic of Joshua Hill is that it is the highest and the closest hill to the sea in Istanbul (200 meters). From the hill the view of the Bosphorus is magnificent. Here there are religious bookshops and places that sell snacks and light meals.

ANADOLU KAVAĞI

Amount of time recommended for visit: **Half a day**

Anadolu Kavağı acts as the entrance to the Black Sea from the Bosphorus and has maintained its character as a fishing village for many years. The village is famous for its beautiful woods and fish restaurants. It is a popular place during the bluefish season in September and October, when Istanbul bids farewell to the summer; here one can enjoy the cool and pleasant autumn days. One can come to Anadolu Kavağı by sea or land. The Bosphorus ferries come here, and this is considered to be the most comfortable mode of transport, and also allows for a relaxed Bosphorus tour. Another way to come here is via the Üsküdar–Beykoz coastal road. There are many fish restaurants on the coast.

One of the important structures in Anadolu Kavağı is Yoros Tower, built by the Genoese to control the Bosphorus. From here one can have a unique view of the Bosphorus and all the ships that enter and exit it. Yoros Tower perched on top of the hill is stunning, with its architecture and the coats of arms on the walls. Anadolu Kavağı was attacked by the Bithynians, Goths and Russians, and for a while was controlled by the Genoese, who constructed Yoros Tower in 1190. It is said that the tower, captured by the Byzantines and then by the Ottomans in the 14th century, was surrounded by twenty-five houses. Evliya Çelebi mentions that there used to be a black tower in Kavak Street that was seized by Yıldırım Khan and repaired by Sultan Mehmed II, who also placed soldiers here. He also says that the circumference of the tower was two hundred feet and it was surrounded by chestnut forests.

CHAPTER 7
PRINCES' ISLANDS

KINALIADA

BURGAZADA

HAGHIOS YORGI
CHURCH

HAGHIA TRIADA
MONASTERY

HAGHIOS NIKOLAOS
ORTHODOX CHURCH

HEYBELİADA

NAVAL HIGH SCHOOL

HEYBELİADA
SANATORIUM

FC

Recommended season for traveling: Spring and summer seasons are preferred.

Amount of time recommended for visit: One day per island should be allowed. If the days left are limited, only Büyük Ada or Heybeli can be chosen.

BÜYÜK ADA (Grand Island)

Büyükada is the largest of the Princes' Islands in both area and population and it acts as the center of the Islands. The island stretches in a north-south direction and is geographically comprised of two hills that are separated by a gorge. Yücetepe (High Hill) rises in the south to a height of 203 meters and to the north İsa Tepesi (Jesus' Hill) reaches 164 meters. Along the western coastline of the island is Dil Burnu (Tongue Point), which is 100 meters wide and 500 meters long. To the south of the headland is Yörüka-

li, while to the north is Nizamkoyu. Karacabey Village stands along the eastern coastline.

Büyükada is the furthest away and the largest of the islands. Its historical wharf and large market place immediately surround you as soon as you get off the ferry. To the left are the famous fish restaurants and to the right are tea gardens and shelters for fishermen, stretching all the way to the Anadolu Kulübü. The horse-drawn carriages wait under the clock tower. No motor vehicles are allowed on the islands, only horses and bicycles. The carriages can be hired for either a "big" or a "small" tour, using different routes from which one can view the beauty of the island. A complete tour around the island takes about two hours by horse carriage. Bicycles can be hired at the square near the carriages. The island has many beautiful places for out-

ings. The Dilburnu picnic area is lovely; here one can drink tea, coffee or soft drinks. Also, barbecues can be rented if you want to have a picnic.

Dilburnu Cafe
Phone: (216) 382 2486

HAMİDİYE MOSQUE

The islands share their history; before the conquest of Constantinople, the majority of the population of the islands was Greek. The first Muslim settlements started to form in 1850. When the Muslim population started to increase , a mosque had to be constructed. The Hamidiye Mosque was built during the reign of Sultan Abdülhamid II in Büyükada, and it was opened to the public in 1895. The mosque is very elegant in appearance.

PANAYIA CHURCH

The gates of the Panayia (Holy Virgin) Church open onto the Arabacılar Square and Çarşı Street. This church is also known as the Arabacılar Church by the residents of Büyükada because of its location. The word Panayia (Saint of the Saints) is another name for the Holy Virgin in Orthodoxy. The belfry was constructed in the 19th century and has a bulbous dome. The feast day of this church is August 15, the day Mother Mary died.

HAGHIOS YORGİ MONASTERY

On the highest hill of Büyükada, the largest of the islands, is Haghios Yorgi, also known as the Haghios Georgios Greek Orthodox Monastery. The monastery takes its name from Saint George of Cappadocia (Anatolia) who was martyred by the pagans when he was a commander of the Roman Army in the 3rd century B.C. His grave is in Palestine. According to some stories, the monastery has a history that dates back over one thousand years and it was constructed by the Byzantine emperor Nikiforos Fokas in 963 A.D. It is an extremely charming monastery with wooden tables, chairs, and small bowers. The prices at the restaurant are reasonable. The menu consists of shish kebabs, French fried potatoes, pastries and salads.

Phone: (216) 382 1333

BÜYÜKADA GREEK ORPHANAGE

The orphanage is located on Hristo Hill of Büyükada. The building was constructed as a hotel between 1898 and 1899 by a French company, led by Count Moris Bostari. The architect of the building was one of the most famous architects of his time, Alexandre Vallaury. The building is empty at the present time and is the property of the Phanar Patriarchate.

HESED LE AVRAAM SYNAGOGUE

This is the only synagogue on Büyükada. It was constructed during the reign of Sultan Abdülhamid II in order to meet the spiritual needs of the Jewish population here. Before this time, Jewish residents, staying on the island for the summer would gather in the houses of the rabbis on Friday and Saturday nights. The land was donated by Avram Fresko Efendi and this is why the synagogue is known as Hesed Le Avraam, or "The good deed of Avram." The synagogue in Büyükada was opened to the public on March 30, 1904.

HAGHIOS DEMETRIOS CHURCH

One of the historical churches on Büyükada is the church dedicated to St. Demetri. The church was opened for worship on May 7, 1856. The architect of the stone building with a brick roof was Fistiki (Fistikos) Kalfa.

HAGHIOS NIKOLAOS MONASTERY

The area where the Haghios Nikolaos Monastery is located is the Byzantine settlement known as Karya (or Karyes). Karya occupies the area on the east coast of Büyükada, across from Sedef island. Haghios Nikolaos Monastery is thought to be located in the center of Karya, an area that was burned down by the Latins who revolted against the Emperor Andronicos Comnenos. Karya was looted by pirates in the 14th and 15th centuries and underwent another fire and an earthquake in the 16th century. An earthquake that occurred in 1509 damaged the islands greatly. Due to the cracks, the bases of the monastery walls sank into the ground. The monastery complex is therefore also known as the "Sunken Monastery."

HEYBELİADA

The reason why this island is called Heybeliada (saddlebag island) is because the island resembles a saddlebag that has been dropped on the ground when seen from a distance. The island is one of the more popular excursion places in Istanbul. It is not only famous for its natural beauty and beautiful weather, but also because of its school, sanitarium and seminary.

The population of the island is around seven thousand and it increases by a couple of multiples of its size every summer. With the visitors, the population of the island reaches about fifty thousand. Ferry transportation to Heybeliada, as well as to other islands, began in the 19th century. Çam Limanı (Pine Harbor), situated on a beautiful cove, and Bahriye Limanı (Navy Harbor) are two of the important places on the island. Other important monuments on the island are the Naval School, Aye Ofemya Ayazması (a spring that is considered sacred by Greek Orthodoxy),

Heybeliada Sanitarium, the first sanitarium in Turkey, which was established in 1924, the Hüseyin Rahmi Gürpınar high school, Abbas Halim Pasha Pavilion, a monastery and other religious and official structures.

Two kinds of tours can be taken, either by riding on donkeys or in horse-drawn carriages. There is a big tour, and a small tour. Unless you choose to walk, you can also rent bikes. Heybeliada is similar to the other islands in Istanbul in that no motor vehicles are allowed.

Ahmed Rasim, a Turkish writer, died on this island; despite the great amount he wrote about Istanbul, he did not produce any works about the island. The song, "Biz Heybeli'de her gece mehtaba çıkardık" (meaning "we would go out in the moonlight on Heybeli") is very well known, written by the grandson of Ahmed Rasim; Yesari Asım. Heybeliada is frequently mentioned in the works of other authors as well.

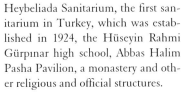

DENİZ LİSESİ (Naval High School)

Until the middle of the 18th century the training of captains for the Ottoman navy was not carried out by any organization, but was rather information that was passed from father to son or from experts to apprentices. The transformation into an education system in the Ottoman Empire started with the opening of the Üsküdar Engineering School in 1734. During the reign of Sultan Selim III, the existing building, originally founded as the Naval Barracks (*Bahriye Kışlası*) on Heybeliada, was rebuilt as the *Mühendishâne-i Bahri Hümayun* (Imperial Naval Engineering School). From 1824 until the end of the World War I the building provided education. Among the students of this school two famous poets emerged, Necip Fazıl Kısakürek and Nazım Hikmet Ran. The Naval High School still functions today.

HAGHIA TRIADA MONASTERY AND CHURCH

The Haghia Triada Monastery is one of the important historical places on Heybeliada. This monastery has one important difference from other places of worship on the other islands. That difference is that the monastery served as a seminary for a long period of time.

The church is situated on the northern part of the island on Papaz Tepesi (Priest Hill). The original name of the church was Siyon, connected to the Sinai Church, probably because the church was affiliated with the Jerusalem Patriarch. Later on, the church was renamed Triada, meaning Trinity. Haghia Triada is the oldest monastery or church on Heybeliada. It is claimed that the church was established in the 9th century by Saint Photius, the patriarch of Constantinople. For this reason, the feast of Saint Photius is celebrated on February 6 every year as the foundation day of the monastery.

According to the marble epigraph written in Greek on the right-hand wall of the monastery the church was opened on Monday, May 1 in 1844 during the period of Sultan Abdülmecid and Patriarch Germanos IV. In the same year, with the support of Patriarch Germanos IV, a seminary was opened within the monastery. One thousand students graduated from the seminary during the time education was given here, between 1844 and 1971.

The monastery was affected by the Cyprus Conflict between Turkey and Greece in 1963. The students who were coming here were not granted visas. At that time, the monastery became a diplomatic matter, and it has as yet not been solved. Other important elements of the monastery are the library that was built as part of the school. The library contains over one hundred and twenty thousand books.

HAGHIOS NIKOLAOS ORTHODOX CHURCH

Haghios Nikolaos Orthodox Church was constructed at the location where Patriarch Samuel I (Byzantios) stayed for the last 4 years of his life; he was buried under the church when he passed away on May 10, 1775. After being severely damaged by an earthquake in 1894, the church underwent extensive renovations during the reign of Sultan Abdülhamid II.

HEYBELİADA SANATORIUM

Tuberculosis used to be treated by providing the patients with rest in clean sea air. Heybeliada was known for being a good place for the treatment of this illness. For this reason, during the early years of the Republic, on an order from Atatürk, a sanatorium was established here. The sanatorium was opened on November 1, 1924 as a small hospital with 16 bedrooms, in a building located at the feet of *Çam Limanı* (Pine Harbor) and *Yeşil Burun* (Green Harbor). Originally, the sanatorium only accepted male patients. Afterwards, a section for women was added. Many famous people have stayed at the sanatorium, including İsmet İnönü. The sanatorium was damaged during the great earthquake on August 17, 1999. The two blocks of the hospital were repaired in 2001. On a decision by the Ministry of Health the sanatorium was transferred to the Süreyya Pasha cardiovascular Hospital in Kartal in 2005.

BURGAZADA

This is the second island that the ferries stop at on their journey from Eminönü. Burgazada is the third largest island, and it consists of one small hill. It is about an average of two kilometers from a seaside spot to the other side of the island. No motor vehicles are allowed. After the conquest of Constantinople, the Turks named this island "Burgaz," derived from the Greek word *Pirgos* (*Prygos*)

meaning "bastion." During the Ottoman period, the island was a popular excursion place for non-Muslims.

Another sanatorium was opened here in 1927. There was only one mosque on the island until 1953. Another small mosque was built in 1953 to celebrate the 500th anniversary of the conquest of Istanbul. The island held the first private zoo in Turkey. One of the great writers in Turkish literature, Sait Faik Abasıyanık, lived here.

AYYANI CHURCH

The church was constructed by Thedora, the wife of the emperor Teophilos, on the location where Methodius was imprisoned. This church was severely damaged during the conquest of Constantinople, but was later repaired in 1759. According to the epigraph, it underwent another restoration in 1817. After the church became so derelict that it could no longer be used, a new church was constructed in 1896. The present church serves the entire Greek population on the island. From the last section of the church, a staircase of ten steps leads down to the cell in which Saint Methodius was jailed.

HAGHIOS YORGI MONASTERY AND CHURCH

This church, famous for its three church bells, was built in the 19th century. On the western side of the island, the church is located on a steep hill on Cennet Yolu (Heaven Road). It is claimed that the monastery was constructed in the 16th century. The monastery burned down while being used by Byelorussian immigrants, between 1920 and 1923. The current monastery is being used by the Greek population of the island.

KINALIADA (HENNAED ISLAND)

There are different views concerning the origin of the name of Kınalıada. One opinion is that the name is derived from the fact that the maquis on the island are reddish in color. According to another view, the island takes its name from the red-colored earth. Both ideas are connected to how the island appears. The easiest way to reach Kınalıada is via the ferries that leave either from Eminönü or Bostancı. Kınalıada is the closest island to Istanbul.

What makes Kınalıada different from the other islands is the lack of horse carriages as transportation. Here there are only bicycles, but the preferred way to get about is on foot. Walking away from Ayazma Beach and heading for the hills, we see Hristo Monastery (Monastery of Christ) situated on the highest hill of Kınalıada. The monastery, located on the highest point of the island, was constructed when the Byzantine emperor Romanus IV Diogenes was exiled here. The monastery can only be visited on Fridays; special permission is needed to visit on other days.

EXCURSION AREAS

Çilingöz

İnceğiz

Fevzi Çakmak

İmrahor

Tayakadın

Odayeri

Göktürk

Ayvat

Kömürcübent

Marmaracık

Bentler

Kurtkemer

M.A.Ersoy

Arnavutköy

Binbaşı

Habibler

Şamlar

Azizpaşa

Beykoz

Mihribat

Göztepe

Yıldız

Gülhane

Fethipaşa

Osmar

Çamlıca

Florya

Harem

Değirmenburnu

Büyükada

N

Avcı

cakçeşme

Hacetderesi

🟢 Woods within the city

🌲 Picnic areas

Roads

GIANT CYPRESS TREES

The two cypress trees in the Subaşı neighborhood of Çatalca are among the giants trees under protection in Turkey. The cypress trees in the Subaşı-Havuzlar region are thought to be between 900 and 1,000 years old and they are fifteen meters tall. These giants trees can easily be reached from the center of Çatalca and are the most interesting examples of giants trees.

AVCI KORU (WOODS) EXCURSION AREA

This is an outing area with a rich collection of trees. It is located on the Üsküdar-Şile TEM Highway, near Ömerli. Inside the area there are disused mines and the park covers an area of six million five hundred and twenty thousand square meters. There is a great variety of plants here. Despite a lack of sitting areas, the forest can be explored via a series of pathways, and various kinds of plants and insects can be seen. The forest is extremely suitable for sports activities such as cross-country trekking or running.

Getting here: From Üsküdar direction, there is an exit to the Avcı Koru Excursion Area 5 kilometers after Ömerli on the Üsküdar-Şile TEM Highway, and 10 kilometers from the Şile direction.

Phone: Alemdağ Nature preservation and National Parks Engineering.

Phone: (216) 413 4015-16

AYDOS EXCURSION AREA

The Aydos Excursion area encircles the beautiful Aydos Hill. Here is an ideal ambiance for resting and sports. The fact that this outing area was used as a hunting place during the Ottoman Empire  indicates the richness of the pine forest. The beauty of the hill, which takes 15 minutes to climb, is worth the effort. For people who want to watch the sun set this is an ideal location.

The pond in the outing area, which covers an area of six million six hundred and twenty square meters, with four different entrances, completes the ecological harmony of the area.

Getting here: Aydos can be reached from the Kartal-Yakacık and Sultanbeyli districts via the E-5 highway (the main artery passing through Istanbul and TEM highway. Public transportation can also be utilized.

Phone: (216) 377 4647

AYVAT BENDİ (AYVAT DAM) EXCURSION AREA

The dam is situated on the Ayvat Stream, which is one of the branches of the Kağıthane Stream. The historical dam, built during the reign of Sultan Mustafa III in 1765, is 13.45 meters high. The reservoir that rests among the small hills offers one of the best views of the Belgrad Forest. The existence of many wild animals means that this is a place of ecological importance. In addition to being an important location from a natural and photographic perspective, there are suitable areas for picnics. Here there are a number of waterways that were constructed for the city of Istanbul in the Ottoman period; the Kurtkemeri aqueduct also attracts a lot of attention.

Getting here: A path leading through the center of the Kurtkemeri Entrance Outing Area, the gateway to the Belgrad Forest from Kemerburgaz, takes one to the Ayvat Bendi Excursion Area.

Phone: (212) 444 3000

AZİZ PASHA EXCURSION AREA

This excursion area is one of the favorite picnic areas in the environs of Istanbul due to its proximity to the districts of Maslak, Gültepe, Levent, Kâğıthane and Eyüp, as well as its interesting flora and great expanse. You can have a break on the fields at the beginning of the area, or choose to go further to climb up the hills; this will help your lungs fill with fresh air. Large groups interested in football can have a match on the football field on the hill. The cafeteria there sells food and goods you will need for a picnic.

Getting here: As one comes down from Maslak, this area is on the right of the road; also as one is coming from Kemerburgaz, turn right and cross over the Hasdal road.

Phone: (212) 360 3085

BAHÇEKÖY NURSERY

Since 1944, the Bahçeköy Arboretum and Nursery has worked with

the Ministry of the Environment and Forestry. Here professional personnel and experts in forestry raise a variety of trees and residents of Istanbul can buy saplings and benefit from the knowledge of the personnel. It is also possible to stroll through the arboretum. The Bahçeköy Nursery makes a significant contribution to the Turkish environment with the work carried out in their laboratories. The arboretum takes up an area of eighty-three thousand square meters while the nursery occupies forty-three thousand square meters of this area. In general, non-deciduous trees, such as spruce, fir, cypress, and juniper are grown, as well as ornamental plants such as laurel, box, cotoneaster, and viburnum. Blue spruce and blue cedar are also produced.

Getting here: The nursery-arboretum is in Bahçeköy and can be reached from the Maslak–Sarıyer road. The left side of the road that leads to the Belgrad Forest belongs to the arboretum.

Phone: (212) 226 1028

BELGRAD FOREST- NEŞET WATER

Neşet Water is an important excursion area established around a fresh water source. The name comes from Professor Neşet (1881–1929), who contributed greatly to the improvement of the Belgrad Forest. This area is popular with locals of Istanbul all year round due to the ease of transport and its location in the center of the Belgrad Forest. In addition to the spring water, there is an eight-kilometer ring around the reservoir

of Büyükbent, which forms an ideal place to walk, as well as picnic areas,

a cafeteria and a carpark. The Neşet Waters Excursion area is used by sports clubs for cross-country running and training programs. It is also of interest to environmental scientists with its rich flora and fauna.

Getting here: Follow signposts to the Belgrad Forest from Levent, Maslak, Bahçeköy or Kemerburgaz. From both directions, one can reach Neşet Water after driving three kilometers along an asphalt road.

Phone: (216) 486 0072

IRMAK (RIVER) EXCURSION AREA

Irmak Excursion Area is an important location that consists of enormous

trees that give the area a great variety of color and fresh air. Immediately at the entrance are tables that have been carefully set up and places suitable for picnics. The clarity of the water and the clean environment immediately noticeable. The track starting from Neşet Suyu goes through the excursion area. The paths take you into the depths of the forest. The area appeals to a wide range of visitors, mainly families or large groups, especially at the weekend.

Getting here: From the sign at the Maslak-Bahçeköy entrance, you need to turn right. At the end of the four kilometer-long road, another signpost greets you, From the Kemerburgaz destination, you turn right. The excursion area is reached after the Binbaşı and Fatih Fountains.

Phone: (212) 559 2549

BELGRAD FOREST – DAMS

This is one of the most beautiful excursion areas in the Belgrad Forest. The Topuzlu Dam (1750), Valide Dam (1796) and Sultan Mahmud I Dam (1839), which were built to meet the demand for water in the Ottoman Empire period, are all situated here. There is a buffet that provides items necessary for picnics. The walking course leads right into the depths of the forest and a cycle path takes you to different areas of beauty with every season. The green cover is stunning in the spring, the coolness is pleasant in the summer, the yellow and red colors of fall are breath-taking, and winter is a quiet world of nature asleep.

Getting here: The asphalt road on the right as one turns at the Bahçeköy entrance of the Belgrad Forest offers an easy and convenient means of getting here.

Phone: (212) 559 2549

BELGRAD FOREST- FALİH RIFKI ATAY EXCURSION AREA

For those who want a calm corner in the Belgrad Forest the excursion area named after the famous author Falih Rıfkı Atay is the place to be. This area measures two hundred thousand square  meters and rests between Neşet Waters and Kömürcübent. The Falih Rıfkı Atay Excursion Area offers ideal opportunities for picnicking in every condition with its wooden benches. The excursion area has ample water resources, while the mini football pitch offers a great chance for children and adults to play. It is possible to see many different examples of local flora and fauna while in the depths of the forest.

Getting here: This area is adjacent to Neşet Waters, after the Bahçeköy entrance of the Belgrad Forest. It can be reached by following the sign-posts to Kemerburgaz, Göktürk and Kurtkemeri.

Phone: (212) 531 5581

BEYKOZ – GÖKNARLIK EXCURSION AREA

Tokatköy–Göknarlık offers a different kind of beauty in Beykoz. The fir trees grow over an area measuring 46.5 hectares and provide a stunning atmosphere. No sunlight can filter through the trees, and walking under them stirs up a variety of emotions. The area, surrounded by chestnut trees, is extremely easy to find because of its proximity to the Beykoz Municipality Center.

COMMANDER'S EXCURSION AREA

Commander's Excursion Area has a wide range of fauna and flora; this can easily be reached from the centers of Kemerburgaz or Belgrad Forest. The area attracts attention because of its running track and sitting areas. There is a legend about this area: During the final years of the Ottoman Empire, a troop of soldiers needed to take refuge here. This was a time of hunger and thirst. The soldiers were discontent, yet they could not leave the camp. The troop commander started to try to solve the problems of the soldiers' thirst and hunger. He began digging a well at night and by morning he had found water; thus his name was given to this area. The cafeteria at the entrance is well equipped to meet the needs of most visitors. There is a charming playground for children in the excursion area.

Getting here: The Commander's Excursion Area is on the road that connects Kemerburgaz to Bahçeköy.

Phone: (212) 280 0147

ÇATALCA MAREŞAL FEVZİ ÇAKMAK EXCURSION AREA

This excursion area is named after Marshall Fevzi Çakmak, one of the founders of the Turkish Republic. It is an important resting and picnic area in the district of Çatalca. The excursion area is filled with pine tree groves, which add to the beauty of the seasonal colors. The swimming pool inside the area is used in the summer months. On the high place near the entrance one can see Rumeli and Çatalca Train Station. Each season the excursion area is flooded with visitors with the advantage of being close to the center of Çatalca.

Getting here: The excursion area is in front of one after turning right from the Çatalca district center, and is easily found from the TEM motorway.

Çatalca Nature Preserve and National Parks.

Phone: (212) 789 6989

ÇİLİNGÖZ EXCURSION AREA

An expansive white beach on the Black Sea coast, a stream that joins the sea among rocks that have been smoothed and shaped by the waves for centuries, a green covering of trees completes this beautiful picture.

Getting here: Follow the road through the forest, and turn right outside the exit from the Binkılıç region on the Çatalca-Saray route.

Phone: Nature Preservation and National Parks Engineering
Phone: (212) 789 1005

DEĞİRMENBURNU EXCURSION AREA

When speaking of the islands, a special kind of beauty comes to mind. Among those, the Değir-

menburnu on Heybeliada has a special charm. One can see the old mill which gives its name to the area, the other islands and the coastline of Istanbul. The scent from the pine trees combines with that of the sea, taking you to a different world. You can also spice up your excursion with horse carriage rides and get something to eat from the buffet. Tours

of the surrounding sea and coves are also offered.

Getting here: One can reach Heybeliada by ferries or private boats; the road that goes to the right leads to the excursion area.

Phone: (212) 601 1188

DİLBURNU EXCURSION AREA

Dilburnu is precious not just to Istanbul, but to all of Turkey. The area is greatly admired due to the unique architecture, the blueness of the sea and the green of the pine trees. Here you can have a picnic, lie on the beach, walk or surf. If you have the time, take the rare pleasure of observing the coves through the pine trees and watch the sunset.

Getting here: It is possible to reach Büyükada by the Adalar–Yalova ferries that leave from Eminönü, Kabataş, Kadıköy, Bostancı and Kartal. After reaching the island, you can walk, cycle or take a horse carriage ride to reach the excursion area.

Phone: (216) 226 3631

ELMASBURNU (DIAMOND POINT) EXCURSION AREA

Elmas Burnu is a precious cove formed from black rocks jutting out of the Black Sea. This is more a holiday resort with its long beach, pine forest, and calm ambiance. It is possible to camp here and greet the rising sun to the sound of the sea. The rocks from the cliffs to the depths of the sea are ideal for spear fishing. This place is extremely popular with fishermen. Right across from the cove, Martı Adası (Seagull Island) is home to various sea birds and dolphins add to the beauty of the island. Once you are in Riva, do not forget to walk along the river and enjoy the surroundings.

Getting here: You can reach the excursion area in 20 minutes by the TEM connection; this lies between Kavacık and Riva. Also, one can go though Mahmud Şevket Pasha Village near Beykoz.

Phone: (212) 651 9891

FATİH FOREST EXCURSION AREA

The word "fatih" means "conqueror" and this area took its name from Sultan Mehmed the Conqueror, who was well known for his love of forests. This forest is quite close to the urban center and it covers a large area. In the depths of the forest there are sitting areas where you can have a great picnic. Fatih Excursion Area is frequently visited by cycling enthusiasts. It is also preferred by families because of the large playground.

Getting here: Follow the Bahçeköy signposts on the Sarıyer route of Maslak Büyükdere Street. It is on the left side after three kilometers. Its other entrance is from the Şişli–Ayazağa direction.

Phone: (212) 299 8475

FATİH CHILDREN'S FOREST-PARK FOREST

Park Forest embraces nature, and it is a location that meets the demands of people of every age. This forest is removed from the typical metropolitan and urban problems and takes one away from the chaos and commotion of

the city. There are several play areas in the sections specially designed for children. There are enjoyable activities 24 hours a day, with sports amenities, musical and artistic events.

Getting here: The forest is on Büyükdere Street as one comes from Maslak. www.parkorman.com.tr

Phone: (212) 328 2000

FATİH FOUNTAIN EXCURSION AREA

This excursion area is built around the fountain that was dedicated to Sultan Mehmed II. The fountain, which is situated at the entrance of the excursion area, has served the public for years and is popular with visitors, particularly in the summer. The small wooden cafeteria at the entrance is a very cozy place. The picnic areas and paths complete the beautiful atmosphere. The oak trees have been planted very close to one another and they surround an area of two hundred and fifty acres. The beautiful colors in every season make the area even more attractive.

Getting here: It can be reached through Kemerburgaz. It takes 6 kilometers from Kemerburgaz in the Belgrad Forest direction. It is on the left side of the road to the fountain of Binbaşı Çeşmesi.

Bahçeköy Nature Preservation and National Parks Engineering.

Phone: (212) 226 2335-37

GAZİ STREET EXCURSION AREA

This is one of the beautiful areas that generally go unnoticed in Istanbul. The excursion area is also known as Alibeyköy Dam and it covers an area of seven hundred and eighty-five acres. Even though there is nowhere to sit down here, the area is beautiful for walking and picnicking. The view of the skyscrapers in Levent and Maslak at sunset add to the variety of colors. The reservoir was opened in 1972. Fishing and swimming are not permitted in the reservoir.

Getting here: It is extremely easy to find as it is close to the center of the city. It can be reached from Gaziosmanpaşa from the center of Gazi Street as well as from Kağıthane-Alibeyköy.

Istanbul Nature Preservation and National Parks.

Phone: (212) 262 7710 / 2484

GÖKTÜRK POND EXCURSION AREA

Göktürk pond was formed to hold the water that comes from the large forests surrounding the excursion  areas and the city of Istanbul. Göktürk Pond, formed on an area of five hundred and sixty acres, is a very beautiful spot. The reservoir is under the control of İSKİ, thus being protected. This beautiful area is ideal for resting and walking in.

Getting here: This area is very close to Göktürk center, which can be reached via the Hasdal–Kemerburgaz route. It is right at the beginning of the İhsaniye road.

Nature Preservation and National Parks Engineering.

Phone: (212) 262 7710/ 2484

GÖKTÜRK NURSERY AND EXCURSION AREA

This is an important nursery serving the provincial directorate of the Ministry of Environment and Forestry since 1969. The nursery covers a fertile area measuring three hundred and twenty-eight hectares. It is flooded with visitors from Istanbul every day of the week.

Getting here: It is easily found by the Kemerburgaz–Göktürk route. It is right across from the shopping mall in Göktürk.

Phone: (212) 322 0014

HACET STREAM EXCURSION AREA

This is one of the popular picnic areas in the Tuzla region; it is small in size, but hosts gigantic pine trees. The park consists of a flat plateau and small playgrounds and sitting areas. The stream that gives its name to the  Excursion area, unfortunately, can at times be polluted, due to the surrounding residential areas. However, the residents enjoy coming here to rest and have picnics. Calabrian pines, that are unique to the islands of Istanbul, can only be seen in Hacet Stream Excursion Area on the Anatolian side.

Getting here: This park is situated in Aydınlık Village that is in the northern section of the Tuzla Distict.

Alemdağ Nature Preservation and National Parks Engineering

Phone: (216) 413 4015–16

İMRAHOR POND

İmrahor Pond was designed to protect the forest and utilize the natural water resources. The flora that started growing in the area has transformed the area into a natural park. The excursion area, where blue meets green, is a great favorite with nature enthusiasts. The sitting and walking areas around the pond are open to the public. This is a very popular place with families at the weekends, and school and work groups have picnics here often. Activities such as swimming and fishing are not permitted in the pond.

Getting here: Turn from the İmrahor Village detour after driving for 5 kilometers on the main road from Gaziosmanpaşa till Tayakadın. The Stabilized road is located in the upper section of the village.

Istanbul Nature Preservation and National Parks

Phone: (212) 262 7710/ 2484

İNCEĞİZ EXCURSION AREA

This is the region where the Çatalca district was established around 2,500 years ago. There are three large caves that were carved into the high rocks in the 9th century by the Genoese.

This is a place where you can find peace of mind. The picnic areas and the stream that runs alongside add to the beauty of the place.

Getting here: The excursion area can easily be found by driving for 6 kilometers after having turned to the left of the asphalt road going from Çatalca to Subaşı after three kilometers.

Phone: (212) 789 1524

KAYMAKDONDURAN EXCURSION AREA

Kaymakdonduran is one of those places that can be described as having a unique atmosphere. The excursion area is located in Beykoz and reaches down to the Bosphorus. The name *Kaymakdonduran* (literally meaning freezing the cream) probably is connected to the coldness of the water. The water that you can drink from the fountain, which was built by the famous Ottoman governor of Kanije, Ahmed Pasha, is wonderful. You can have a great picnic in the fields set out with picnic tables. The giant trees, two hundred years old, are growing on an area that measures six hundred and fifty acres.

Getting here: The excursion area detour is located after 3 kilometers on the Beykoz–Akbaba village destination and the entrance is located 1 kilometer after that. You can reach the area after five minutes along the gravel road.

Alemdağ Nature Preservation and National Parks Engineering

Phone: (216) 413 4015-16

KİRAZLIBENT EXCURSION AREA

This area is a great work of nature. The thin winding paths, the tall trees and the historic reservoir all add to the atmosphere. The reservoir in the upper section is an object of admiration and was

built by Sultan Mahmud II in 1818 on the Kirazlı Stream; it is 11.25 meters deep and is 59.45 meters wide.

Getting here: It is across from the Irmak Excursion Area on the road through Bahçeköy turning left to Kemerburgaz.

Nature Preservation and National Parks Engineering

Phone: (212) 226 2335

KÖMÜRCÜ BENDİ (RESERVOIR) EXCURSION AREA

This area is a great example of how the Ottomans were a civilization preoccupied with water. The reservoir, also known as Karanlıkbent (dark reservoir) was built by Sultan Osman II in 1620 on the Topuz Stream. The Küçüksu reservoir hosts various living things. Close to the reservoir is a deer-breeding center. It is possible to see these charming animals from afar. The terrain is a little uneven and has a unique beauty with trees reaching to the skies. The picnic and rest locations are very well tended. The asphalt road that goes through the excursion area leeds to Kısırkaya village.

Getting here: You can reach Kömürcü Reservoir Excursion Area by following Neşet Suyu and Falih Rıfkı Atay Excursion Areas from the Bahçeköy entrance of the Belgrad Forest. The wild animals breeding center is right next to it.

Phone: (212) 221 4537

KURT KEMERİ EXCURSION AREA

This is considered to be a continuation of the Belgrad Forest. There are many different locations for picnicking here. This area is frequented by residents of districts in Eyüp, Kâğıthane, Kemerburgaz and Göktürk. There are paths and running and walking tracks.

Getting here: It is on the point of connection of the road to the Belgrad Forest.

Phone: (212) 530 7016

MARMARACIK EXCURSION AREA

It is here that the pounding Black Sea takes a breather. You can either run and play or go fishing or listen to the silence of nature here. Because of all the activities on offer—the camping area, the wooden houses, the country houses, the restaurants, beaches, golf courts, and surfing opportunities—this area attracts many visitors. The buildings have been constructed completely out of wood and natural stones, with a thought for the environment. This area was once famous as it was the head lodge for VW Beetle enthusiasts. It is also a wonderful place for photography with its natural beauty.

Getting here: It is situated at the end of the road at the left turn from the Rumeli Kavağı, which is reached from Sarıyer. E-Mail: info@altunbas-turizm.com
Phone: (212) 325 5583-85

MEHMET AKİF ERSOY EXCURSION AREA

This area was established under the name of the poet Mehmet Akif Ersoy who wrote the words to the Turkish national anthem. His closeness to Sarıyer and Levent make it a popular place. The elegant restaurants and well-tended picnic areas make this a good place for large groups. The mini football court is suitable for players of all ages. The excursion area has a different atmosphere every season and is well known for its very tall trees.

Getting here: It is located on Çayırbaşı Street that goes down to Sarıköy from Bahçeköy. Right next to it, there is a bus stop.

Phone: (212) 226 3631

MİHRABAD EXCURSION AREA

This area is part of the natural heritage of Kanlıca, which has witnessed all the colors of Istanbul. The excursion area is situated on a hill that dominates the Bosphorus. It hosts a wide range of trees, such as  pines, redbuds, plane trees and cypresses. Particularly in the spring it is a special pleasure to wander among the beautiful flowers here. The region, along with the pavilion at the wharf, which belonged to Sultan Abdülhamid I, was donated by Necibe Hanim, the wife of the Ambassador to Germany, Sadullah Pasha to Rukiye Hanim as part of her dowry. The princess then had the pavilion rebuilt in its current state. This park is frequented by a large number of visitors because of the largeness of the space (200 acres), the sitting areas, the buffet, the racecourse, playground, and other sections.

Getting here: Mihrabad Excursion area can either be reached from the coast (Kanlıca Direction) or from Kavacik Tekke Region via TEM connection road.

Alemdağ Nature Preservation and National Parks Engineering

Phone: (216) 413 4015-16

ODAYERİ EXCURSION AREA

If you want to escape the urban commotion, the stress of every day life and get a chance to take a breather, come to the Odayeri Excursion Area. Here there are a number of hardwood trees surrounding the fields. If you want to have a picnic, you can bring your own ingredients or buy them from the nearby village. The ponds formed from mining excavations add to the beauty of nature, yet it should not be forgotten that they can be treacherous.

Getting here: Odayeri Excursion Area is situated on the Ağaçlı Road 6 kilometers away from İhsaniye Köyü (İhsaniye village) after exiting Hasdal, Kemerburgaz, and Göktük. Istanbul Nature Preservation and National Parks Engineering

Phone: (212) 262 7710

POLONEZKÖY (POLISH VILLAGE) NATURAL PARK

Polonezköy is a colony established by Polish refugees in 1842. The wide variety of trees and plants is a reason for great admiration. The majority of the population here are of Polish extraction. It is possible to see diverse cultures and lifestyles here. The camping areas are ideal, especially at weekends. The beauty of this area is widely known and the region has hosted famous people such as Mustafa Kemal Atatürk, Franz Liszt, and Gustav Flaubert.

Getting here: Polonezköy (Polish village) Natural Park can be reached via various routes, because of its popularity. You can either follow the signs from the Kavacık–Çavuşbaşı or from Beykoz–Riva and Alemdağ–Şile destinations.

SAZAKÇEŞME EXCURSION AREA

This is one of the important excursion areas on the Anatolian side of Istanbul, where one can indulge in activities like resting, walking and picnicking. Despite having a small entrance area, the forest area grows larger as you move up the hill. The paths inside the forest can take you to the corner of your choice and there are special places for children. While you can rest among pine trees that stretch up to the sky, your children can have a fun time playing in the specially prepared areas. You can observe the forest on the Anatolian side of Istanbul from a wide perspective while sipping a glass of tea in the wooden cafeteria of the excursion area.

Getting there: It is on the right side of the Üsküdar–Şile TEM route. It is about twenty-five kilometers from the center of Üsküdar

Phone: (532) 717 1442

TAŞDELEN EXCURSION AREA

A variety of trees cover the *Taşdelen* Excursion Area. What makes this area outstanding is the *Taşdelen* water that runs through the eight hundred acres. This is an attractive excursion area on the Anatolian side with a natural beauty, friendly and approachable personnel, well-kept areas, and easy transportation. You can picnic here or eat at the convenient restaurant.

Getting here: It is 1 kilometer away from the *Taşdelen* center which you can reach via the Üsküdar–Şile TEM route. You can use either private or public transportation.

Phone: (216) 312 1368

TAYAKADIN EXCURSION AREA

This is an important location on the European side of Istanbul, famous for its green fields, well-maintained sections, and the good quality of service. Families, student groups, or other large groups can spend a pleasant time in the forest. The oxygen generated by the pine and oak trees will definitely take away your weariness. You can choose to enjoy a self- prepared picnic or utilize the facilities and the menu at the cafeteria. There is an interesting variety of wild animals, including foxes, squirrels, eagles and falcons. After seeing Tayakadın Excur-

sion Area, you can go on to see Terkos Lake as well as many other locations.

Getting here: The excursion area runs parallel with the road on the left after passing by Gaziosmanpaşa–Arnavutköy.

Phone: (212) 614 2824
(535) 763 9069

BOSPHORUS TOUR–GOLDEN HORN TOUR

Sarayburnu: Every day except Monday and Thursday.

Itinerary: All the magnificent palaces on both sides of Istanbul: Dolmabahçe, Beylerbeyi Palaces and Küçüksu Pavilion can be visited and you can transfer between them on the Sultan Kayıkları (Sultan's boats), the symbol of power and majesty in the Ottoman Period. To do this a ticket can be purchased from the ticket booth at the entrance to Dolmabahçe Palace.

Wharf: Dolmabahçe

Tour of the Golden Horn: Every week day at 17.30 and at the weekends 13.30–17.30

Itinerary: You can observe the historical locations that display the cultural wealth of Istanbul; the tour lasts for forty-five minutes. You can see Pierre Loti, the Phanar Greek Patriarchate, the Bulgarian Church, Eyüp Mosque, the Greek Boys School (also known as the Red School), the district of Fener (Phanar), Feshane, Galata Tower, Topkapı Palace, and Haghia Sophia.

Wharf: It departs from the Sultan's Boat Harbor at Eyüp.

Phone: (212) 296 5240 pbx

Bosphorus Tour: Every week day at 19.30 and weekends from 13.30 to 19.30. Itinerary: You can spend a pleasant hour accompanied by music, with Asia and Europe on both sides of you. On the tour you will see Dolmabahçe Palace, Çırağan Palace, the Bosphorus Bridge, Feriye Pavilion, Esma Sultan Mansion, Beylerbeyi Palace, Topkapı Palace, the Selimiye Barracks, the Maiden Tower, Salacak and Çamlıca.

Wharf: It departs from Dolmabahçe. For reservations
Phone: (212) 296 5240

MUSEUMS

Adam Mickiewcz Museum
Harbiye
Phone: (212) 253 6698

Archeology Museum
Gülhane
Phone: (212) 520 7740

Aşiyan Museum
Rumelihisarı-Beşiktaş
Phone: (212) 263 6986

Atatürk Museum
Şişli
Phone: (212) 240 6319

Haghia Irene (Aya İrini) Museum
Sultanahmet
Phone: (212) 512 0480

Haghia Sophia (Ayasofya) Museum
Sultanahmet
Phone: (212) 588 4500

Press (Basın) Museum
Çemberlitaş
Phone: (212) 513 8458

Beylerbeyi Palace
Beylerbeyi
Phone: (216) 321 9320

Tiled (Çinili) Kiosk
Gülhane
Phone: (212) 520 7740

Naval (Deniz) Museum
Beşiktaş
Phone: (212)261 0040

Divan Literature Museum
Tünel (Beyoğlu-Karaköy short subway line)
(212) 245 4141

Dolmabahçe Palace
Beşiktaş
(212) 236 9000

Eastern Antiquities Museum
Gülhane
(212) 520 7740

Carpet Museum
Sultanahmet
(212) 518 1330

Ihlamur (Linden) Pavilion
Beşiktaş
(212) 259 5086

Fire Brigade Museum
Fatih
(212) 524 1126-27

Museum of Caricatures and Humor
Fatih
(212) 521 1264

Kariye Museum
Edirnekapı
(212) 631 9241

Maslak Pavilions
Maslak
(212) 276 1022

Museum of Mosaics
Sultanahmet
(212) 518 1205

Rahmi M. Koç Industrial Museum
Hasköy
(212) 256 7133

Painting and Sculpture Museum
Beşiktaş
(212) 261 4298

Rumeli Hisarı (Rumeli Fortress)
Beşiktaş
(212) 265 0410

Sabancı Museum
Emirgan
(212) 277 7153

Sadberk Hanım Museum
Büyükdere
(212) 242 3813

Şehir Müzesi (city museum)
Beşiktaş
(212) 258 5344

Tanzimat Museum
Sirkeci
(212) 512 6384

Topkapı Palace Museum
Sultanahmet
(212) 512 0480

Turkish and Islamic Arts Museum
Sultanahmet
(212) 518 1805

Turkish Foundations Calligraphy Museum
Beyazıt
(212) 527 5851

Yapı Kredi Bank Vedat Tör Museum
Beyoğlu
(212) 252 4700

Yerebatan Sarnıcı (Basilica Cistern)
Sultanahmet
(212) 522 1259

Yıldız Palace - Şale Pavilion
Yıldız
(212) 259 4570

SHOPPING MALLS

Akmerkez
Etiler
Phone: (212) 28201/ 70
www.akmerkez.com.tr

Atrium
Ataköy
Phone: (212) 661 1233
Fax: (212) 560 3665
Web: www.atrium.com.tr
E-Posta: atrium@bistek.net.tr
Address: 9-10. Kısım, Ataköy

Bauhaus
İçerenköy
Phone: (216) 448 0344
Address: E-5 Karayolu Eski Gen Oto Arkası, Hal Giriş Yanı, İçerenköy

Capitol
Altunizade
Phone: (216) 391 1920
Address: Mahiz İz Cad. Altunizade

Carousel
Bakırköy
Phone: (212) 570 8434

Fax: (212) 538 6676
Web: www.carousel.com.tr
Address: Halit Ziya Uşaklıgil Cad. No:1
Bakırköy

Carrefour
Carrefour / Büyükçekmece
Phone: (212) 852 0606
Address: Londra Asfaltı Haramidere Mevkii, Yakuplu Köyü, Büyükçekmece

Carrefour / İçerenköy
Phone: (216) 448 0296-97
Address: Eski Gen Oto Arkası, Hal Giriş Yanı, İçerenköy

Carrefour / Ümraniye
Phone: (216) 525 1050-51
Address: İnkılap Mahallesi Küçüksu Caddesi, No:68 Vega Ümraniye

Cevahir
Büyükdere Cad. No: 22 Şişli/İstanbul
Open between 10:00–22:00.

Colony Outlet ve Yaşam Merkezi
Sefaköy
Phone: (212) 580 4575
Address: E-5 Londra Asfaltı Bağlar Mevkii
Bağlar Caddesi, Sefaköy
Open between 10:00–22:00

Galleria Ataköy
Phone: (212) 559 9560
Fax: (212) 560 0538
Web: www.galleria-atakoy.com.tr
Address: Sahilyolu, Ataköy Kanyon
Büyükdere Cad. No:185 Levent
(212) 281 0800
www.kanyon.com.tr

Kule Çarşı
İş Kuleleri 4. Levent
Phone: (212) 316 1015
Open between 10:00 - 22:00

Maxi City
Phone: (212) 323 5666
Web: www.maxi.com.tr
E-Posta: info@maxi.com.tr
Address: ABC Yolu Boğaziçi A Blokları
Önü 34460 İstinye

Mass Alışveriş ve Eğlence Merkezi
Gaziosmanpaşa
Phone: (212) 616 2265 - (212) 616 2264
Fax: (212) 616 2266

Address: Eski Edirne Asfaltı No: 34 Gaziosmanpaşa

Mayadrom
Phone: (212) 284 5706
Web: www.mayadrom.com.tr
Address: Yıldırım Göker Cad. Etiler

Metro
Güneşli
Phone: (212) 478 7000
Kozyatağı
Phone: (216) 317 1274
Büyükçekmece
Phone: (212) 886 1386

Millenium Metrocity
4. Levent
Phone: (212) 282 4951
www.metrocity.com.tr

Mr. Bricolage
Güneşli
Phone: (212) 630 0807
www.mrbricolage.com.tr

Olivium Alışveriş Merkezi
Zeytinburnu
Phone: (212) 547 7453 (pbx)
Fax: (212) 582 0626
Web: www.olivium.com
E-Posta: musteri@olivium.com.tr
Address: Prof.Dr. Muammer Aksoy Cad.
No:1/1 Zeytinburnu

Polcenter
Levent
Phone: (212) 270 6331
Fax: (212) 270 4721
Web: www.polatholding.com.tr
Address: Büyükdere Cad. Eczacı Ali Kaya
Sk. No: 4 Levent Levent

Praktiker Yapı Marketleri AŞ.
Address: Küçüksu Cad. No:115
Ümraniye- Istanbul
Phone: (216) 522 8888
Fax: (216) 522 8986
Alo Praktiker: (212) 343 1313
Web: www.praktiker.com.tr

Profilo Alışveriş Merkezi
Mecidiyeköy
Phone: (212) 216 4400
Fax: (212) 216 4410
Web: www.profiloalisverismerkezi.com.tr
Address: Cemal Sahir Cad. 26/28 Mecidi-
yeköy

Tekzen
Phone: (212) 660 1011
Address: Çırpıcı Yolu 34720 Merter
Bakırköy/ISTANBUL
Web: www.tekzen.com.tr
Fax: (212) 572 8120

Tepe Nautilus Alışveriş Merkezi
Kadıköy Acıbadem
Address: Fatih Caddesi No:1 Acıbadem
34650 Kadıköy
Phone: (216) 339 3929
Fax: (216) 339 3920

Town Center Alışveriş Merkezi
Bakırköy
Phone: (212) 466 0770
Address: Town Center Alışveriş Merkezi
İncirli cad. No:11 Kat:5 Bakırköy

HOSPITALS

Aksaray Vatan Hospital
Aksaray
(212) 525 9395

Acıbadem Hospital
Acıbadem
(216) 544 4444

German Hospital
Taksim
(212) 293 2150

American Hospital
Nişantaşı
(212)311 2000

Dünya Eye Hospital
Levent
(212) 281 1111

Florance Nightingale Hospital
Çağlayan
(212) 224 4950

International Hospital
Yeşilköy
(212) 663 3000 (30 lines)

Metropolitan Florance Nightingale Hospital
Mecidiyeköy
(212) 288 3400

Sema Hospital
Maltepe
(216) 444 7362

STATE HOSPITALS

Cerrahpaşa Medical Faculty Hospital
Cerrahpaşa
(212) 588 4800 (60 lines)

Çapa Medical Faculty Hospital
Çapa
(212) 534 0000 (10 lines)

Haydarpaşa Numune Hospital
Haydarpaşa–Kadıköy
(216) 345 4680

Marmara University Medical
School Hospital
Koşuyolu
(216) 327 1010

Siyami Ersek Kalp ve Göğüs
Cerrahisi Hospital
Haydarpaşa-Kadıköy
(216) 349 9120

Taksim İlkyardım Hospital
Taksim
(212) 252 4300

AMBULANCE SERVICES

Clinix (Ambulance)
(216) 349 8090

Çapa Private Ambulance
(212) 585 6184
(212)587 4611

International Hospital Ambulance
(212) 663 3000

International SOS
Assistance (Ambulance)
(212) 247 2560
(212) 247 9779
(Air Ambulance)

Marmara Ambulance
(216) 341 2727
(216) 474 8282

Med-Line
(Fully Equipped Ambulance)
(212) 282 0000
(212) 329 1212
(212) 444 1212

Özel Ambulance
(212) 240 1342
(212) 240 6886
(212) 247 2006

SOS Alarm (Ambulance)
(212) 505 7272
(Air Ambulance)

Teşvikiye Ambulance
(212) 247 0781
(212) 231 1144
(212) 302 1515

EMERGENCY NUMBERS

110 Fire
112 Ambulance-First aid
118 telephone directory service
154 Traffic warden
155 Police

TIPS FOR TRANSPORT WITHIN ISTANBUL

The buses of the Havaş organization take you and your luggage from both of the airports to two central spots of the city, Kozyatağı on the Anatolian side and Taksim on the European side; it is far cheaper means than taking a taxi (for details, see www.havas.com.tr). "Metrobüs" is the name given for the special buses running on their separate road and their major route is along the E5 highway passing through Istanbul. Having a very long route, the Metrobüs is one of the fastest means of transport immune to traffic except for passing the Bosphorus Bridge. The railed systems also offer alternative ways of being saved from heavy traffic. Most of these services are available on the European side, where the historical peninsula and most of the tourist attractions are—though the cars can sometimes be too crowded. The "Hafif Metro" runs between the Atatürk Airport and Aksaray, whereas the "Hızlı Tramway" runs between Zeytinburnu and Kabataş. If you come to the Atatürk Airport and do not mind transferring your luggage from one vehicle to another, you can take the Metro until Zeytinburnu station and then pass to the Tramway. Thus, you will not have to take a taxi if you are going somewhere in Beyazıt, Sultanahmet, Sirkeci etc. If you wish to pass from the Metro to Metrobüs, the Şirinevler station will provide the easiest switch.

AIRPORTS

SABİHA GÖKÇEN AIRPORT

Transport:

The airport is on the Anatolian side in Pendik/Kurtköy district. It is 40 km to Kadıköy, 12 km to Pendik and 50 km to Taksim. The 1.5 km road maintaining connection with TEM highway makes transport easy. The Pendik sea buses port is 14 km away.

ATATÜRK AIRPORT

Transport:

Atatürk Airport is located on the European side of Istanbul in Yeşilköy. The Distance to the city center Sirkeci is 28 km and the distance to the sea is about 4-4.5 km. Subway (hafif metro) is available from the airport to Aksaray.

BUS TERMINALS

ESENLER BUS TERMINAL

Located on the European side, Esenler is one of the largest bus terminals in Turkey. It is possible here to find buses to/from every city in Turkey.

Transport: the subway (hafif metro) maintains connection with Aksaray or Atatürk Airport.

There are public transportation buses to Taksim, Beşiktaş, Mecidiyeköy, Eminönü, Bakırköy, and Avcılar, but these are rather rare. There are also blue buses (Halk Otobüsü) which go to Bostancı, Sarıyer, or Arnavutköy.

THE HAREM BUS TERMINAL

This is the main inter-city bus terminal on the Asian side. Most buses coming from or going to the Esenler Bus Terminal stop over the Harem Terminal. Public buses are available to places like Kadıköy and Pendik. You can pass to Sirkeci or Kabataş on the European side by ship from the Üsküdar port (10 minutes by walking from the Harem Terminal). If you are traveling via the Harem terminal, taking a taxi is a sensible option.

EMBASSIES AND CONSULATES

German Embassy
Phone: (212) 334 6100
Fax: (212) 245 2624
Web: www.germanembassyank.com
E-Posta: infomail@germanembassyank.com
Address: İsmet İnönü Caddesi No:16
Gümüşsuyu, Istanbul

American Embassy
Phone: (212) 335 9000
Fax: (212) 335 9102
Web: www.usemb-ankara.org.tr
Address: İstinye Mahallesi Kaplıcalar
Mevkii No.2 İstinye, Sarıyer 34460 Istanbul

Albanian Embassy
Phone: (212) 296 2428
Fax: (212) 296 2427
Address: Valikonağı Cad. Ekmek Fabrikası
Sok. No: 4, Nişantaşı Şişli, Istanbul

Australian Embassy
Phone: (212) 257 7050 - 52
Fax: (212) 257 7054
Web: www.embaustralia.org
E-Posta: ausemank@ibm.net
Address: Tepecik Yolu No: 58, Etiler, Istanbul

Austrian Embassy
Phone: (212) 262 9315
Fax: (212) 262 4984
Web: www.austria.org.tr
Address: Koybaşı Caddesi No:46
Yeniköy, Istanbul

Azerbaijani Embassy
Phone: (212) 279 5400, 269 1343
Fax: (212) 284 9579
E-Posta: arzist@superonline.com
Address: Alt Zeren Sokak No:13
1. Levent, Istanbul

The Bahamas Consular Agency
Phone: (0216) 493 8000
Fax: (0216) 493 8080
E-Posta: moliva@turk.net
Address: Aydıntepe Mah. Tersaneler
Caddesi 50.Sokak No:7
Tuzla, 81700 Istanbul

Hasan Kemal YARDIMCI
(Consular Agent)

Bangladeshi Consular Agency
Phone: (212) 315 5200
Fax: (212) 347 0083
E-Posta: soyakint@turk.net
Address: Büyükdere Caddesi No:38
Mecidiyeköy, Istanbul
Mehmed Rasim SENGİR
(Consular Agent)

Belgian Embassy
Phone: (212) 243 3300
Fax: (212) 243 5074
Web: www.diplobel.org
Address: Sıraselviler Cad. No: 73
Beyoğlu, Istanbul

United Arab Emirates Embassy
Phone: (212) 279 6349
Address: Konaklar Mah. Meşeli Sok. No.11
4.Levent, Istanbul

Bolivia Consular Agency
Phone: (212) 272 2402
Fax: (212) 267 2647
Address: Altan Erbulak Sokak No:3 Kat:3,
Mecidiyeköy, Istanbul
Karlo Yakup MİLOVİÇ (Consular Agent)

Bosnian Embassy
Phone: (212) 245 1616 / 245 1619
Fax: (212) 245 1620
Address: Beyaz Karanfil Sok. 45,
3.Levent, Istanbul

Brasilian Consular Agency
Phone: (212) 251 4735
Fax: (212) 293 9129
E-Posta: ist.brasil.cons@superonline.com
Address: Bankalar Cad. 31/33 K:2
Karaköy, Istanbul
Silvyo BENBASSAT (Consular Agent)

Bulgarian Embassy
Phone: (212) 269 0478
Fax: (212) 264 1011
Address: Ulus Mahallesi Adnan Saygun
Cad. No:44, 2. Levent, Istanbul

Burkino Faso Consular Agency
Phone: (212) 213 0650
Fax: (212) 212 8263
E-Posta: cgandur@seahorsenet.com
Address: Kore Şehitleri cad. Mithat Ünlü
Sokak no:23 Zincirlikuyu, Istanbul
F. Cemil GANDUR (Consular Agent)

Algerian Embassy
Phone: (212) 327 8980-81
Fax: (212) 327 8983
Address: Süleyman Seba Cad. No:124,
(Akaretler Yokuşu) Beşiktaş, Istanbul

Czech Embassy
Phone: (212) 234 1366 - 230 9597
Fax: (212) 231 9493
Address: Abdi İpekçi Cad. 71, Maçka
Nişantaşı, Istanbul

Chinese Embassy
Phone: (212) 272 5200
Fax: (212) 274 7733
Web: www.chinaembassy.org.tr
E-Posta: chinaemb_tr@mfa.gov.cn
Address: Ortaklar Caddesi No:14
Mecidiyeköy, Istanbul

Danish Embassy
Phone: (212) 359 1900
Fax: (212) 359 1902
Web: www.danimarka.org.tr
E-Posta: info@denmark.org.tr
Address: Meygede Sokak No.2 TR-80810
Bebek, Istanbul

Dominican Republic Consular Agency
Phone: (212) 248 3613
Fax: (212) 231 3065
E-Posta: sahipak@superonline.com
Address: Teşvikiye Caddesi No: 172 İzgü
Apt. Kat 4 Da:6 Nişantaşı, Istanbul
Sahip AKOSMAN (Consular Agent)

Embassy of Ecuador
Phone: (212) 257 4788, 257 5116
Fax: (212) 287 5924
E-Posta: ecuadorist@na-plus.com
Address: Seher Yıldızı Sokak 33/12
Etiler, Istanbul
Fadi NAHAS (Consular Agent)

El Salvador Consular Agency
Phone: (212) 567 4760 (5 lines)
Fax: (212) 565 3070
E-Posta: info@tekstiplik.com.tr
Address: Çırpıcı Yolu No:2 34020 Istanbul
Jeki Levi (Consular Agent)

Indonesian Consular Agency
Phone: (212) 287 0008
Fax: (212) 287 0009
Address: Seheryıldızı Sokak No:22/11
Etiler Istanbul
Semih TEZCAN (Consular Agent)

Estonian Consular Agency
Phone: (212) 315 7071-72
Fax: (212) 232 6291
E-Posta: rana.ozduzenciler@abank.com.tr
Address: Alternatif Bank A.Ş. Merkez Şubesi,
Cumhuriyet Cad. No:22-24 80200 \
Elmadağ, Istanbul
Tuncay ÖZİLHAN (Consular Agent)

Ethiopia Consular Agency
Phone: (212) 299 1120/36
Fax: (212) 223 9581
Address: Nuri Paşa Caddesi No:84 Tarabya
Sarıyer, Istanbul
Atilla YURTÇU (Consular Agent)

Philippines Consular Agency
Phone: (216) 331 4344
Fax: (216) 537 0234
E-Posta: rzaimoglu@etas.com.tr
Address: Cumhuriyet Cad. Ak İş Merkezi
No:1 Kat: 5-6 Kavacık Beykoz, Istanbul
Rasim Zaimoğlu (Consular Agent)

Finnish Consular Agency
Phone: (212) 283 5737 - 38
Fax: (212) 283 5739
Address: Yeni Çamlık Caddesi Ayaz Sokak
No: 5 4. Levent, Istanbul
Ural ATAMAN (Consular Agent)

French Embassy
Phone: (212) 243 1852-53, 293 2460-
61, 292 4810-11
Fax: (212) 249 9168
Web: www.ambafrance-tr.org
Address: İstiklal Cad. 8, Taksim, Istanbul

Gabon Consular Agency
Phone: (212) 260 7178
Fax: (212) 280 0071
Address: Nispetiye Cad. Korukent Yolu,
Aydın Sok. No: 10 Levent, Istanbul
Tuğrul ERKİN (Consular Agent)

Gambian Consular Agency
Phone: (212) 259 1742
Fax: (212) 258 4365
Address: Yıldız Sarayı , Seyir Köşkü,
Barbaros Bulvarı Beşiktaş, 80700 Istanbul
Ekmeleddin İHSANOĞLU (Consular Agent)

Ghanaian Consular Agency
Phone: (212) 346 0112
Fax: (212) 346 0121
E-Posta: merkez@ustay.com
Address: Maslak Polaris Plaza, Kat:11 Ahi
Evran Cad. No: 1, Istanbul
Ali Haydar ÜSTAY (Consular Agent)

Guinean Consular Agency
Phone: (216) 550 9401
Fax: (216) 550 9403
E-Posta: consulatdeguinee@yahoo.fr
Address: Poyraz Sok. Sadıkoğlu Plaza 1 Kat:
3/69 Kadıköy, Istanbul
Orhan ARGÜN (Consular Agent)

South African Consular Agency
Phone: (212) 227 5200
Fax: (212) 260 2378
Web: www.southafrica.org.tr
E-Posta: ialaton@alarko.com.tr
Address: Alarko Holding A.Ş. Muallim Naci
Caddesi 113-115 Ortaköy, Istanbul
İshak ALATON (Consular Agent)

Georgian Embassy
Phone: (212) 292 8110
Fax: (212) 292 8112
Address: İnönü Caddesi No : 55 Marmara
Apt. Da:2 Gümüşsuyu Taksim, Istanbul

**The Hashemite Kingdom of Jordan
Consular Agency**
Phone: (212) 274 7543-44
Fax: (212) 274 7562
Address: Büyükdere Caddesi Lalezar İşhanı
No:101 Kat.2 Mecidiyeköy, Istanbul
Osman Mehmed Mithat ÖZBEK
(Consular Agent)

Croatian Embassy
Phone: (212) 293 5467-68
Fax: (212) 293 5476
E-Posta: croconis@netone.com.tr
Address: Meşrutiyet Caddesi No: 163/2
Tepebaşı Beyoğlu, Istanbul

Indian Embassy
Phone: (212) 296 2131 - 32
Fax: (212) 296 2130
Web: www.indembassy.org.tr
Address: Cumhuriyet Cad. 18, Dörtler Apt.
Kat:7 Harbiye-Taksim, Istanbul

Dutch Embassy
Phone: (212) 251 5030-33
Fax: (212) 292 5031
Web: www.dutchembassy.org.tr
E-Posta: nlgovist@domi.net.tr
Address: İstiklal Cad. 393, Beyoğlu, Istanbul

British Embassy
Phone: (212) 334 6400
Fax: (212) 334 6401
Web: www.britishembassy.org.tr
Address: Meşrutiyet Cad. No:34 Tepebaşı,
Beyoğlu, Istanbul

Iranian Embassy
Phone: (212) 513 8230 - 32
Fax: (212) 511 5219
Address: Ankara Cad. 1/2, Cağaloğlu
Eminönü, Istanbul

Irish Consular Agency
Phone: (212) 246 6025
Address: Cumhuriyet Cad. 26,
Harbiye, Istanbul
Dr. James Geary (Consular Agent)

Spanish Embassy
Phone: (212) 270 7410 - (212) 270 7414
Address: Karanfil Aralığı Cad. No:16
Levent, Istanbul

Israeli Embassy
Phone: (212) 317 6500
Fax: (212) 317 6555
Web:www.israel.org.tr
Address: Büyükdere Cad. Yapı Kredi Plaza C
Blok 7. Kat 80620 4. Levent, Istanbul

Swedish Embassy
Phone: (212) 243 5770
Fax: (212) 252 4114
Web: www.swedenembassy.org.tr
Address: İstiklal Cad. 497, Tünel
Beyoğlu, Istanbul

Swiss Embassy
Phone: (212) 283 1282
Fax: (212) 283 1297, 283 1298 (Vize)
E-Posta: Vertretung@ist.rep.admin.ch
Address: 1. Levent Plaza, A Blok, Kat 3,
Büyükdere Cad.No:173,34394,
Levent, Istanbul

Italian Embassy
Phone: (212) 243 1024-25, (212) 252 5436
Fax: (212) 252 5879
Web:www.italyancons.org.tr
Address:Boğazkesen Cad. Tom Tom Kaptan
Sok. 15, Galatasaray Beyoğlu Istanbul
Visa: (212) 244 32 59

Iceland Consular Agency
Phone: (216) 394 3210
Fax: (216) 394 3208
E-Posta: iceconsulist@hotmail.com
Address: Okul Yolu No : 9, 81474
Orhanlı, Istanbul
Kazım Münir HAMAMCIOĞLU
(Consular Agent)

Jamaican Consular Agency
Phone: (212) 288 6351
Fax: (212) 266 4221
E-Posta: batadıs@superonline.com
Address: Altan Erbulak Sok. Eken Apt. 6/3,
Mecidiyeköy, Istanbul
Hikmet Aykut EKEN (Consular Agent)

Japanese Embassy
Phone: (212) 393 2010-13
Fax: (212) 393 2008
Web:www.mofa.go.jp/embjapan/turkey
Address:İnönü Cad. No: 24, Gümüşuyu
Taksim, Istanbul

Canadian Embassy
Phone: (212) 251 9838
Fax: (212) 251 9888
Web:www.dfait-maeci.gc.ca/ankara
Address: İstiklal Cad. No. 373/5

Beyoğlu, Istanbul
Phone: (212) 662 5347-48
Fax: (212) 662 5349
E-Posta: consulkzist@superonline.com
Address: Florya Cad.No:62,Yeşilköy,
Bakırköy, Istanbul

Kirghiz Embassy
Phone: (212) 235 6767
Fax: (212) 235 9293
Address: Lamartin Caddesi Altınay Apt.
No:7 Kat 3 Taksim Istanbul

Northern Cyprus Turkish Embassy
Phone: (212) 227 3490
Fax: (212) 227 3493
Address: Emirhan Cad. Yeni Gelin Sok. 8,
Balmumcu Beşiktaş Istanbul

Colombian Consular Agency
Phone: (212) 279 9828-29
Fax: (212) 268 4895
Address: Birlik Sokak.Manolya Apt.3/3 1.
Levent, Istanbul
Martha P. Ardila De ÜLKÜMEN
(Consular Agent)

Congo Embassy
Phone: (216) 425 3777
Fax: (216) 425 3777
E-Posta: kdcist@yahoo.com
Address: Çubuklu Caddesi No 52/3 kat 2,
Pembe Yalı-Kanlıca-Beykoz
Consular Agent: Belkıs Gümüş Sever

South Korean Consular Agency
Phone: (212) 256 4970
Fax: (212) 256 4414
E-Posta: alikibar@kibarholding.com
Address: Tersane Cad.Bakır Sokak.No:19,
Karaköy, Istanbul
Ali Kibar (Consular Agent)

Costa Rican Consular Agency
Phone: (212) 528 6819
Fax: (212) 527 5777
E-Posta: hkitapcı@aidata.net.tr
Address: Tahmis Kalçın sokak No.15
Eminönü, Istanbul
Ender KİTAPÇI (Consular Agent)

Latvian Consular Agency
Phone: (216) 358 8298
Fax: (216) 302 6442
E-Posta: latvia@netone.com.tr
Address: Caddesi No: 367/7
Erenköy, Istanbul
Ahmet ARBATLI (Consular Agent)

Liberian Consular Agency
Phone: (212) 230 1331
Fax: (212) 225 0644
Address: Cumhuriyet Caddesi No:269
Harbiye 80230 Istanbul
Ceylan PİRİNÇÇİOĞLU
(Consular Agent)

Libyan Embassy
Phone: (212) 251 8100
Fax: (212) 252 5515
Address: Miralay Şefik Bey Sok. No:13,
Gümüşsuyu, Taksim

Lithuanian Consular Agency
Phone: (216) 425 0500
Fax: (216) 425 0497-98
Address: Çavuşbaşı Cad. No: 33 81640
Kavacık, Istanbul
Tayfun UZUNOVA (Consular Agent)

Lebanese Embassy
Phone: (212) 236 1365-66
Fax: (212) 227 3373
Address: Teşvikiye Cad. 134/1, Teşvikiye
Şişli, Istanbul

Hungarian Embassy
Phone: (212) 225 5501 - 225 5519
Fax: (212) 248 2783
E-Posta: huconsist@domi.net.tr
Address: Poyrazcık Sok. No: 35,
Beyoğlu, Istanbul

Madagaskar Consular Agency
Phone: (212) 211 9206, 216 8513
Fax: (212) 211 7701
E-Posta: aftuexport@superonline.com
Address: Büyükdere Cad. Kral Apt.
No:75/10 80300 Mecidiyeköy, Istanbul
Nesrin KARAARSLAN KARADAĞ
(Consular Agent)

Macedonian Embassy
Phone: (212) 249 9977, 251 2233
Fax: (212) 293 7765
Address: İnönü Cad. No: 20/3, Gümüşsuyu,
Taksim, Istanbul

Malawian Consular Agency
Phone: (216) 521 3850
Fax: (216) 521 3855
E-Posta: mfbal@hotmail.com
Address: Alemdağ Caddesi No: 48/4 Kat 3
Çamlıca Üsküdar, Istanbul
Mehmed Fatih BALTACI (Consular Agent)

Maldivian Consular Agency
Phone: (212) 241 7372
Fax: (212) 230 3697
E-Posta: kamera@turk.net
Address: Cumhuriyet Caddesi No: 257 Kat.3
Harbiye 80230 Istanbul
Nihat BÖYTÜZÜN (Consular Agent)

Malaysian Consular Agency
Phone: (212) 247 1728
Fax: (212) 247 1375
E-Posta: nusreta@koc.com.tr
Address: Halaskargazi Cad. No: 266 Çanka-
ya Apt. Kat 4 Daire 7 Şişli, 80020 Istanbul
Nüsret ARSEL (Consular Agent)

Malian Consular Agency
Phone: (212) 296 8131, 296 9139
Fax: (212) 232 1661, 247 1341
Address: Vali Konağı Cad. Mim Kemal 2.
Apt.No:72/12 Nişantaşı, Istanbul
Faruk CENGİÇ (Consular Agent)

Maltese Consular Agency
Phone: (212) 244 2895,
249 8162, 243 0328
Fax: (212) 252 9796, 293 3514
Address: İstiklal Caddesi Korsan Çıkmazı
Akdeniz Apt. K..2 80074
Beyoğlu, Istanbul
M. Oğuz TEOMAN (Consular Agent)

Mexican Consular Agency
Phone: (212) 227 3500
Fax: (212) 227 3504
Address: Teşvikiye Caddesi Teşvikiye Palas
No: 107/2 Nişantaşı, Istanbul
Varol DERELİ (Consular Agent)

Egyptian Embassy
Phone: (212) 263 6038, 265 2440
Fax: (212) 257 4428
Address: Cevdet Paşa Cad. no 173
Bebek, Istanbul

Monaco Consular Agency
Phone: (212) 262 4148
Fax: (212) 266 4745
Address: Köybaşı Arkası Sok. No:4 Park
Apt.Daire 2, Yeniköy, Istanbul
Tuna Aksoy KÖPRÜLÜ (Consular Agent)

Nepalese Consular Agency
Phone: (212) 246 6104-05
Fax: (212) 240 2199
Address: Vali Konağı Caddesi YKB İşhanı
Nişantaşı, Istanbul
Fatma Günseli MALKOÇ (Consular Agent)

Norwegian Consular Agency
Phone: (212)-249 9753 - 252 0600
Fax: (212) 249 4434
Address: Bilezik Sokak No:2 Fındıklı Istanbul
Selim BİLGİŞİN (Consular Agent)

Omani Consular Agency
Phone: (212) 240 1166
Fax: (212) 234 2204
E-Posta: dmagripli@national.com.tr
Address: Rumeli Cad. 16/11, 82220,
Nişantaşı, Istanbul
Kenan MAĞRİPLİ (Consular Agent)

Uzbek Embassy
Phone: (212) 323 2037, 229 0075
Fax: (212) 323 2040
Address: Şehit Halil İbrahim Cad. 23,
İstinye, Istanbul

Pakistani Embassy
Phone: (212) 358 4506
Fax: (212) 358 4508
Address: Nispetiye Cad.Gülşen Sok.No:3,
Beyaz Ev, Etiler, Istanbul

Panama Consular Agency
Phone: (212) 223 3267
Fax: (212) 223 3267
Address: Acar Sokak Kubilay Sitesi Mimoza
Apt. 26/4 Tarabya, Istanbul
İrma Ah Che DE FİRUZ
(Consular Agent)

Peruvian Consular Agency
Phone: (212) 294 2300
Fax: (212) 294 2304
E-Posta: consulperu-ist@diplomats.com
Address: Ayazma Yolu, No:23, 34403,
Kağıthane, Istanbul
Jak HAYİM (Consular Agent)

Polonese Embassy
Phone: (212) 291 0300-1
Fax: (212) 233 0618
Address: Büyükçiftlik Sok. 5-7,
Nişantaşı, Istanbul

Portuguese Consular Agency
Phone: (212) 251 9118
Fax: (212) 251 7348
Address: Muradiye Cad. 49/5 Sirkeci Istanbul
Aron NOMMAZ (Consular Agent)

Romanian Embassy
Phone: (212) 292 4125-26-27
Fax: (212) 293 8261
Address: Sıraseviler Cad. No:55
Taksim, Istanbul

Russian Embassy
Phone: (212) 244 1693
Fax: (212) 249 0507
E-Posta: visavi@turk.net
Address: İstiklal Cad. 443,
Beyoğlu, Istanbul

San Marino Consular Agency
Phone: (212)352 0697
Fax: (212) 352 0554
Address: Maya Rezidans, M Blok, D/13,
Etiler, Istanbul
Mehmed Bercis MOROVA
(Consular Agent)

Senegal Consular Agency
Phone: (212) 241 7372
Fax: (212) 230 3697
E-Posta: senegalconsulate@turk.net
Address: Cumhuriyet Caddesi No: 257
Kat.3 Şişli 80230 Istanbul
Nihat BÖYTÜZÜN (Consular Agent)

Seychellois Consular Agency
Phone: (212) 325 2624
Fax: (212) 325 2620

E-Posta: altunc@destekfinans.com
Address: Yapı Kredi Plaza C Blok Kat 13
Levent, Istanbul
Altunç KUMOVA (Consular Agent)

Serbian Embassy
Phone: (212) 248 1004
Fax: (212) 248 3534
Address: Valikonağı Cad. No: 96/A
Nişantaşı Istanbul

Singapore Consular Agency
Phone: (216) 358 0133, 302 7044
Fax: (216) 350 8619
Address: Kazım Özalp Sokak No:28/8 Şaş-
kınbakkal, Istanbul

Slovenian Consular Agency
Phone: (216) 321 9000
Fax: (216) 321 9013
Address: Hacı Reşit Paşa Sokak No:7,
Çamlıca, Istanbul
Mustafa Başar Arıoğlu (Consular Agent)

Sri Lankan Consular Agency
Phone: (212) 232 4700
Fax: (212) 231 0035
E-Posta: cerrahgil@cerrahgil.com.tr
Address: Abdi İpekçi Caddesi
No.33 Teşvikiye, Istanbul
Eşref CERRAHOĞLU (Consular Agent)

Sudanese Consular Agency
Phone: (212) 287 6850
Fax: (212) 287 6851
E-Posta: zqe@erdem.com.tr
Address: Etiler Sokak No:1 , 80630,
Etiler, Istanbul
Zeynel Abidin ERDEM (Consular Agent)

Surinamese Consular Agency
Phone: (212) 291 0626, 231 2550
Fax: (212) 219 3964
E-Posta: habaconsultant@superonline.com
Address: Cumhuriyet Caddesi No:317/9 ,
80230, Harbiye, Istanbul
Haşmet BAŞAR (Consular Agent)

Syrian Embassy
Phone: (212) 232 6721 - 232 7110
Fax: (212) 230 2215
Address: Maçka Caddesi Ralli Apt. 59/3
Teşvikiye, Istanbul

Saudi Arabian Embassy
Phone: (212) 281 9140
Fax: (212) 281 9141
Address: Akıncı Bayırı Sokak No : 8
Mecidiyeköy, Istanbul

Tanzanian Consular Agency
Phone: (212) 233 8291 – 246 6142
Fax: (212) 234 5679
Address: Şakayık Sok. Park Palas Apt.
No:49/1 Kat 3 Teşvikiye, Istanbul
Ziya KARAHAN (Consular Agent)

Thai Consular Agency
Phone: (212) 292 8651-52, 292 8366
Fax: (212) 292 9770, 249 4309
E-Posta: info@thaicons-ist.org
Address: İnönü Caddesi No: 90 Dersan Han
Gümüşsuyu Taksim, Istanbul
Refik GÖKÇEK (Consular Agent)

Togolese Consular Agency
Phone: (216) 342 7821
Fax: (216) 342 7821
Address: Mesut Baban Sitesi, No: 68 A Blok,
Daire 20 Altunizade, Istanbul
Sitou GNASSOVNOU (Consular Agent)

Tunisian Embassy
Phone: (212) 293 9578-86
Fax: (212) 293 9576
Address: Meşrutiyet Cad. No:99/1, Tarhan
Han, Tepebaşı, Istanbul

Turkmen Embassy
Phone: (212) 662 0222-23
Fax: (212) 662 0224
Address: Gazi Evronos Caddesi Baharistan
Sokak No: 13 Yeşilköy, Istanbul

Ukrainian Embassy
Phone: (212) 662 2541, 662 2735
Fax: (212) 662 1876
Address: Adakale Sokak No:13 Şenlikköy
Florya Bakırköy, Istanbul

Uruguayan Consular Agency
Phone: (212) 352 1067, 351 2316
Fax: (212) 351 0871
Address: Zeytinoğlu Cad. Yeşerti Sok. Hayat
Apt. 1. B /15 Daire 8, 80630
Etiler, Istanbul

Elvira Alonso de Barghi
(Consular Agent)

Vietnamese Embassy
Phone: (212) 274 6908
Fax: (212) 274 6909
Address:No: 3/1, Itri Sok., Balmumcu,
Beşiktaş, Istanbul

Yemeni Consular Agency
Phone: (212) 231 2705, 248 2046, 231 5366
Fax: (212) 240 6808
Address:Halaskargazi Caddesi Oral Apt.
No:107/2 Harbiye, Istanbul
Mohamed Ahmed AL-MASHARI
(Consular Agent)

New Zealand Consular Agency
Phone: (212) 244 0272
Fax: (212) 251 4004
E-Posta: nzhonconist@hatem-law.com.tr
Address: İnönü Cad. 92/3 Taksim, 80090
Istanbul İzzet HATEM (Consular Agent)

Greek Embassy
Phone: (212) 245 0596-97-98
Fax: (212) 252 1365
Address: Turnacıbaşı Sok. No:32
Galatasaray,
Beyoğlu, Istanbul

CULTURAL ATTACHÉS

German Cultural Attaché
Phone: (212) 251 5404
Fax: (212) 249 9920
Address: İnönü Cad. No:16 80090
Taksim, Istanbul

American Cultural Attaché
Phone: (212) 251 2589, 251 3606
Fax: (212) 251 5254
Address: Meşrutiyet Cad. No:104-108
80050 Tepebaşı, Istanbul

Austrian Cultural Attaché
Phone: (212) 236 1581, 262 4984
Fax: (212) 258 0222
Address: Teşvikiye Cad. Belveder Apt.
No: 101 K:2 80212 Teşvikiye, Istanbul

Belgian Cultural Attaché
Phone: (212) 243 3300

Fax: (212) 243 5074
Address: Sıraselviler Cad. No:73 80060
Taksim, Istanbul

Chinese Cultural Attaché
Phone: (212) 272 5201
Fax: (212) 27 6906
Address:Ortaklar Cad. No:14 80290
Mecidiyeköy, Istanbul

French Cultural Attaché
Phone: (212) 243 4387, 245 3835
Fax: (212) 243 7738
Address: Nuru Ziya Cad. No:22 80050
Beyoğlu, Istanbul

Indian Cultural Attaché
Phone: (212) 248 4864
Fax: (212) 230 3697
Address: Cumhuriyet Cad. No:257/3
80230 Harbiye, Istanbul

Dutch Cultural Attaché
Phone: (212) 251 5030, 251 5031
Fax: (212) 251 9289
Address: İstiklal Cad. No:393 80050
Beyoğlu, Istanbul

Iraqi Cultural Attaché
Phone: (212) 230 2933
Fax: (212) 234 5726
Address: Halide Edip Adıvar Mah.
İpekböceği Sok. No: 1 80270
Şişli, Istanbul

British Cultural Attaché
Phone: (212) 252 7474, 252 7478
Fax: (212) 243 7682
Address: İstiklal Cad. No:251-253 K:2
80050 Beyoğlu, Istanbul

Iranian Cultural Attaché
Phone: (212) 513 8230
Fax: (212) 511 5219
Address: Ankara Cad. No:1
34410 Cağaloğlu

Spanish Cultural Attaché
Phone: (212) 225 2099
Fax: (212) 225 2088
Address: Valikonağı Cad. Başaran Apt.
No:33 K:3 80220 Harbiye

Italian Cultural Attaché
Phone: (212) 293 9848
Fax: (212) 251 0748
Address: Meşrutiyet Cad. No:161
80070 Tepebaşı

Russian Cultural Attaché
Phone: (212) 244 2610, 244 1693
Fax: (212) 249 0507
Address: İstiklal Cad. No:443
80050 Beyoğlu

Greek Cultural Attaché
Phone: (212) 245 0596, 245 0597
Fax: (212) 252 1365
Address: Turnacıbaşı Sok. No:32
80060 Beyoğlu

CULTURAL OFFICES AND CENTERS

Austrian Cultural Office
Palais Yeniköy
Köybaşı Cad. No: 44 Pk.13 34464
Yeniköy - Istanbul
Phone: (212) 223 7843
Fax: (212) 223 3469

E-Posta: istanbul-kf@bmaa.gv.at

French Cultural Center
Phone: (212) 334 8740
Fax: (212) 334 8741
web: www.infist.org/
Address: İstiklal Cad. No:8 Beyoğlu

Spanish Cultural Center
Tarlabaşi Bulvarı Zambak Sokak 33
34435 Taksim, Istanbul
Phone: (212) 292 6536
Fax: (212) 292 6537
web: cenest@cervantes.es

Italian Cultural Center
Phone: (212) 293 9848
Address: Meşrutiyet Cad. No:161,
Tepebaşı, Taksim, Istanbul

Japanese Office of Culture
and Information
Phone: (212) 251 1580-81
Address: İstiklal Cad. Fransız
Konsolosluğu arkası Ana Çesme
Sok. No:3, Istanbul